T0326428

TOWARDS a KNOWLEDGE BASED ECONOMY?

PETER LANG
New York • Washington, D.C./Baltimore • Bern
Frankfurt am Main • Berlin • Brussels • Vienna • Oxford

TOWARDS a KNOWLEDGE BASED ECONOMY?

Knowledge and Learning
in European Educational Research

Michael Kuhn • Massimo Tomassini • P. Robert-Jan Simons
EDITORS

PETER LANG
New York • Washington, D.C./Baltimore • Bern
Frankfurt am Main • Berlin • Brussels • Vienna • Oxford

Library of Congress Cataloging-in-Publication Data

Towards a knowledge based economy?: knowledge and learning in European
educational research / Michael Kuhn, Massimo Tomassini, P. Robert-Jan Simons editors.
p. cm.
Includes bibliographical references.
1. Information technology—Economic aspects—Europe. 2. Information society—Europe.
3. Intellectual capital—Europe. 4. Knowledge management—Europe.
I. Kuhn, Michael. II. Tomassini, M. (Massimo). III. Simons, J. Robert-Jan.
HC240.9.I55T69   658.4'8'094—dc22   2005017863
ISBN 0-8204-7470-3

Bibliographic information published by **Die Deutsche Bibliothek**.
Die Deutsche Bibliothek lists this publication in the "Deutsche
Nationalbibliografie"; detailed bibliographic data is available
on the Internet at http://dnb.ddb.de/.

The project "Towards the Learning Economy—Conclusions from FRP 4 and 5 Projects
to Shape European Policies in Education and Training" has been funded
by the European Commission, DG Research, Framework Programme 5.

The paper in this book meets the guidelines for permanence and durability
of the Committee on Production Guidelines for Book Longevity
of the Council of Library Resources.

© 2006 Peter Lang Publishing, Inc., New York
29 Broadway, New York, NY 10006
www.peterlangusa.com

Printed in the United States of America

Table of Contents

CHAPTER ONE

European Educational Research— Contributions to the Discourse about the EU as a 'Knowledge Based Society'

MICHAEL KUHN

The EU—towards the unknown knowledge based society

It is meanwhile common sense that the EU has set out to become a knowledge based society, even the *"the most competitive and dynamic knowledge based economy in the world....* (European Commission, 2000). Which knowledge—last but not least about the knowledge based society or economy—guided the decision of the EU towards this strategic aim, one feels attempted to ask?

The E&T Cluster project was initiated in 2000 and started in October 2001 in a situation, when the idea of a "learning economy" had started to play a major role in designing European policies in general and to influence the discourses in EU research, also in the realm of educational research. While the previous discourses in social sciences in the context of EU research programmes at that time where rather dominated by the technology driven idea of an "information society", the concept of a "learning economy" introduced reflections about the future of the project Europe which were much more related to social phenomena. Due to the fact that the European policies in general were traditionally very much geared towards economic goals, last but not least mirrored in the introduction of a joint EU-currency, reflections about strategic economic issues attracted the attention of a broad range of social sciences engaged in European research.

The outcomes of the first generation of educational research projects funded under FRP 4 and the interim findings of some FRP 5 projects had shown already in their titles and in the research topics they were addressing, that the research agenda of European educational research had widely been influenced by this economically dominated social science discourse about the project "Europe". However, at that time the debate about the EU as a "learning society" was discussed, at least among researchers, still with a slight question mark, also due to the rather vague meaning of what a learning society is supposed to be.

Due to political decisions by the highest political bodies of the EU this question mark had been then replaced by most decisive and powerful exclamation marks. Since then the idea of the now called "Knowledge based Society" has become the strategic aim of the EU and also the exclusive research topic of social sciences research under EU research programmes, directing any social European research towards the abbreviations of a "KBS".

The current main social research programme of the EU in the Priority 7 of FRP 6, "Citizens and Governance in an knowledge based Society", documents two most remarkable positions about the policy agenda of the EU "in a knowledge based society" (further on KBS) (EU Commission, http://www.cordis.lu/citizens/ home.html): firstly, the extend to which the concept of a KBS is now guiding policies in all relevant policy areas of the EU, including European social sciences research policies; and secondly, the complete lack of any knowledge about this society concept guiding European policies for and towards a knowledge based society.

The policy areas dominated and geared towards the idea of making Europe a KBS become apparent via the policy fields requiring further research according to the above mentioned EU research programme. Policy areas addressed in the research programme, which the EU has decided to re-shape towards the requirements of KBS are:

—   "Growth, employment and competitiveness in a knowledge based economy"

—   the "dynamic growth regions and their role in a global economy"

—   "The relations between the labour market, employment and welfare regimes"

—   "Educational strategies for inclusion and social cohesion and their relation to other policies."

—   "Societal trends, quality of life and public policies"

—   "Inequalities in society and their consequences"

– "Governance for sustainable development."
  (EU Commission, http://www.cordis.lu/citizens/ home.html)

Given the portfolios of EU policies, in fact no major policy domain is missing on the EU research agenda. Finally, as if the Commission wants to prove the complete absence of any knowledge about the society model guiding her policies, the research programmes also mentions

– "Understanding knowledge"

– "Knowledge based policies for the knowledge based society"

as research topics about which knowledge is not available and thus requires further research.

Taking into account the limited scope of EU policies compared to the policy domains of member state governments, the policy domains in this list of social policy areas covers more or less the major policy agenda of the EU. The policy areas to be restructured towards a learning society concept are the policy areas of economics, labour market, social policies, education and sustainable development; in other words almost all key policy areas of the EU are subject of social science research in order to gain knowledge about how they are affected by the vision of a society model governed by knowledge towards which they are geared to!

Just as if the Commission also wants to prove, that the decision to restructure her entire policy agenda towards a society based on knowledge is not based on any knowledge about the knowledge based society, the same research programme documents in the research priorities of the "Work Programme" a revealing list of research topics, in which knowledge about the society and the according policy domains governed by knowledge are lacking. Knowledge is not available for all above policy areas which are supposed to be re-shaped towards a society governed by knowledge and so future European research efforts must help

> "...to understand the ways in which policy-making organisations learn and to assess the role of knowledge in the formulation and implementation of policies, with a view to promote learning and knowledge based policies."

> "...to develop improved concepts and theories on the knowledge based economy, and provide a comprehensive understanding of its characteristics and to the determinants of competitiveness, economic growth, aggregate demand and conditions for full employment."

> "...to analyse emerging growth regions in terms of the factors underlying their growth performances as well as shifting comparative advantages and changing roles in the world economy, with special attention to the role of knowledge and the implications for the EU."

"...to examine the public and private good characteristics of knowledge and to better understand its function in the European economy and society."

"...to significantly improve understanding of these relations, how they operate within different social models, the roles played by knowledge, and how policies might better take account of these relations."

"...to assess the role of education and training , in interaction with other areas of social policy in addressing social inequalities, vulnerability, marginalisation, disengagement and as a means of fostering social cohesion."

"...to expand the knowledge base concerning the relations between , on the one hand, current societal and policy trends, and on the other, the quality of life (or well-being) of individual citizens, as well as the implications of these relations for public policies."

"...to examine and provide a better understanding of the social, economic and cultural issues that affect intergenerational relations with particular focus on the attitudes , lifestyles and forms of participation adopted by European youth and on their consequences for European society and the economy."

"......to explore the interactions between governance modes and sustainable development within a European knowledge based society."

(EU Commission, http://www.cordis.lu/citizens/ home.html)

The exhaustive quotation of the research topics in Framework Programme 6 is noteworthy, since the long list of policy areas in which knowledge about the knowledge based society is required is in fact confessing that any knowledge about the society concept is lacking, which is though guiding the policy agenda of nothing less but a major global policy entity, the European Union. If this is the case, one might raise the question, which knowledge guided the European Commission to decide to become a society guided by knowledge?

In an interim summary, the research priorities inform us firstly that most fundamental knowledge about the knowledge based society concept is lacking. There is no knowledge about fundamentals of competitiveness, economic growth and their relation to employment; there is also no knowledge about the interplay of the three European policy levels both in a European as in a global context; there is no knowledge about the interplay between private and public knowledge production, knowledge transfer and knowledge, including political interventions; there is no knowledge about the contribution of education and training to a KBS also in relation to other policy fields like employment and social exclusion; the is no knowledge about the impact of a KBS on the life of European citizens and related policy interventions; there is no knowledge about the affect of a KBS of "intergenerational relations" and about "sustainable development". Does the EU have any knowledge about any aspect of a knowledge based society, one feels attempted to ask? The answer given by the EU via her research programme is definitively: no.

Thus, a rather bizarre phenomenon accompanies the idea of variations of society or economy models dominated by knowledge and learning, may they be called a "knowledge based economy" or in an broader version a "learning society". A first conclusion that can be made here is that the EU admits via her research agenda that there is hardly any substantial knowledge in any policy domain about the society governed by knowledge, a society model that is though governing the strategic policies of the EU and re-shaping the whole societies in the EU towards this aim!

However, as a matter of fact, the concept of a "knowledge based economy" has been presented as the major strategic aim of the European Union, making Europe *"the most competitive and dynamic knowledge-based economy in the world...."*. (ibid) In other words the idea of a KBS *is* the strategic aim of the EU, not only in a global context for any policy relations between the EU and the world outside of the EU, but the concept of a KBS *is* also governing the agenda for re-shaping the EU-countries and their policy agendas and the societies inside the EU; a rather totalitarian policy vision, preparing the European *societies and economies via also accordingly re-shaped policies* for nothing less but to become the winner in world wide competition; a policy agenda, which aims at re-structuring the totality of the social reality in the EU—the individuals, societies and economies and policies—governed by their functionality for global economic competitiveness.

Though lacking most relevant knowledge about all those policy domains which are to be re-structured towards the perspective to become the winner in global competition, the EU presents these global ambitious aims as the aim of a society governed by knowledge. Since the Commission admits that her decision to become a knowledge based society is based on no knowledge at all it becomes obvious that the policy agenda of the EU becoming a knowledge based society is neither governed by knowledge nor geared towards knowledge. The KBS is the ideological title for most ordinary and most ambitious global economic competitiveness governed by the most ordinary profit capitalistic calculation of companies and their shareholders, in which knowledge is one means among other calculation factors. It is though a crucial factor for those world regions like the EU, who announce via the aim to become the winner of global competition that they are trying *to set the terms of trade in global competition*. This is what the ideology of a KBS really means: the KBS is not only announcing that the EU wants to become the winner of global competition, but that the EU plans to dictate the conditions of global capitalism, namely the conditions of what economist call innovation based growth. Very consequently the very latest policy documents of the new Baroso Commission frankly considers the notions of economic competitiveness and the notion of a knowledge based society as simply the same thing.

Thus, a second conclusion can be drawn: the KBS presents a policy agenda re-shaping the totality of our social reality via a society governed by knowledge, which at the same time is lacking any knowledge about any aspect of the social reality as any knowledge about the vision the agenda is geared to. If it is obviously not knowledge that is governing the move towards the knowledge based society, what is really governing this totalitarian and imperial ideology? Most obviously, the means for restructuring the European societies towards knowledge based societies are not all kind of seminars for the European citizens on which KBS experts discuss the society model with the citizens. The introduction of a KBS has never been a subject for any bottom up decision process in which the citizens were involved. Rather the opposite is the case. Recent reforms of labour market policies across the EU, dealing with those who prove via the status of being unemployed in this knowledge based society their lacking employ-*abilities*, "persuade" European citizens rather with means economists usually call "economic incentives", than with knowledgeable arguments about the needs of a knowledge based society. How could they, since we have learned from the latest EU research programmes that they have only very recently become a subject of contemporary European social science research! The KBS is internally a rather violent society concept, which *sanctions* any deviations with deteriorating life qualities of its citizens instead of exchanging different views with the citizens.

Finally, a third ideological aspect of the EU as a knowledge based economy becomes apparent via the EU policy agenda and the research programme of the EU, putting this society concept into practise: namely European policy makers, strongly supported by political analysts complain frequently about the deterioration of the influence of the nation states in general and the lacking power of national policies intervening in a globalising world. Policies within the EU restructuring the social, economic and political life of EU citizens towards a knowledge based society are therefore usually presented as a *response* to globalisation.

It should be mentioned, that the policy agenda of the EU documented in the Lisbon summit presents the EU not at all as a powerless victim of the most powerful "global players"; the Lisbon strategy envisages the EU as a quite un-modest global super *power* not only interested in promoting nothing else but a "competitive and dynamic knowledge based economy". The policy agenda of the EU is exclusively directed to also re-shape the inner social life of the EU with all possible political and very powerful instruments of the EU policy bodies towards a service of its citizens for a competitive European economy to make the EU even the *winner* of globalisation. This is anything else, but the poor response of a powerless victim of globalisation.

The global competition rather appears to be the *result* also of EU policies as of other political entities promoting global competition. Presenting the potential winner of globalisation as a powerless victim of globalisation is another bizarre image about the knowledge based society vision. The EU is not a powerless victim of global economies, as they state mainly towards their citizens when confronting them with the requirements of a knowledge based society. The idea, that restructuring the inner life of the EU towards a knowledge based society as a unavoidable response to globalisation is obviously the third major ideology of the EU as a knowledge based society.

Thus, the policy agenda of the EU *"the most competitive and dynamic knowledge-based economy in the world..."* allows some general conclusions:

- the ideology of a knowledge based society circumscribes the strategic policy agenda of and for the EU in all EU policy domains directed towards global competition;

- the policy agenda to re-shape the EU towards the knowledge based society is not based on any substantial knowledge about the knowledge based society nor geared or even governed by knowledge;

- the knowledge based society is an ideological title for a society governed by the subordination of its citizens under the calculation criteria of capitalistic companies in global competition;

- the knowledge based society driven policy agenda is directing the totality of social, political and economic life in the EU towards making the EU a winner in global economic competition;

- the knowledge based society driven policy agenda presents the EU as a powerful political entity re-shaping the inner social life towards a EU serving a globally competitive economy;

- EU citizens are governed towards services for global competitiveness not via knowledge but the whole range of powerful political and economic instruments of European nation states;

- the EU policies re-shaping the social, political and economic life of European societies is not the response of a powerless victim of globalisations, but rather globalisation is the result of the very powerful EU-promotion of the global players in and for global competitiveness.

The E&T Cluster Project

The recent research programme for social sciences in FP 6 also expresses a remarkable concept of social science research: different from FP 5, in which the research agenda was phrased in a more open way allowing to interpret the aims of the research efforts by the research community research carried out under FP 6 is perceived as a service to carry out a given policy agenda, the implementation of the KBS in Europe.

Despite of this fundamental difference conceptualizing social science research and the interplay between a European research community and European policies the research agenda of the EU and the accordingly designed policy measures showed also already in FP 5 that the move of the EU towards a learning economy driven society concept also affected education and training in a very fundamental sense. And most importantly, regarding the discussions of changes needed in education and training policies, economists have also held a stronghold in the provision of new ideas about knowledge-related issues to the European Commission.

Both the political and scientific discourse in the EU about the "learning economy" as a guiding idea for shaping European policies in general as the discourse about education and training policies were already under FP 5 widely influenced by a group of "learning economists" engaged in EU-research, who had published their ideas in a booklet with the title "The globalising learning economy: Implications for innovation policy" (Lundvall, B.-A. (1997). The above research agenda of FP 6, designed after the publication of those economists views on the future of the EU as a learning economy, proves that even the wording of some research priorities appear to be almost copied from that booklet and thus also prove the actuality of this debate as the intervention into that discourse by the E&T Cluster project.

This book presents some outcomes of this E&T Cluster project with the title "Towards the Learning Economy—Conclusions from 4 and 5 FRP Projects to Shape European Policies in Education and Training", conducted under Framework Programme 5, "Accompanying Measures", funded by the European Commission.

The E&T Cluster project aimed to complement the conceptual schemes based on *economic* thoughts with ideas and research derived from *other social disciplinary domains* and approaches, such as sociology, psychology, educational studies or anthropology. While the latter may be less clear-cut and coherent for macroeconomic decisions, they offer a deeper understanding of the contents of policies influencing the micro economic and social dimensions. They were considered as important and critical contributions to the discourse about a knowledge economy concept, which by definition is populated by actors operating in idiosyncratic ways, at local levels, responding to specific cultural stimuli. They also offer perspectives beyond an economic understanding of learning that might be more adequate on the level of the learning actors.

Objectives of the E&T Project Cluster

The E&T Cluster project aimed to collect insights into how educational research conducted under the research programmes of the EU were in influenced by and responded to the rather economy driven discourses about the Learning Economy concept. Projects performed under FP 4 and 5 in the realm of education and training were selected for an interdisciplinary discourse between project partners. The objectives of the E&T Cluster were:

- to discuss the outcomes of 29 previous and current European socio-economic research projects in the field of education and training carried out under the European framework programmes 4 and 5 with respect to their contribution to the learning society debate;
- to initiate a European and international dialogue among different research disciplines related to the issue of learning in learning economies/learning societies;
- to critically review the scientific debate, concepts and research practice relating to issues of learning economies/learning societies;
- to contribute to the dialogue among practitioners and policymakers about the future model of the EU as a learning society or learning economy.

Thematic Domains of the E&T Project Cluster

As mentioned before, in the context of European research the notion of the "learning economy" was elaborated upon and propagated by Lundvall & Borras (1997), Lundvall (1997), and Archibugi and Lundvall (2001). The learning economy concept is "based on the hypothesis that during the last decades an acceleration of both knowledge creation and knowledge destruction has taken place. Individuals as well as firms need to reconstruct their competences more often than before, because the problems they face change more rapidly than before. Therefore, what constitutes success is not so much having access to a stock of knowledge. They key to success is, rather, rapid learning and forgetting." (Lundvall 1997)

According to this theory, in a fast changing environment the acquisitions and transfer of knowledge gains crucial importance. Information and communication technologies enable the convenient storage, retrieval and transfer of information at low costs, and worldwide. In the light of easy availability of information, competitive advantage of individuals and companies increasingly rests on *tacit* knowledge. In contrast to codified knowledge, tacit knowledge signifies person-bound knowledge which cannot easily be digitalised. Tacit knowledge (know-how, and know-who) is thus not immediately transferable and remain rooted in specific organisations and locations.

From this viewpoint, the competitive advantage of enterprises depends on the effective uses of (i) explicit knowledge, especially through the exploitation of opportunities offered by new information and communication technologies and infrastructures, and of (ii) tacit knowledge, in terms of facilitation of organisational learning processes and continuous rebuilding both of skills of individual and of firm technological and organisational competencies (European Commission, 1999). Regarding these challenges, the 'learning organisation' appears as the ideal model of such an organisation that is continuously improving itself on the basis of the (both tacit and explicit) knowledge of its members. 'Learning organisations' can thus be regarded as building blocks of a learning economy.

The *Thematic Domain 1"Knowledge and Competencies in the Learning Economies"* of the Cluster therefore investigated concepts of knowledge and competences with special regard to the practice of learning organisations.

Thematic Domain 1 looked at:

- the ways in which the integration of tacit knowledge and explicit knowledge is the basis of learning processes that create competitive advantages and new levels of effectiveness for organisations;
- the ways in which Human Resource Development practices can be based on emerging concepts of knowledge at work;
- how the new meanings of knowledge should be taken into account by educationalists and decision makers in E&T;
- which methods are the most suitable for identifying and valorising the knowledge contents of competencies in organisational and territorial contexts.

However, learning is not restricted to educational or organisational contexts only. In a learning economy or society learning becomes the all pervasive, governing principle of a society. Whereas Lundvall (1997) defines learning as "the acquisition of competences and skills that make the learning agent—be it an individual or an organisation—more successful in pursuing his/its goals", a more general concept of learning seems to be needed that transcends the limits of (rational) goal orientation. If lifelong learning becomes reality, an increasing number of people of all age groups will engage in learning activities. The learning society vision therefore not only demands to develop new knowledge and competences, but also to develop new concepts of learning and new teaching methods. ICT increasingly plays a role in innovative learning environments. E-learning opens up possibilities for flexible, self-organised learning that follows the aims and agenda of the learner rather than that of the teacher. ICT provide easier access to learning opportunities, especially at work places and facilitates lifelong learning. Reflecting this important role of ICT, the Thematic domain 2 of the Cluster addressed new roles of learning and ICT in the learning society.

The *Thematic Domain 2 "Learning and Information and Communication Technologies (ICT)",* asked:

- how can ICT support and stimulate learning in the new economy
- what kinds of software are needed, and what is a suitable software development strategy for the European Union
- how can ICT based learning environments be implemented in education and training
- what are the important competencies for the new economy that can be promoted with the help of ICT and how these can be assessed.

Globalisation, changed forms of organisations, and the arrival of ICT have resulted in changes of biographies, living conditions and life plans of individuals. Facing the challenges of a highly competitive labour market, learning becomes mandatory in order not to be marginalized or "socially excluded". In a learning society, people have to acquire a learning attitude to life, reconstructing their competences in the face of ever changing requirements (Lundvall 1997). In the Thematic Domain 3 the Cluster therefore investigated the position of the learning citizen, thus recognizing the "pivotal role of the individual in the construction of the learning society" (European Commission, White paper on education and training 1995, p. 7).

Under *Thematic Domain 3 "Living, Working and Learning in the Learning Society—the Perspective of the Learning Citizen"* the following questions were raised:

- what concepts of learning, working and subjectivity are used in FP projects?
- what is the concept of the learning citizen, how is he/she addressed by research projects?
- is the learning society becoming a reality for people, and in which respect?

E&T Cluster activities

E&T Cluster has conducted its work through discourses among European scholars along those three thematic domains and their research topics.

The domains were worked upon over five thematic workshops in which representatives of FRP-projects participated together with external European and other international experts, who discussed in a dialogistic evaluation along a set of prepared Leitfragen and presentations the major concepts and theories used in educational research projects.

Focus topics discussed at the five workshops were:

- "Learning in the Learning Economies"
- "Knowledge and Competencies in the Learning Economy"
- "Learning and ICT in the Learning Economy/Learning Society"
- "Living, working and learning in the Learning Society—the perspective of the learning citizen in EU funded research"
- "Educational Research in the European Research Area—the Learning Society in European Research".

Overview of this book

The book does not present a complete picture about the numerous papers presented on the five project workshops. It selects some major contributions, underpinning the need to reflect the concept of a learning society from the perspective of the European learning citizen.

The book is divided in three main sections. After presenting some background information about the E&T Cluster project in chapter 1 section 1 discusses the issues of "Conceptualizing the LS: Knowledge, Learning and Subjects". This section reflects on the underlying ore declared concepts of knowledge, learning and subjectivity as they are articulated in EU educational research projects.

In this section 1 chapter 2 "The 'learning economy'—the Theoretical Domestication of Knowledge and Learning for Global Competition" by Michael Kuhn presents some critical reflections about the fundamental concepts of knowledge in the learning economy approach on which the knowledge based society or similar society models are based.

Chapter 3 "Concepts of Knowledge and Learning in Findings of FRP 4 and 5 Projects" by Ronald Sultana considers the ways in which learning in European educational research projects has been re-interpreted towards a 'moral imperative' and how knowledge is equated with 'competence' and 'skills', where instrumentalist or performative knowledge' is privileged to serve the needs of an rather one dimensional economistically interpreted learning society approach.

Referring to the Foucault distinction of subjects in the double sense both of bodies of knowledge and subjectivities chapter 4 titled "Intellectual Technologies in the Constitution of Learning Societies" by Richard Edwards looks at the multiple meanings of 'subject' and 'discipline' used in EU- educational research projects. The concept of subjects and their according location in certain disciplines shows a lack of reflexivity in the policy focused research in this area either adopted through choice and disciplinary affiliation or through contractual compliance to those who fund research.

Section 2 is devoted to the issue of "Learning in a working context". Chapter 5 "Knowledge, Learning and Competencies in Organisations: Lessons from Projects Under 4TH and 5TH Framework Programmes", by Massimo Tomassini is looking at the organisational dimension of knowledge and learning. This is crucial in the learning economy for assuring learning and cooperation in informal organisational and inter-organisational settings. Chapter 6 "The Knowledge Economy, Work Process Knowledge and the Learning Citizen—Central but Vulnerable", by Nick Boreham, critiques the opposition between binary knowledge concepts which are equally problematic and reinforce the separation of school and workplace in the formation of vocational competencies. Boreham suggests a conceptualization of work-based knowing as a socio-cultural activity—one in which 'knowledge' and 'learning' are constitutive of the work process itself and which allows creating and sharing knowledge as a potentially conflictual activity. After looking at the paradigmatic assumptions and purposes of the learning economy agenda applied in particular to its implications for work and workers conceiving work as solely or principally economic utility, chapter 7, "Work and Workers in the Learning Economy: Conceptions, Critique, Implications" by Catherine Casey, analyses the extent to which and how educational research projects apply the paradigmatic assumptions of the neo liberal learning economy approach to the world of work, workers and work related learning. Based on the findings of the project "Vocational Identity, Flexibility and Mobility in the European Labour Market (FAME)" chapter 8 "The Subject and Work Related Identity" by Gabriele Laske reflects on the problems of identity formation of workers responding to both flexible and changing working conditions and to an increasing mobility and how employees respond, adjust or refuse to meet these identity formation demands of workers.

Section 3 discusses ICT and Learning and the manner in which European educational research projects reflect on new roles for ICT within education, in work contexts and outside of those two. Chapter 9 "Learning and ICT in the Learning Economy / Learning Society" by P. Robert-Jan Simons presents reflections about new conceptions of learning and knowledge in a learning society approach, the role of ICT within education, ICT and complex learning environments in and between organisations, about ICT outside of education and work and finally about the interplay of ICT and collective learning. Chapter 10, written by M. Beatrice Ligorio, "Computer Supported Collaborative Learning (CSCL) contributions to the E-Learning economy" presents some reflection about how artifacts can promote collaborative learning. Considering learning as a collaborative activity, learning is no longer seen as reproduction of knowledge only. Instead, new views of learning emphasize deeper processing of knowledge are discussed along the findings of three EU funded research projects in this chapter. Finally, Chapter 11 "Developing Synergies among Researchers and Teachers to Support ICT-related School Teaching and Learning Innovations" by Andreas Kollias and Kathy Kikis present consideration which should strengthen links, collaboration and develop shared understanding and action among teachers and researchers in the design, implementation and further utilisation of pedagogic innovations with the use of information and communication technologies. The ideas discussed here result from the Sypredem project[1] and from a number of research and development projects on ICTs-related innovations in the field of education and training. They are also based on experience gleaned from collaboration between research institutes, universities, schools, teachers and students from several EU countries.

As the discourse about the KBS is divided in views opposing the KBS vision or promoting its implementation this book is also divided in chapters which more or less advocate the ideas of a KBS and those which critique the vision about a society model instrumentalizing knowledge and citizens for global competition. It must though be mentioned that also those chapters, which rather discuss ways to implement the concept of a "knowledge based economy" also criticize an economic reductionism of a economy model, in which major aspects even of citizenship are reduced to economic functionalism—and thus do not even function within the reduced world of economics!

Note

1. Sypredem: Synergy between Practitioners' needs and opportunities, Research orientations and Decision Making on the usage of ICT in primary and secondary education. See http://promitheas.iacm.forth.gr/sypredem.

References

Archibugi, D. & Lundvall, B.-A. (eds.) (2001). The Globalizing Learning Economy. Oxford: Oxford University Press.

European Commission (1995) *White paper. Teaching and Learning: Towards the Learning Society*. Web document.

European Commission (1997) *Towards a Europe of Knowledge-Commission outlines action on education and training*. Web document.

European Commission (2000) *A Memorandum on Lifelong Learning*. Web document.

European Commission (2000) *Presidency Conclusions of the Lisbon European Council* . Web document.

European Commission (2002) FP 6 Integrating Programme. Priority 7: Citizens and Governance in a knowledge based society. Web document.

European Commission (2005), Communication to the Spring European Council,

Working together for growth and jobs, A new start for the Lisbon Strategy, Web document

Lundvall, B.-A. (1997). The globalising learning economy: Implications for innovation policy. Luxembourg, Publication of the European Communities.

1

Conceptualizing the Learning Society: Knowledge, Learning and Subjects

CHAPTER TWO

The 'Learning Economy'—The Theoretical Domestication of Knowledge and Learning for Global Competition

MICHAEL KUHN

'So far it is only in science fiction that mad criminals manage to get physical control of the brains of eminent scientists.' — Lundvall, B.-A, Borras, 1999, 46

Introduction:
Discovering knowledge as an issue for economic theory

In the field of social research it can meanwhile be taken as common sense that knowledge and learning are constitutive aspects of any variation of so called post-modern societies. These may be 'post industrial', 'knowledge-based economies', 'learning societies' or 'information societies':

> 'A knowledge driven economy is one in which the generation and the exploitation of knowledge has come to play the predominant part in the creation of wealth... It is argued that the knowledge economy is different from the traditional industrial economy because knowledge is fundamentally different from other commodities, and that these differences, consequently, have fundamental implications both for public policy and for the mode of organisation of a knowledge economy.' Joseph Stiglitz (1999), for instance, suggests, the 'movement to the knowledge economy necessitates a rethinking of economic fundamentals because, he maintains, knowledge is different from other goods in that it shares many of the properties of a global public good.' (Peters, 2004, 2)

Re-thinking economic fundamentals is not only the response of the economists' academic community, committed to the ideas of a 'learning economy' in a globalizing world. The ideas of the 'knowledge-based economy' have also become the foundation for designing the strategic aims of the policy agenda of the European Union making Europe *'the most competitive and dynamic knowledge-based economy in the world'*. (European Commission, 2000).

Although other countries do not devote such importance to the concept of a learning economy in their policy programmes, the ideas of a learning economy or a learning society also play a major role in the policy agendas of at least most EU countries.[1]

The question about the extent to which the policy agendas either of the European Commission or of European countries have been influenced by the academic learning economy discourse is not such an issue here. However, many topics of the social research agenda in 'Priority 7' of FP 6 sometimes appear to be phrased word for word along the theories of the 'learning economy'.

More important is the fact that both the policy and the research agendas of European policies are based on the same set of economic fundamentals, namely on a new conceptualization knowledge and learning and their dominating role in designing policy strategies.

The purpose of this paper is not to discuss the different post modern society models. However, it should be mentioned that unlike Bell's 'post-industrial society' or Toffler's 'information society' (and his successors Drucker 1993, Castells 1989 etc), who as so many others derive their society models from technological change, the concept of the 'knowledge-based economy' (KBE) as the seemingly broader notion of the learning society or knowledge-based society (KBS) motivate their reflections about a fundamental change. This justifies nothing less but the appearance of a new society model or at least a new economy type, not in relation to technology but in relation to a *social* phenomenon. This is noteworthy for two reasons: The idea to construct the immaculate appearance of a subject-less and aimless technology which creates its subjects and aims to serve the requirements of the deus ex machina revealed its ideological purposes too obviously for many social scientists. Thus, by eliminating any societal conflicts of previous theories and allowing the construction of a harmonic society united in serving technology constraints, mainly post-marxist Sociologists warned of the 'risks' (Beck, 1992), or a 'legitimacy crisis' (Habermas, 1996) of such purely technology based society models and the policy models supervising those 'risky' social constructs.

In fact, the knowledge-based models are different in this respect. They do not only motivate the occurrence of a new economy or society model through fundamental changes of the social phenomena 'knowledge', which is—on top of this—*the* distinctive characteristic of human beings; the idea that knowledge and learning are governing the economy and society as a whole and thus the life of mankind within this emerging society clearly sounds most appealing, not only for the social scientist.

Economists, habitually state that 'scarcity' rules our lives of ever increasing productivity and periodically dumped, overproduced goods and that we need to limit our demands for what is left. In this instance, the same professional sceptic and ever warning thinkers present us with a concise vision of an economy in which knowledge and learning—maybe even wisdom—is governing the world of work, society and—according to their hypothesise— even politics. The harmony of this society vision is not disrupted by social conflicts between classes, warnings about the ever existing risks of economic growth, or the ambiguities of political power.

Not surprisingly, social scientists from other disciplines are also attracted by this rather unusual economistic view. This view has not only borrowed knowledge as the key term of human related sciences but has also put knowledge into the centre of economic reflections, which usually deal with less sophisticated and more materialistic matters. It is no surprise that many social research disciplines feel impelled to contribute various reflections based on their re-definition of knowledge and learning. Economists who have set agendas in European social science research in this manner are offered knowledge contributions from other social disciplines in response to the questions raised through the introduction of new society models, despite the fact that they are supposed to be constructed by knowledge.

Not surprisingly, disciplines which claim the issues of knowledge and more specifically learning as their inherited disciplinary topic are flattered by the economists' new-found attention and devotion to knowledge, which to the humanistic mindset of education researchers has always dominated human lives.

The prominent role that knowledge is playing in new society models is more or less being welcomed by all concerned. This is illustrated by Stigglitz with his quote from Peters, stating that knowledge now constitutes a new era known as the 'knowledge-based economy'. And, as we heard before, this '...movement to the knowledge economy necessitates a rethinking of economic fundamentals' (Peters, 2004, 2)

So far, knowledge-based economy or society models have not attracted any fundamental critiques comparable to the technology driven predeceasing new society models. In fact, rather the opposite is the case: The economic re-definitions of knowledge and learning have invaded the category systems of most social sciences.

Notwithstanding the major appreciations of the economic re-definitions of knowledge and learning, a critique also exists. But this critique neither really manages to question the rationale of the learning economy, nor to substantially critique their re-definitions of knowledge and learning. It also seems as if so much appreciation for knowledge and learning by economists, (who normally prefer to talk about hard fact and figures, their ups and downs, relations and quotients—as required by the economy as their research objectives—and who tend to disregard or even discredit other social sciences as purely normative and speculative), who suddenly discover knowledge and learning as a relevant topic for economic reflections, succeed in irritating social scientists. The critique of the learning economy, namely of their concepts of knowledge is strikingly silent and rather poor.

One critical attempt does not even try to seriously disprove the rationale of a learning economy, namely their rationale of knowledge and learning. Instead it simply reveals their thoughts as a 'free floating utopia' that 'degenerates into an ideology' (Rikowski, G, 225, 226). However, if ideologies are not critiqued by disproving their arguments and purely rejected as ideology, this critique is scientifically no better than any ideology, whatever their political intentions and motivations might be.

The second major approach to critique the knowledge-based or learning economy, preferably but not exclusively practised among economists, is to prove that knowledge and learning empirically do not play that dominant role as implied in the notion of that theory. (See Hirsch- Kreiensen, 2003). Methodologically, such a critique is somewhat bizarre, as it finally shares what it pretends to critique. Is the statement about a fundamental new role of knowledge in globalising economies true dependent on the number of companies practising that economy model? If this is their critique about the learning economy, then they admit that it *is* the case, where it is the *case*. Is it their critique, that the learning economy ideas are correctly analysing the role of economies and knowledge, but just not everywhere? What then is the critique of the learning economy, if it is correct, but only here and there? In fact, what Learning Economists even explicitly claim (Lundvall, B.-A, Borras, *1999, p 35)* is that the statements of learning economists is not to say that the majority of industries are dominated by knowledge or are based on 'knowledge intensive' industries or work places. They do state that knowledge and learning principally play a new role in today's post industrial economies, regardless of the extent to which the production process is knowledge intensive or not. In that case the role of knowledge is less relevant and consequently leads learning economist to the conclusion that they are still old industrial production processes and on their way towards their knowledge-based economy. Their statement is not about an extended role of knowledge, which could be measured along any units of knowledge spreads; their statement is about a 'fundamentally' new role of knowledge and this, and only this principally new role of knowledge 'in a globalising economy' makes it—according to the learning economists—necessary to state that globalizing economies are based on knowledge. Such a statement cannot be disproved by counting the number of knowledge intensive jobs. It can only be disproved via reflecting if their rationale about the fundamental role of knowledge in that economy approach is consistent or not.

This discussion about knowledge and learning appreciated by economists might also show that the appreciations learning economists devote to knowledge and learning *is* an appreciation for knowledge and learning: But which knowledge and which learning? Appreciating knowledge and learning as such, namely by social sciences, might also be an ideology, and lead to that silence or rather naïve critique of the learning economy among social sciences.

These economic redefinitions of knowledge and learning, which constitute new economy as[2] society models, are the subject of this chapter's consideration.

Re-thinking knowledge for the knowledge-based economy: Tacit and codified knowledge

The re-thinking of knowledge as fundamental in the rationale for a learning or knowledge-based economy is based on a discourse about the category set 'tacit' and 'codified' knowledge. Since those terms have been introduced into the social sciences by Polanyi (Polanyi, M., 1962) as part of a 'spiral of knowledge' and then applied to the context of organisation development by Nonaka and Takeuchi they have attracted enormous attention, mostly from sociologists. There is hardly any paper today namely in the realm of European socio-economic research that does not positively refer to the distinction of these two knowledge types. As Neuweg (Neuweg, G.H., 2001, 139) rightly mentions, the concept of 'tacit knowledge' was only scantly used by Polanyi. He preferred to talk about 'tacit knowing' and his reflections are focused on a theory of thinking rather than of knowledge. More importantly Neuweg also rightly stresses that Polanyi's version of implicit knowledge has been widely misinterpreted towards a diminishing, if not discriminating role of explicit or codified knowledge and- strange enough - even more of scientific knowledge. As we will see, learning economists not only also prioritise tacit knowledge. Due to their interest in new knowledge for innovations, they implicitly also disvalue if not discredit scientific knowledge even in the realm of science and technology in a very principle sense, if it does not contribute to their agenda of continuous innovation, while promoting a knowledge-based economy. It would be worthwhile tracing how and why Polanyi's reflections about implicit knowledge have been misinterpreted as undervaluing any forms of explicit or codified knowledge. This might be in fact due to the economic perspective looking at knowledge as an ingredient of 'change', in which last but not least only 'new' knowledge counts. This is the view on knowledge of theories not only in micro-economic contexts, namely organisational theories. Interestingly enough, this is also the case in the more macro-economists' re-thinking of knowledge as a rationale for a new economy, which is explicitly based on those two Polanyi's forms of the knowledge.

Anyway, as we shall in fact see in due course, the discourse among learning economists about tacit and codified knowledge does not really discuss the two Polanyi's terms. These terms are rather misinterpreted for their macro-economistic re-interpretations of knowledge in the context of re-thinking economic fundamentals, justifying the emergence of the learning economy and the need for political interventions in knowledge and learning arising from this new economy model.

As shall soon become apparent, they also put a certain preference on tacit knowledge and disvalue the codified knowledge components. This will also shed some light on the above question as to *why* the rationale for a society or economy based on knowledge tends to undervalue codified knowledge components, including scientific knowledge.[3]

Especially in the context of European socio-economic research the ideas of the fundamentally new 'learning economy model' and the justification of political actions for the sake of a learning economy is the work of a group around Lundvall and Borras. This work is based upon contributions from seven projects under the TSER programme, published in a booklet entitled 'The globalizing learning economy: Implications for innovation policy' *(Lundvall, B.-A, Borras, 1999)*. These reflections focused on European innovation policies for global competitiveness have widely influenced the European scientific discourses as the formation and design of policy strategies in the European Union.[4] The Lisbon declaration and the research priorities of FRP 6 document the influence that those ideas have on designing European policies in general and on research policies in particular.

Although investigations into the extent and ways in which the learning economy approaches has influenced the practice of European socio-economic research were worth it to be carry out, it is certainly not an exaggeration to say that the European agenda for socio-economic research of the major European research programme is almost exclusively devoted to issues related to the idea of the 'Citizens and Governance in a Knowledge-based Society' (European Commission, http://fp6).

Reflecting on the economic fundamental re-thinking of knowledge and learning also seems to be of some importance since generations of European social research programmes and projects—especially those in the in the realm of learning and education—widely refer to this category duo in a positive manner. Last but not least, the more sociological interpretations of tacit and codified knowledge also play a major role in the twin concept of the learning economy, the vision of a learning society.[5]

This chapter though neither discusses the influence of the learning economy ideas on the European research, the overall policy agenda, nor how European research has been affected by the ideas of this economy concept. This is the case in several of the following other chapters in this volume. In this chapter we just focus on some aspects of re-thinking the fundamentals of economic theory, justifying the emergence of an economy model that is—according to this approach—based on a new role of knowledge and learning and is called after these terms.

After this introduction, in the second section of this chapter the reflections are focused on the fundamentally new thoughts about tacit and codified knowledge reasoning the learning economy concept. In the first part of the following section 3 we discuss the political conclusions drawn by the learning economists from the distinction about tacit and codified knowledge, advocating political interventions in knowledge and learning for the sake of the learning economy. In the second part of section 3 the conceptualisations of knowledge and learning implied in the policy agenda of the learning economy approach are reflected. Finally, in section 4 we discuss what these learning economies concepts of knowledge and learning and the policies related to knowledge and learning imply for European citizens.

Tacit and codified knowledge

> 'When discussing the role of knowledge and knowledge production in economic activity it is important to distinguish between tacit and codified knowledge.' (ibid, 31)

What is this distinction between these two knowledge types and why is this distinction important?

Tacit knowledge. The most common interpretation about the major difference between tacit and codified knowledge is that codified knowledge is transferable, tacit knowledge is not, or is not 'easily' transferable.

> 'In contrast to codified knowledge, tacit knowledge... cannot be easily transferred because it has not been stated in an explicit form. One important type of knowledge is skill' (ibid, 31)

Since numerous social researchers seem to share both the distinction of those two knowledge types and the notion that tacit knowledge, different from codified knowledge, cannot be transferred easily, it would be worth it to discuss the issue of transferring knowledge and what are the problems transferring knowledge at this point. In fact, one could raise the question, if it was the case that for example skills—an important variation of tacit knowledge —could not be 'easily' transferred, how did mankind manage to survive? One could also discuss the question: What is the problem about tacit knowledge if the trainer trains his trainee the knowledge the trainer owns as his tacit knowledge? Or better: The fact that the trainer has tacit knowledge that the trainees does not have, is the point of departure for any learning; if it was already the trainees knowledge, why should the trainer 'transfer' his tacit knowledge to a trainee? Moreover: If it was true, that tacit knowledge cannot be easily transferred, how could we even face a knowledge-based economy or society today, if that was so difficult to 'transfer' tacit knowledge?

Ironically one could also add, that fortunately the idea if tacit knowledge is not only the tacit knowledge of the learning economists. Apparently, not only to economists the tacit knowledge about tacitness had been quite easily transmitted.

Elaborating on all these questions about tacit knowledge, the transferability of tacit knowledge, and any factors that make it difficult to transfer tacit knowledge, elaborating on them is an important issue. However, in the context of the learning economy rational this fundamental discussion does not make very much sense, since the first statement that knowledge cannot be transferred easily, is immediately followed by the second opposite statement about tacit knowledge.

Learning economist does not even make any attempt to explain which factors make the transferability of tacit knowledge easier or more difficult. But this seems not to be of any interest for an economy named after learning. Instead, we are told the sheer opposite about the transferability of tacit knowledge:

> '...tacit knowledge can be learnt ...tacit knowledge can be shared through interaction
> and co-operation... Interactive learning is the key to sharing tacit knowledge.'
> (ibid, 46)

This is somewhat confusing: Firstly, we were told, in contrast to codified knowledge, tacit knowledge is not easily transferable; now we are told that it 'can be learnt' or 'shared' through 'interactive learning'. But is learning not by its nature 'interactive' and is interactive learning not the most normal, or even the only possible way to 'transfer' knowledge? What is the problem with tacit knowledge? Who does not want to say that learning of any knowledge is 'not easy'? Learning is learning and always requires some intellectual 'loops', as not only pedagogies know. (Argyris G., Schoen D. A., 1978).

Any *learning* is 'not easy' and any knowledge must be acquired, because the learner does not have it, so it needs to be 'transferred'. However, any difficulty to acquire any knowledge is not a matter of the nature of knowledge but dependent on various components, which determine the process of learning and the learning subject. To conclude from the fact that learning certain knowledge might not be not easy for certain learning subjects that this is due to the specific nature of the learned knowledge, can be easily disproved by the fact that learning the same knowledge *is* easy for another learning subject. The difficulties to learn cannot be devoted to the *object* of learning, the learned knowledge, be it 'easy' or not, but are a matter of the components of learning and the learning subject. The difficulties to acquire knowledge are not dependent on a type of knowledge, but on the various components, which constitute the preconditions for the process of learning or for the learning subject. Although 'information' can be easily transmitted, it is not 'easy' to learn through the process of their transmission. This is also dependent upon the components of learning, not on the quality of information nor the substance of what is learnt.

However, according to the re-thinking of economic fundamentals there seems to be serious cases, in which tacit knowledge cannot even 'not easily' be shared via learning:

> 'Basically, knowledge remains tacit if it is complex or variable in quality: in situations where several different human senses need to be used at the same time, when skilful physical behaviour is involved and understanding social relationship is crucial.' (ibid, 14)

This statement about tacit knowledge consists of one obvious contradiction in adjecto: Thanks to the fact that the re-thinking of economic fundamentals is not as complex and variable in quality, it does not permanently 'remain' the tacit knowledge of learning economists. It thus can be easily transferred and it does not even require 'several human senses' to realize that this statement about knowledge is disproving itself, whatever the 'social relationships' might be.

If the tacitness of knowledge is the same as its non-transfer-ability, then it would remain tacit, if it is tacit and could not be transferred. Or if it is the case that it can only be 'not easily' transferred, then it does no longer make any sense to any further discuss a categorical distinction of tacit and codified knowledge along their abilities to be transferred, if after all both knowledge types can be transferred more or less easily. Distinguishing different categories of knowledge due to different levels of difficulties in the process of the acquisition of knowledge does not make any sense. Logically, the relations of the learning subject to the object of learning cannot justify the creation of distinctive features of the object of learning.

The secret of the economic considerations about tacit knowledge and its transferability is that the learning economist does not really talk about learning nor about knowledge, not to mention certain Polanyi's knowledge types and its characteristics, when they talk about 'transmitting' knowledge and when they reason the transmission difficulties with the quality of tacitness. When they talk about transmitting knowledge, they do not talk about transferring knowledge via learning, but about economic transmission forms of knowledge and they try to prove that the concept of tacit knowledge is responsible for *economic* knowledge transfer problems, which are in fact not at all easy, as we will see later.

In fact, after discussing the economic interpretations of the sister category 'codified knowledge', we will find out why the economist equals tacit knowledge with 'not easily' transferable knowledge and why the notion of transferable knowledge in the rational of economists has nothing much to do neither with learning nor with knowledge, nor with tacit or codified knowledge.

We now examine what economists try to 'transfer' to the reader about codified knowledge.

Codified knowledge. After discussing the distinction between the two knowledge types not in terms of their characteristic forms of knowledge and what distinguishes them as different ways of knowing, but in terms of their different transfer-abilities, it is hardly surprising that codified knowledge, the other sub-specie of these new concepts of knowledge which forms the basis of the new learning economy, is the sheer opposite of its sister category, tacit knowledge:

> 'Codified knowledge can normally be transferred over long distances and across organisational boundaries' (ibid, 31)

Discussing the transferability of knowledge, in this case of codified knowledge as a matter of transfer over distances and over 'organisational boundaries' reveals that Lundvall/Borras are not really discussing the knowledge transfer or the knowledge transfer difficulties of two kinds of knowledge via learning.

What they do discuss under the labels of tacit and codified knowledge is the transfer of knowledge in the economic sense of buying and commanding knowledge. With this in mind distances and organisational boundaries do play a role for that kind of knowledge transfer. With this meaning of transfer in mind they equal the Polnyia's *categorical* distinction of tacit and codified knowledge as grades of difficulties to transfer knowledge, trying to prove that the economic knowledge transfer problems to buy knowledge originate from (the Polnanyia's) knowledge features. With this in mind, they can also equate knowledge with information: 'codified knowledge may be equated to information...' (ibid, 45)

In fact, both transferring knowledge and information economically contains the same *economic problems* and in this respect knowledge and information are the same. However, this has nothing to do neither with information nor with knowledge, but a lot with buying knowledge as buying information. And this is also why it is no problem for learning economists 'to take the extreme case, the phone book', while they discuss the philosophical terms tacit and codified knowledge! In fact, this is an extreme case, proving how little learning economists know about knowledge.

Given this view on knowledge transfer as buying and selling knowledge, as knowledge that can be 'bought from the shelf' (ibid, 46) or not, they can ultimately 'easily' ignore any distinctive knowledge attributes. From that *economic* point of view the distinction between knowledge and information does not really matter as does the distinction between tacit and codified knowledge.

Consequently, the distinction between tacit and codified knowledge and their transferability introduced to us as most important and fundamental distinctions for the rationale of the learning economy is more and more blurring. The 'fundamental' re-definitions of knowledge to justify a knowledge-based or learning economy finally vanish. After we had been told, that in contrast to tacit knowledge, codified knowledge can be 'normally transferred' (ibid, 31), we are now told:

> 'Most codes relating to science, technology and innovation can only be decoded by experts who have already invested heavily in learning the codes' (ibid, 33)

In other words, to decode—a precondition to be transferred—codified knowledge, tacit knowledge about codified knowledge is required. A really bizarre catch 22 logic: Not or at least 'not easily' transferable knowledge (tacit) is the precondition to transfer transferable knowledge (codified).

The fact that we have been lead by the learning economists towards a completed circle of their economic fundamentals reasoning an economy based on knowledge is frankly acknowledged by them:

> 'In fact, the clear distinction made above between tacit and codified knowledge my be misleading in some regards' (ibid, 33)

With a determined opening line: 'in fact', they let us know that they are not irritated by their conclusions. Instead, they make the reader believe, that he should not have trusted the distinction made at the beginning and that it was the readers misunderstanding to arrive at these un-resolvable contradictory concepts of knowledge.

However, the definitions of tacit and codified knowledge as being both 'conditional' and 'exclusive' is an inconsistent theory, in not only 'some', but in all regards. They do not reveal, why they firstly mislead the reader by making that clear distinction although it seems not to be clear at all. Instead, they invite us to a remarkable way out of their contradictory knowledge theory.

The way out of the theoretical mess is as striking as the way they admit that they have lead the reader into the confusion. We are now informed that tacit and codified knowledge must not only be distinguished, but that their exclusive and conditional attributes are what they are:

'...codified and tacit knowledge are complementary and co-exist in time.' (ibid, 33)

Complementarity and, to a greater extent, co-existence are certainly ideas, promising peaceful and neat relationships. They also somehow express the intention of the authors to get rid of the mess of their contradictory theory in which they now find themselves. However, co-existence does not bring us any further since the substance of what co-exists extinguishes the difference between the co-existing knowledge types. 'Time' might heal many things, but does not heal the contradiction of distinctive attributes of something of which the opposite attributes are a precondition to achieve what that something is!

If it is—as we remember—firstly 'important to distinguish... when discussing the role of knowledge and knowledge production in economic activity' (ibid, 31) between tacit and codified knowledge; if secondly tacit knowledge is the precondition to decode codified knowledge and codified knowledge the precondition to transfer tacit knowledge, then we end up in this contradictory mess of our re-thinking of the fundamentals of the learning economy—whatever dialectic logic, the learning economists might call for help.

Nevertheless, this is not at all a problem for the learning economists: Their way out of the inconsistent theory about tacit and codified knowledge is to state that the theoretical contradictions at which we have arrived are not at all discrediting their re-thinking of economic fundamentals. Rather the opposite is the case: The reader is now lectured that this contradiction is not due to the learning economists thoughts about knowledge, but due to the nature of knowledge. Stating the contradicting interrelation of the conditional *and* exclusive attributes of tacit and codified knowledge as the complementary nature of knowledge, is in fact theoretically rather adventurous and certainly not a Polanyi's idea. The rationale of a new type of economy based on these contradicting interpretations of tacit and codified knowledge and all the economic and political strategies derived from this inconsistent theory is deemed politically rather irresponsible.

Before going towards the learning economists' calls for political intervention in knowledge and learning resolving his theoretical mess, some brief interim conclusions might be useful:

1. Any knowledge is 'transferable' due to its nature. Distinguishing between tacit and codified knowledge with regards to their transfer-abilities in the sense of acquiring or learning knowledge does not make any sense and ends in extinguishing the distinctive knowledge attributes of any knowledge type. Different levels of intellectual demands to acquire knowledge more or less easily are not an attribute of the knowledge, but a matter of the preconditions or attributes of the subject acquiring or learning knowledge.

2. Equalizing the acquisition of knowledge with economic modes of buying and commanding knowledge as knowledge transfer misinterprets tacit and codified knowledge as transferable and not transferable knowledge. The idea to conclude from the distinction of the two knowledge types as transferable and not, or not easily transferable knowledge, a fundamental shift towards a knowledge-based economy has nothing to do with the nature of knowledge, but with the problems occurring from the impossibility to buy knowledge *and* to subordinate knowledge under the command of the knowledge owner via buying. Through this act of buying knowledge, the knowledge owner is though not the knowledge holder and the knowledge owner is not interested in knowledge as such. His interest in knowledge is very conditional and instrumental. This clearly differs from the knowledge holder.

3. Deriving any economic or political conclusions, namely related to knowledge and learning from this inconsistent rationale for what is thus wrongly called a learning or—more recently—knowledge-based economy or knowledge-based society is theoretically un-reasoned and politically irresponsible and does not justify a political conclusion to intervene in knowledge and learning.

The conflicting natures of knowledge and goods

The problems implied in the economic transfer of knowledge attributed to the nature of two different types of knowledge have nothing to do with the nature of knowledge, as the learning economists want us make to believe. They have something to do with the conflicting nature of knowledge on one hand and using knowledge as economic goods or commodities in capitalistic economies on the other.

Since the economy interpretation of the distinction of tacit and codified knowledge along a transferability equalize the acquisition of knowledge with buying knowledge, the economic reflections about tacit and codified knowledge are accompanied by a second strand of considerations in the learning economy rationale. This is in order to reason the re-definition of economic fundamental towards a politically governed approach of a learning economy. As will soon become apparent these more explicit economic considerations are last but not least only introduced to arrive a second time at a new variation of the conflicting natures of knowledge and its economic use in a market economy. This time, the disobedience of knowledge to the rules of capitalism motivates the learning economists to call for political interventions to domesticate the resisting attributes of knowledge for serving the purposes of capitalistic economies.

The commodity codified knowledge. In contrast to the distinction between tacit and codified knowledge, where we started with an appreciation of tacit knowledge, the distinction between tacit and codified knowledge as economic goods starts with an economic appreciation of the commodity-codified knowledge.

> 'Codification is an important process for economic activity and development for four main reasons. Firstly, codification reduces some of the costs of the process of knowledge acquisition and technology dissemination.
> Secondly, through codification, knowledge is acquiring more and more the properties of a commodity.' (ibid, 32)

According to the learning economy approach, codified knowledge contains an attribute which allows that form of knowledge to freely enter the world of economic thinking, not entirely, but at least 'more and more'.

Knowledge, acquiring the 'properties' of a commodity is important, due to the fact that 'market transactions are facilitated by codification' (ibid, 32). In other words, in contrast to tacit knowledge, codified knowledge can be 'bought from the shelf' (ibid, 46). This even 'reduces some of the costs for knowledge acquisition and technology dissemination.' (ibid, 32)

One can read between the lines, the extent to which economists seem to wish there was only codified knowledge in the world of knowing; it acquires 'more and more' the attributes of a commodity, thus can be bought! In addition, buying *is* a mode of transferring knowledge that is also much closer to economic activities and economic 'eyes', than learning or acquiring knowledge. Above all, codified knowledge is inexpensive. Codified knowledge must be the perfect commodity! But—it is not! We remember, we were already warned by a relativating 'more and more': In fact, exactly these celebrating considerations about this almost perfect commodity and about the ideal transfer modalities of codified knowledge and finally the cheap price of codified knowledge, announces the arrival of a serious and disappointing problem. The pleasure in knowledge in its codified version does not last long, although it seems to provide only attractive attributes for economists. If it is cheap, everybody can afford it and it can be transferred and bought. And exactly the same positive attributes are at the same time precisely the problem of codified knowledge as a good:

> 'There are several reasons why codification does not have this major effect on the transferability of knowledge. The most fundamental one is the rapid rate of change. When the content of knowledge is changing rapidly it is only those who take part in its creation who can get access' (ibid, 34)

It does not make sense that only those who take part in its creation are supposed to gain access to codified knowledge. As we were told, accessibility of knowledge is the nature of codified knowledge. But, getting access to knowledge whilst it is being created is not getting access to codified knowledge, because it is not yet codified. That knowledge is—tacit knowledge! Not *yet,* codified knowledge is not codified knowledge, but tacit knowledge.

The intention to now discredit the just appreciated attributes of codified knowledge via a not outspoken comparison with tacit knowledge is quite obvious. Discrediting now a *market* effect of codified knowledge—though it can be bought and is cheap—does make sense for the learning economist, since —this is his implicit logic—the time it takes to codify knowledge does make it cheap, but for the very same reason also without any value for those who bought it. Why is this?

> 'It may be true that codification increases the possibility of transforming knowledge into a commodity, but the value of this commodity will be limited for all those who do not have the necessary basis for understanding and using the knowledge.' (ibid, 34)

'It may be true': One feels attempted to say, but if it now turns out to be not true, after we have been told all those positive factors about codified knowledge, why have we been told that it was true? Anyway, the problem associated with codified knowledge begins to get clearer: During the time it takes that knowledge acquires the status of a transferable commodity via its codification it looses it value. In other words, it is cheap; everybody can buy it. Thus, it *only* has value for those who took part in its *creation*. But again, is not that tacit knowledge and not codified knowledge? Exactly, one can 'easily' sense the discrete appearance of tacit knowledge—to compensate the negative aspects of codified knowledge: Does codified knowledge only acquire 'more and more' the attributes of a commodity if it is more and more, not codified, but tacit knowledge? One feels reminded of the previous methodological construct to resolve the problems of the rationale of a learning economy by attributing the contradictory *definitions* of the learning economy theory about the object knowledge to an attribute of the *object's nature*!

In fact, knowledge seems to be a true nightmare for economist reasoning a knowledge-based economy: Codified knowledge, almost achieving the attributes of a commodity only has a value—as long as it remains tacit!

Knowledge transfer and *thus* codified knowledge in the eyes of economists is a very ambiguous concept. It attributes knowledge an economic format, which makes it simpler for 'economic activities'. In other words, it can be bought. Buying knowledge in the format of a commodity—this the idea of economic thinking—allows to get hold of an economic ingredient, which is 'embodied in people' (ibid, 44). Despite the fact, that knowledge cannot be bought, but only created, acquired or learned, the economic construct of codified knowledge circumscribes the ideal knowledge to make knowledge available by economic means for economic activities in the market economy— at least for the market as a whole.

The nightmarish implication is that knowledge that can be bought has a value as a *commodity but no value as knowledge*, because it is not exclusively owned knowledge. If it can be bought, it can be owned by anybody. And knowledge that is 'cheap' is not at all a positive attribute but another word for its non-exclusive use and thus the positive attribute 'cheap' is transferred to the attribute of a low value. In fact, what counts in market economies for an *individual enterprise* is to own knowledge exclusively. Only this gives an advantage in competition compared to other competitors.

In other words, looking at the *economy as a whole*, codified knowledge allows an economic access to the knowledge embodied within human brains; looking at the driving forces in economic competition codification is of very limited value, limited to those who created that knowledge; in other words codified knowledge counts in this respect only—as long as it is: tacit!

The commodity tacit knowledge. What is it that qualifies tacit knowledge as the true value-able knowledge, although it cannot be bought and thus has no value, since it is 'a not tradable commodity'? (ibid, 46)

> 'The experts are outstanding in their field because they have skills and competencies that cannot be codified.... This tacit knowledge cannot be bought off the shelf and while the services of the expert can be bought it is difficult to prevent others from getting similar access to his or her skills.' (ibid, 46)

This quotation contains a couple of statements which provide some clarifications about the re-thinking of economic fundamentals in a knowledge-based economy.

Firstly, we now hear that the knowledge economists are preferably interested in the tacit knowledge of 'outstanding experts', which *cannot* be codified. The explicitly made conclusion that it cannot be 'easily transferred' since it cannot be codified, is not only no longer a problem, but is now even seen as an advantage, since it helps to get along with the difficulty 'to prevent others from getting similar access to his or her skills' (ibid, 46) and 'that the firm does not give too much away in terms of information to competitors.' (ibid, 50)

One can conclude as an interim summary, that the almost-commodity codified knowledge can be bought, but has no value, whereas tacit knowledge, which is not a tradable commodity, has value, although it cannot not be bought. The fact that it cannot be bought constitutes its value, since it almost guarantees exclusive ownership; ownership, not over the knowledge, but at least over the 'services of the experts'. (ibid, 46) Indeed: 'Incorporating knowledge into standard economic production functions is not an easy task' (OECD, ibid, 11)

However, this is not all about the not tradable, good tacit knowledge: Although *it is not* transferable, it is difficult *to prevent* the transfer, because— although the tacit knowledge *cannot* be bought—one can buy 'the services of an expert' (Lundval/Borras, 1997, ibid); this means that the ownership of knowledge remains in the experts' brain and that is why it is problematic to prevent others from getting hold of the exclusive ownership of knowledge. In other words: Transferable knowledge, even when it cannot be bought off the shelf, is a serious problem because the company pays for the services of the outstanding experts but the knowledge is still not under the control of the buying company:

> 'So far it is only in science fiction that mad criminals manage to get physical control of the brains of eminent scientists.' (ibid, 46)

One could almost hear the mental closeness between the rejected unrealistic dreams of the economists and the fictions of the 'mad criminals'. However, this would be the ideal knowledge-based economy world: Tacit knowledge, although not tradable, but accessible by buying the service of the knowledge expert and managing to exclusively own the knowledge compared to other competitors! This is a dream—but only a dream.

However, economists are no dreamers and admit that the idea of harmonising the nature of knowledge and commodities and to re-interpret knowledge for its fundamental role in a knowledge-based market economies is a true disaster:

- If it has any value, then it should be kept for the exclusive use of a competitor;
- this is difficult enough, because one competitor can buy the service of the experts, but the knowledge is still in his brain, under his control. Who knows if he might misuse his control and sell his knowledge via a discrete means to a competitor?
- from the view of the market as a whole, the exclusive ownership of the services of the outstanding expert is a serious problem. This is due to the fact that his knowledge is under the exclusive ownership of one company and not available for the other competitors, it cannot be bought off the shelf by others;
- the transferability of codified knowledge makes it an economic good which can be bought from the shelf and makes it accessible for all competitors;
- but it has no value, since it cannot be owned exclusively;
- thus, it can be dumped as soon as it has acquired the status of a decent economic commodity!

One should add that the nature of knowledge and commodities are indeed conflicting concepts: Knowledge means sharing—not owning; knowledge is a social item—goods are private items; 'goods' are owned—to not be shared; knowledge can be generated—but not bought. You do not buy goods that you produce; knowledge counts in substance—goods count in quantities; goods are replaceable by other goods—whereas knowledge is unique.

As contradicting as knowledge and goods are as contradicting are the according subjects involved in knowledge and business affairs: Knowledge holders compete about knowledge progress by exchanging knowledge; commodity holders exclude others from the knowledge they have. The nature of knowledge and the nature of the market economy are conflicting even in terms of the way representatives of knowledge—academics—on one hand and representatives of goods—business people—behave or present themselves in their opposing social habits of their according social communities:

> 'In general, honesty is fundamental for the quality and efficiency of academic knowledge production. If a professor systematically steals his/her colleagues' ideas and does not contribute his (her own ideas through open exchange in seminars he/she will be excluded from academic networks. It is obvious that the world of academia is where pure instrumentalistic behaviour does not pay.... On the other end of the scale there might be a company lawyer...His/her main concern will be that the firm does not give too much away in terms of information to the competitor.' (ibid, 50)

In fact, reflecting the 'interdependence between the globalisation process and the nature of knowledge creation and learning' (ibid, 31), Lundavall/ Borras are struggling with the opposing natures of knowledge and commodities and accordingly with the opposing 'social nature' (ibid, 30) of the knowledge and business communities, representing the business priorities in trading commodities on one hand and the non tradable knowledge on the other. They struggle with the fact that knowledge is not a commodity and does not obey the rules of the market, on either level of economic interactions. Knowledge defies the rules and objectives of economic competition both as a subject of 'inter-firm collaborations and industrial networks' (ibid, 30) and as a subject of 'functional integration and networking inside firms' (ibid, 30).

In the hand of economic competitors knowledge becomes only *one* ingredient of strategic capitalistic calculations among others. These calculations with knowledge conflict both with other competitors and with the interests of the 'outstanding experts':

1. Companies are interested in the exclusive ownership of outstanding knowledge—experts with outstanding knowledge are interested in exchanging their knowledge with other outstanding experts.
2. Companies create knowledge only in relation to the extent to which knowledge contributes to the companies' economic success—intellectual curiosity is attempted to cross the boarders of existing knowledge without limits.
3. Companies dump knowledge as knowledge products, if they do not promise to contribute to business for the sake of 'change'. 'Forgetting' knowledge and knowledge products is the major attribute of 'knowledge-based economies'—fostering and preserving knowledge is the subject of any scientist.

In addition, all subjects dealing with knowledge in market economies mirror the contradictive nature of knowledge and goods in their conflicting interests:

The individual capitalist is interested in buying the services of an expert, but that costs and it might not pay off because others might do the same or are quicker in either increasing the productivity of a given good or in producing a new product. But this only becomes apparent after the services have been purchased, so it is an insecure investment; the expert is not primarily interested in the profit of his employer, but in his salary, which increases the costs for his service and the risk factor for the company, as to whether his services will pay off or not. The service provider creates knowledge to increase knowledge and the more he disseminates his knowledge, the more attractive he becomes both among knowledge holders and for other capitalists. This is why the capitalist paying for the service of the knowledge holders is interested in avoiding other individual capitalists accessing their individuals' knowledge.

The skills of people producing the goods are crucial for productivity, but their creation is costly. The employers' interest is therefore to avoid investing in skills, but they are needed to increase productivity. The employee may not be fazed by this fact, since the use of his skills is for the production of goods, which only belong to the employer. The employee becomes more interested when he succeeds raising his salary by use of his skills. When an employee utilises his specialist skills, costs for production increase and therefore diminish their effects on the productivity.

In summary, knowledge and the use of knowledge for the sake of knowledge creation conflict in all aspects with the calculations of competitors in market economies. All in all, in the words of the learning economist, knowledge does not obey the rules of the market economy: '....this factor defies some fundamental economic principles.' (OECD, ibid, 11).

And this is what Lundvall/Borras—whilst advocating the 'learning economy'—finally also conclude:

> 'The problem with using the market failure concept in the context of the learning economy is that almost all aspects of knowledge creation and learning are characterised by market failure... These characteristics make information/codified knowledge a very peculiar commodity characterized by elements of market failure. Tacit knowledge is a in plain market failure in the sense that it cannot, as such, be transacted in the market.' (ibid, 49)

We summarize: Codified knowledge is not a 'plain market failure' as tacit knowledge is. But as codified knowledge is not information, which 'characterized' only 'by elements of market failure', both codified and tacit knowledge do disobey the practical rules of a market economic; just as they disobey the attempts of the knowledge-based economy approach to make knowledge the fundament of the knowledge-based economy! Knowledge is simply in-conform to market economy principles. And the above statement characterizing both knowledge types as market failures confesses unwillingly this in-conformity, whilst the learning economists try to prove that their model of a market economy is based on knowledge.

A remarkable conclusion indeed: Trying to justify the need to re-consider economic fundamentals in the light of a new knowledge-based economy approach the rethinking of a knowledge-based economy ends in a statement about their exclusive nature: Any kind of knowledge is a market failure!

For the rationale of a learning economy the conclusion of the exclusive nature of knowledge and market economies does not at all prove the theoretical failure to prove a market economy model based on knowledge. Arriving at the proof of the incommensurability of what is governing the world of tradable goods and non-tradable knowledge, we witness a surprising explicit confession:

'This being the case, we can conclude that the market failure is not a useful concept in the learning economy.' (ibid, 49)

It is obviously not only no problem for an economist proving his model of a knowledge-based economy if the market failure concept applied to the commodity knowledge proves the incommensurability of the market economy and knowledge. It does also not matter, if all the previous reflections about the 'economic fundamentals' prove any kind of consistency between knowledge and market economies or not.

To understand this straight forward rejection of achieving any consistency in academic thinking it helps to remember, that only *'academia is a world where pure instrumentalistic behaviour does not pay...'* (ibid, 50) This is seemingly not the case in the *world of* academia of economics, at least not in their discourse about the economic role of knowledge. It must be the intellectual neighbourhood of the research subjects in the world of academia of learning economists and their research objects, that allows them to welcome the disprove of the coincidence of knowledge and market as a prove of their theory about a market economy based on knowledge. It must be this neighbourhood that justifies not only a 'pure instrumentalistic' conclusion from the insight about knowledge as a market failure, towards the justification of a knowledge-based economy; the obvious political ambitions of the learning economists motivate a view, which frankly admits, that economic theory about knowledge has turned out to be an obstacle to prove the needs of political interventions to create their 'knowledge-based economy':

'Since this applies wherever innovation matters it gives little help in locating a need for policies.' (ibid, 49)

'Locating a need for policies'! This is what the learning economy theory should 'give little help in'! That is why we call our economy after a true market failure, to help the learning economist to prove that only political interventions can help to construct his idea about a knowledge-based economy! Why should we be concerned with all our previous reflections upon what is 'fundamental' to reason the occurrence of a new 'knowledge-based economy'; what is the use of all those 'most important' considerations about tacit and codified knowledge, if they after all 'give little help in locating a need for policies'! *This* is what our reflections about economic fundamentals, tacit and codified knowledge and whatever finally should 'give help in'. Let us ignore what has previously been discussed, about knowledge being a market failure—if it 'is not useful' and does not lead us where we want to arrive at; let us ignore the fact that learning economists do not achieve any theoretical control over the knowledge of people in their rational for the learning economy. Let us call for political intervention to make practically become true what we have proved to be impossible in our economic theories about knowledge. This is a true masterpiece of economic knowledge about a knowledge-based economy: *Because* economy theory has proved that knowledge and capitalistic economies are contradicting concepts, we must 'call for public action' (ibid, 43). Not since but because our theory failed to unite the market failures with the market, the failure of our economic theory proves the need for a 'little help' of political power to unite the market failure and the market. Simply impressing unique economic knowledge that proves via the failure to prove an economy based on knowledge the need for political power to practically make become true that they are right!

Scientifically, this 'little help' is achieved much more 'easily' than all those demanding reflections about knowledge in a knowledge-based economy. And, not to forget, their call has been heard.

The political domestication of peoples' brains for global competition

Learning economists are in fact no 'mad criminals', but—as they told us—they appreciate their role as realistic policy consultants, who of course do 'not give recipes for policies' (ibid, 16), while the distance between new theoretical results and new policy ideas has been shrinking'. (ibid, 42)

Neither knowledge nor learning plays a major role in their further considerations about innovation *policies* in their learning economy. The conclusion that knowledge causes the need 'calling for political action' and their considerations about knowledge and learning as ingredients for innovation policies contain though some important implications for policies related to knowledge and learning. These political implications for *learning and knowledge as a subject of policies* and what they mean for the learning citizens in the knowledge-based economy approach are the subject of our following reflections. They briefly focus on the *political* re-definition of *knowledge and learning* implied in the vision of the learning economy approach.

Knowledge as a 'public good'

Failing to justify the distinction between tacit and codified knowledge as a 'basic concept' for learning economies, the learning economists simply call for 'political intervention' (ibid, 55) to handle practically through political power, what could not be settled via economic theory. It is now the task of the political intervention to handle the conflicting nature of knowledge and the market economy and to disclose the 'locked in knowledge' (Rutherford, D. (1992), 272) in order to guarantee its economic functionalities.

'Learning and knowledge are tied to people, and if people cannot keep pace, there is little point in having access to advanced machinery or advanced computer programmes. ...The need to stimulate investment in human resources and organisational change at the firm level has become more widely recognised by policy makers.' (OECD, 1996a, 60)

The true reason for the detection of Polanyi's terms of tacit and codified knowledge is finally revealed when it comes to call for political interventions and the making of policy suggestions regarding how 'to shape ... policies taking into account factors characterising a learning economy' (ibid, 59): The real problem experienced by learning economists about what they discuss under the issue of 'knowledge transfer' is, that 'knowledge and learning are tied to people'!

It is not the nature of knowledge, but the learning economists that 'call for public action' (ibid, 43). Knowledge must be untied from people and become a 'public good' (ibid, 43).

This is a remarkable confession for an economy preferably called 'learning economy': Learning and knowledge in particular are viewed as potential obstacles for an economy based on knowledge and learning. And to make policy makers 'recognize' these as obstacles for a learning economy it is thought that political intervention is required to domesticate peoples' knowledge for the economy.

This is least as notable as the justification to make knowledge and learning a subject of policy attentions and actions is the reasoning for the statement about knowledge 'tied' to peoples brain: Knowledge cannot not keep pace with the knowledge products!

We are not told by the learning economists how it can happen that 'people' cannot catch up with their own knowledge incorporated in their own knowledge products. It is too natural for economists to make an unspoken implicit *distinction among the inhabitants of their learning economy:* Those who are the 'outstanding experts', of course including outstanding learning economists, whose knowledge contributes to the knowledge products and those whose knowledge is considered as a potential obstacle for a society based on knowledge, if their knowledge 'cannot keep pace' with the knowledge economy.

Knowledge and learning, politically untied from people—distinguished in re-thinkers and learners

Whereas the outstanding experts, who *re-think* knowledge, are 'stimulated' by paying their attractive services for exclusive use in firms or universities, other inhabitants of a learning economy, who 'learn and forget' and also called 'human resource' cause a several problems for the learning economy, which deserve the specific attention of the academic learning policy consultants. This group is not yet sufficiently 'recognized' by political and other human resource management experts. And the learners and forgetters might not be sufficiently aware of their responsibility for their 'crucial role of learning in the economy' (ibid, 61). This is why these knowledgeable inhabitants of the knowledge-based economy require most realistic policy interventions in order to gain control over the knowledge 'tied to peoples' (ibid, 60) minds.

It is not at all the case that the learning economy only cares about their eminent scientists. The part called human recourse experiences special attention by the learning economists, in order to get control of these brains of these learners, who learn and forget. Their knowledge must be unlocked and directed towards its crucial role for the learning economy. As a subject of political interventions, their knowledge must be re-defined with the help of 'incentives' both in terms of the knowledge format, its contents as in terms of its use.

Knowledge beyond the command of knowledge holders. In terms of its *format* this *knowledge,* politically untied from people, is a true dialectic challenge for these knowledge holders. Firstly, politically untied knowledge is no longer a private, but a 'public good'. It therefore no longer belongs to individuals, but to political bodies and their policy agendas. It *is* knowledge in the minds of these knowledge holders, but it is *neither from nor for them, thus not their knowledge.* It is knowledge untied from any substance for the individual or private use of people. It is knowledge untied from individual minds, prioritised and re-defined as knowledge according to public interests in knowledge, which—according to the learning economy—is knowledge for economic competition, 'adapting constantly to the new demands and conditions of the economy' (ibid, 61).

This knowledge appears to these knowledge holders as an alien *challenge*, if not a threat, at least a moral imperative[6]. It is knowledge, that is always a risk to hinder 'change'; thus, knowledge appears to these knowledge holders as something that they no longer own or share, but that they have to 'constantly' adapt themselves to. This is then a life long process of *subordination knowledge by acquiring knowledge*, applied to an alien use, which is not a matter of their own commands about *their* knowledge. Knowledge is no longer a tool of and for people to design and master their life affairs, but an alien demand for alien purposes they have to follow. It does not matter if it pays off for them, but '…it pays an economy to have a large proportion of well-trained people in the labour force.' (ibid, 51)

Not surprisingly, numerous educational experts have been invited to establish merocratic knowledge and learning systems, rewarding to acquire this alienating knowledge. And, as if their materialistic learning motivations still leave some suspicions about their commitments to learning, the creation of a 'learning climate' must help to warm up the learning motivations of these alienated learners, to make knowledge and learning *though* attractive for the learner in a society and economy devoted to knowledge or learning.

Whereas the outstanding experts produce knowledge-based products and theories about 'knowledge-based economies' and *re-think* economic fundamentals, the steeple chasers of the knowledge-based economy are advised not to re-think but to 'absorb change' (ibid, 99) and to subjugate themselves proactively under alien knowledge changes. A relationship towards new knowledge, which learning economists rightly call 'learning and forgetting' (Lundvall, B.A., Johnson, B, 1994). Characterizing the process of building 'new' knowledge as 'forgetting' 'old' knowledge presents an idea about these knowledge holders and their particular knowledge in which knowledge appears to be a kind of mind equipment, a knowledge without knowing. The acquisition of knowledge appears accordingly as a process of consuming and dumping alien insights produced elsewhere. And this impossible idea of *building* knowledge as *consuming and dumping* is required as the *active effort* of the alienated knowledge holders. More concretely this type of knowledge, in contrast to academic knowledge holders, does not re-think knowledge in the light of new knowledge. Instead, it continuously copes with the cognitive monster of *proactive continuous knowledge adaptations.*

This idea of feeding in and out without knowing neither the reasons nor the objectives of the 'old' nor the 'new' knowledge bits makes these knowledge holders in the words of learning economists true knowledge absorbers. *Their* knowledge is not made for them, but for the use of those who are interested in the locked-in knowledge of these knowledge holders. This knowledge holder acquires new knowledge, which has not been created by or for him. *He has to forget his knowledge* if it is no longer requested though he does not know why and *he* has to acquire knowledge which is not his nor for him. This is his contribution to what learning economists call the mysterious subject 'change'. A true and revealing image of a concept of *knowing as subordination to knowledge!*

The ideal knowledge content: Knowing how to forget knowledge. The *contents of this knowledge* is decided, not according to the practical or other needs of these knowledge holders, but along the functionality of the knowledge for use beyond the objectives of that knowledge holders that he must though acquire: Either for his 'employability' whilst unemployed or the needs of being a 'human resource' for his employer as long as they want to benefit from the knowledge of the employee.

Not surprisingly, knowledge in the learning economy is in fact most 'fragile' (Boreham, The Knowledge Economy, Work Process Knowledge and the Learning Citizen—Central but Vulnerable, see chapter 6) as Boreham rightly notices. For the very same reason it is also not surprising that science and research have such a negative image among these knowledge holders who are not invited to rethink knowledge and to build new knowledge, but who learn and forget.

However, any knowledge, even if it is purely defined by its functionality for economic use, is still seen as a potential risk for the learning economy. On the side of these knowledge holders, no concrete knowledge really counts. Rather any substantial knowledge is a risk to absorb new knowledge. What therefore really counts as knowledge is the meata-knowledge about how to adapt knowledge. Consequently, the knowledge concepts for these knowledge holders in the learning economy climax in a knowledge concept in which knowledge has been deliberated of any substantial contents, that could become a risk for learning and forgetting. In the ideal learning economy any substantive knowledge is replaced by a meta-knowledge content that—in the mind of learning economists—represents in its content less contents the final aim of knowledge in the learning economy: it is knowledge about a method to adapt any knowledge to the alien subject 'change'.

> 'In a complex and rapidly changing context there will be more demand for knowledge aimed at solving a wider range of problems than for narrowly defined substantive knowledge.
> Employees need skills that make it possible for them to cope with change in an interaction with others'. (ibid, 91)

The ideal employees of a learning economy are knowledge holders, who are deliberated from any 'narrowly defined substantive' knowledge and instead are equipped with knowledge, for which no employer would ever employ them, since their knowledge is completed useless for any concrete real workplace. No workplace even in a learning economy is about 'interactions with others to cope with change', but to do any very substantive job requiring substantial knowledge or skills. This peculiar job profile and the according 'skills' *are* the *fiction* of the learning economist representing the ideal worker in a learning economy. Such an employee does not have any substantive knowledge to conduct any substantial work, but has the abilities to practise the ideal worker of a learning economist. This knowledge holder would in fact not be employed by anybody, except by the learning economist to solve the 'mad' contradictions of his theory about knowledge for the proactive and knowledgeable adaptation of knowledge.

Learning to learn to forget. Learning is an activity of those knowledge holders who do not (re-)think knowledge, but 'learn and forget'. As knowledge, learning in the learning economy approach is transferred into a public good and has become the subject of political interventions governed towards the knowledge acquisition of human resources serving the learning economy. Politically conceptualized and supervised, learning in the learning economy is *the* key activity of the Lundvallien ideal worker, who himself has to untie his knowledge from his own individual purposes via learning. This worker devotes his knowledge acquisition to fulfil the ideal of a learning economist about learning and who devotes his mind to adopt his knowledge to 'change'. All aspects of learning in the learning economy represent a fundamentally contradicting concept of learning: In terms of the means of acquiring knowledge, the modes of learning, the contents of learning and in terms of the ways that the learning process is organized and managed.

Learning to never know. The specific *form of learning* in the learning economy has nothing in common with what learning substantially is. Learning appears not as acquiring knowledge to use it for achieving the aims of the learner, but as the submission of the learner's mind *under* knowledge, representing objectives of an abstract alien subject. This subject is called 'change', which people do not govern, but it is a demand, they are confronted with as a continuous burden, creating the continuous threat to learn. Learning is not about improving the abilities of peoples' minds to govern their life, but about the submission of their minds under knowledge, which represents the threatening aims of the learning economy that they have to *proactively* adopt *themselves* to *as if* it was their own individual life agenda.

Within this concept of learning, learning is only carried out in the very formal sense that a given knowledge is being acquired via the activity of the subject learner. It is the learning subject who learns, but the substance and the modes of learning that are governed by using the acquired knowledge for *being* the object of and for other subjects. Thus learning, the most subjective activity of humans becomes a service, an 'investment'—but never a service for the learner.

Learners learn, because others are interested in the knowledge they acquire. Therefore they acquire the knowledge they demand from the learner. Learning, the acquisition of knowledge thus is not making the learner more knowledgeable. Since their acquisition of knowledge is based on forgetting their previous knowledge, learning is about updating the *potential functionality of their knowledge* with alien knowledge for alien purposes. In the words of the learning economy: 'Competition pressure must match with the ability to absorb change'. (ibid, 99) To continuously absorb change via learning causes the life long pressure for the learner to make his knowledge match with the demands of the alien abstract subjectless subject, the learning economist discretely sometimes calls 'change' or more concretely the 'growth of regions and nations.' (ibid, 53)

The concept of learning for these knowledge holders is in fact totalitarian in all regards. If it is true that 'there is no 'economic sphere' that can be strictly isolated from the social sphere' (53) it is also true, that there is no social sphere which is not strictly geared towards 'interactive learning' for 'industrial dynamics and growth of regions and nations' (ibid). Through political interventions, these learners are deprived of the power to decide about which knowledge they wish to learn. There decision power is replaced by knowledge that is now politically directed and thus made beneficial for the 'growth of regions and nations' (ibid).

Creating this workforce of knowledge absorbers, '... government policy has an important role to play in this area' (ibid, 90), since this also '...puts new demands on education and training institutions....focused on making students capable of confronting and solving problems as they appear. ...much of the training and learning has to take place at the work-place or in close connection with firms.' (ibid, 94)

The totalitarian vision of learning economists about learning of the knowledge absorbers is gaining shape. This type of learning exclusively subordinates and instrumentalises their minds of these knowledge holders by use of 'government policies' under the needs of firms, regions or nations.

Learning to be a subjectless subject. Consequently, also the *contents as the modes and ways of learning reflect* the idea of learning as a sheer adaptation of alien knowledge for alien purposes.

The curriculum for learners also becomes a public good and thus a matter of political priorities. As a public good, learning is directed towards economic functionalism. The contents of learning are politically domesticated towards a meta-vocationalistic functionalism in a twofold sense.

Firstly—and this is most visible in all current reforms in all education sectors—the economically functionalistic learning agenda clears the curriculum from all knowledge contents, which do not serve the world of work and economics. In other words, learning, just contributing to private objectives of people, or—as in the case of the academic sphere learning for intellectual curiosity—is successively taken from the learning agenda. Recent reforms of education in the EU are in fact[7] successively fulfilling the ideas of a learning economy and skip any curricula which are not contributing to this economic functionalism. They thus represent an example of putting the policy agenda of the learning economy about politically 'untied knowledge' and the accordingly designed learning of people into the practise of current reforms in the education sector.

Secondly, as a public good, learning is subordinated under the strategic political considerations of a broader economistic untilitarism. Previous concepts of education aimed at knowledgeable citizens in a more humanistic sense and tradition are replaced by considering knowledge and learning as an investment in global competitiveness and from now on are exclusively judged along the criterion to contribute to this aim and nothing else. Thus learning becomes one factor among others on the policy agenda to become the most competitive economy in the world, on which 'education' is no longer a service for citizens, but an economic factor. Learning, after gaining the status of a public good, becomes a factor for political considerations and priorities about and devoted to economic competitiveness.

Driven by their fear, that change could be hold up by lacking abilities to absorb change, knowledge economists are theoretically even more radical than current policy reforms and promote the totalitarian submission of learning under their concept of a learning economy.[8] It is not any substantive knowledge that counts as a subject of learning. As already knowledge for these knowledge holders was defined as meta-knowledge about how to change knowledge learning economists also define learning as a meta concept of methodological learning and suggest:

> '...that employees have the background necessary to absorb and to be creative in combining old pieces of knowledge in new ways.' (ibid, 94)

The totalitarian ideal of the learning economists' untied learning consists of the shear adaptation abilities 'to cope with change'. Learning thus is consequently imaged as a knowledge 'absorbing' ability, for which any concrete learning substance is a risk to be absorbed. Consequently the ideal learning is *learning without knowing*, a cognitively impossible idea about what the untied learning means after being untied from people and directed towards economic functionalism through political interventions: Whereas usually learning progresses by building new knowledge on the knowledge acquired in previous learning loops, the ideal learning for learning economies requires to forget the existing knowledge fundament as a basis for building new knowledge—building on what? The learning economist is so obsessed with his idea that knowledge tied up in people could hinder them 'to cope with change' that they even create the impossibility to replace any substantial learning by a meta ability—here for good reasons vaguely called 'background'. This learning does not consist of anything else but the abstract meta ability to practise learning as the adaptation ability to pick up and dump knowledge. This is the ideal learning ability of the therefore called learning economy: The ideal of learning is to acquire the objectives of an alien economic untilitarism as ones' own abilities, in terms of its contents format and its modes of learning.

Learning campaigns. Learning untied from the motivations of the learner to learn, from the interest of the learner in the knowledge content and from the use of the acquired knowledge for any learners' individual objectives is demanding for the learner. Learning as a burden and a threat requires what the learning economist call 'incentives'.

As if the threat behind losing the race catching up with change was not threatening enough, not only for the losers of this learning race, economic incentives are linking learning activities to deteriorating living conditions. Thus current reforms of labour market policies rewarding learning and punishing non-learning, reflect the current political practice of treating learning as a public good. These are the political actions the learning economist was calling for after detecting knowledge as a 'true' market failure.

However, as much learning is politically domesticated towards the economic instrumentalism as is promoted by learning economists, learning by its nature remains an activity of the learning subject however the learning contents and objectives might be untied from the learner. The subjectivity required for the process of acquiring knowledge cannot be replaced by any economic or political intervention. It is the learner who learns.

This is why the more learning is politically untied from the learning subject and its private motivation and objectives to learn, the more learning is politically organized as a kind of 'political campaign'. This campaign about 'learning climates'[9], creating learning as of kind of second societal nature compliments the pressure to learn via economic 'incentives' with a moral pressure[10] on the learner as a societal responsible citizen. Learning becomes a duty and not learning excludes citizens from their societal communities. Interpreting the acquisition of alien knowledge for alien purposes as a second human societal nature completes the totalitarianism of the conceptualisation of the learning subject in the learning economy.

Living for learning. Finally, from these concepts of knowledge learning as a public good and the learning campaigns for the alienated knowledge holders, nobody can ever escape: 'This implies that all categories of employees and management need to renew their skills and capabilities from time to time…' (ibid, 94) Learning economists are also very much aware, that 'the result of this is the exclusion of citizens from active participation' (ibid, 99). The learning economist, promoting learning as a second societal nature knows, that the continuous threat to become excluded from the society, if you do not to absorb change, does not prevent you from being excluded.

'Giving special incentives to low-skilled workers to go on leave in order to develop general and specific skills, and to bring in unemployed of the same category in their place could be part of such a programme... it is especially difficult to motivate older worker to engage in training... However, the main strategy should be to create a cohesive labour market and, as far as possible, to avoid exclusion and polarisation.' (ibid, 100)

Learning economists, experts in knowledge and learning, anticipate possible problems arsing from the lacking absorption abilities of this 'category' of knowledge holders, the 'low skilled workers', who also seem to be normal inhabitants of an economy, which does not aim at anything else but learning. But even after giving them the treatment of 'special incentives' the learning economies has to deal with knowledge holders, who do not manage to absorb change, how hard they try and how inspiring these special treatments might be. And this is a problem for the learning economists:

'When the workforce is required to master more skills than they are capable of learning, the result is the exclusion from active participation.' (ibid, 99)

If it was just true that any inhabitant of this totalitarian learning society could ever escape the agenda of a learning economist 'mastering skills' and 'absorb change'. It was at least true, one could escape this torture by refuse from learning and thus being deliberated from this never-ending live long learning fight. It is not, there is no chance:

'For this very reason, as well as for social reasons, a whole set of specific measures to support the low skilled workers and slow learners is needed.' (ibid, 99)

The vision of science fictions how to get hold of the brains is a rather modest idea compared to this obsession, that any body might escape to be 'supported' via specific measures to contribute to the learning economy.

The reason why the risks of people, who do not master more skills than they are capable of learning, are not characterized by the economists as utterly poor living conditions in the middle of a society, which is overwhelmed by innovations for the wealth of regions and nations, but are identified as a risk to be excluded from 'active participation' in the agenda of absorbing knowledge for change, is that he is concerned, anybody might not share his totalitarian vision, devoting his life to a learning economy. In other cases, for example the 'inflationary bottleneck problems' the economists know how much it counts to count money. In this case of the 'low skilled workers', they count their skills and find them 'low' to thus create a 'category' of 'low skilled' humans and—more coincidentally—a kind of learning based racism. And after these people have been identified as not low paid, but low skilled, they are the subject of 'a whole set of specific measures to support'... To support what? To support, 'transferring' finally the totalitarian economy concept on the society as a whole and on any of its citizens, if they like it or not. This is why those who cannot master more skills, than they are capable to learn, are now supported to prevent 'exclusion from active participation' in the un-escapable agenda of the learning economy.

However, this 'whole set of specific measures' for this 'category' is also problematic for the learning economist—not for the low skilled knowledge holders, but for the growth of regions and nations.

> 'Trying to bring unemployment rates down in such a situation will give raise to inflationary bottle neck problems in the labour market. Safeguarding a high level of trust in a strongly and permanently polarized economy may also be difficult... However, the main strategy should be to create a cohesive labour market and, as far as possible, to avoid exclusion and polarisation.' (ibid, 100)

But this is not difficult for a learning economist. To avoid 'inflationary bottle-neck problems in the labour market', in other words, to avoid that the precious workforce is becoming too expensive and diminishing via the de-valuation of the national currency the growth of regions and nations, 'specific measures to support the low-skilled and slow learners are needed' by means of a next set of 'special incentives' (ibid, 100).

As we can witness, current labour market reforms across the EU are trying with those 'specific measures' and 'special incentives' to 'create a cohesive labour market and, to avoid exclusion and polarisation' especially for those 'slow learners'. Thus, via these 'special measures' they are attempting to avoid these inflationary bottleneck problems and reduce the costs for their labour force, proving that at least European policies, which '(should) itself be a learning process', have learned their lessons from the learning economy about knowledge and learning and how to treat some categories without any bottleneck problems. They certainly did.

> 'The latest editions of the different country reports show that most countries are beginning to shape their policies taking into account factors characterizing a learning economy.' (ibid, 59)

At least, this is a correct observation. But what about this prudish: 'As far as possible'? One feels attempted to raise the question: Which political interventions do learning economist recommend for those for whom even the reduction of labour costs or—in the language of learning economists—for whom the 'special incentives' have failed and will continue to fail, who thus are 'excluded' and for whom further 'investments' causes that inflationary bottle neck problem? We know the criteria for what *is* possible and what is not. It is the effect of employment policies on inflating the value of the growth of regions and nations. We also know how to calculate the limits for these 'incentives': What is possible and what is not is indicated by the rate of inflation.

But still, what do they recommend beyond this 'as far as possible'? The answer is concise and to the point: 'a new 'new' deal' (ibid, 99).

For those for whom learning is not forgetting, the historical comparison of the learning economist suggestions with an 'old' new deal is not only polishing up the importance of the learning economists to historical dimensions; substantially it is not an error, but very consequent, though not at all new in any respect. For those who have never heard about any old or new deal: in the language of another metier, old as new deals are deals which cannot be rejected.

From the point of view of a European citizen, this raises still one remaining question: What is the difference between the 'bad' neo-liberal economists and the 'good' learning economists?

Conclusions: The learning economy—promoting the totalitarianism of economic utilitarianism

1. Scientifically, the rationale of the learning economy is a theoretical failure. The learning economy theory is full of contradictions and does not justify characterising a market economy as an economy governed by knowledge and learning.

    The concept of the 'learning economy' is theoretically inconsistent and not convincing. If tacit and codified knowledge, presented as fundamental categories to justify a market economy based on knowledge, are both *market failures,* they are not fundamentals of a market economy. With this in mind, knowledge and market economy have conflicting natures and consequently the market economy, however equipped with the labels of a knowledge-based or learning economy, cannot be presented as based neither on knowledge nor on learning.

    Knowledge and learning do play an instrumental and conditional role in market economies and between companies, they are one means for competition among many others. In the context of political actions for learning economies, learning plays an even more instrumental, conditional and economically restricted role. To invest in a competitive workforce as one means for the competition between countries and this investment is measured against its impact on inflation. Thus, reducing the investments in learning and increase the learning activities is one, but also only one means for the competition between countries to attract capital. This minor and most conditional role does not justify the construction of life around learning under the label of 'learning economies'.

Rather the opposite is revealed and proved from the rationale of the learning economy theory: Market economies create all kind of problems for the creation of knowledge as for learning. Under the governance of economic competition, knowledge is conditioned and subordinated for its use for economic success. This is measured in units of abstract growth, may it be for regions or nations, and certainly not in units of increasing wisdom. And if the investments in knowledge and learning in a learning economy have to be measured against the impact of these investments in inflating the wealth of regions and nations, the learning economy considers learning and knowledge in particular as the workforce in general as problematic costs, which tend to diminish the wealth of regions and nations, the higher the cost for knowledge and learning are. Lowering the investments in knowledge and learning is the strategy of learning economies. Current labour market reforms across the EU put this idea of the learning economy into practice.

Thus, this conditional status of knowledge in economies geared towards and measured in abstract wealth units rather *restricts* the creation of knowledge both in terms of its contents and in terms of the extent, which is exclusively dependent on its promises for profit. This subordination of knowledge and learning under the criterion to promise profit implies to waste and dump knowledge in unique historical dimensions whenever this promise fails to be proved.

2. Whilst the learning economy theory does not prove the concept of an economy based on knowledge and learning, it calls for and justifies political intervention into knowledge and learning, also in historically unique dimensions. From the declaration of knowledge and learning as   a 'public good' the learning economy concept motivates policies disempowering citizens from governing their knowledge and from their individual objectives for knowledge and learning. Instead, it advocates both knowledge and learning as issues for the agenda of public policy bodies according to their political priorities. They promote 'untying' knowledge and learning from people both in terms of its contents and of its use to re-redirect domesticated knowledge and learning for the use of the economic growth of market economies and nations in the context of global competitiveness. Thus knowledge and learning are no longer means of citizens, but appear in front of the learners as a life long moral imperative, threat and burden.

3. The knowledge-based economy is thus a misleading and disorientating concept for European citizens. The conflicting natures of knowledge and market economies as revealed in the learning economy approach do not

allow one to take for granted that knowledge is a means for citizens to intervene in the mechanisms of market economy for their own sake through knowledge and learning. The learning economy concept makes citizens believe that market economies are governed by knowledge and thus insinuates that knowledge as the acquisition of knowledge allow citizens to play a decisive role via the acquisition of knowledge. There is no justification to focus all activities of European citizens on knowledge and learning for economic success. Likewise, there is no justification that focussing citizens' lives on learning pays off—for the citizens.

Rather the opposite is the case. Both the concepts of knowledge as the concepts of learning lead to a subordination of people's life under the needs economic competitiveness, not because they lack knowledge, but via the acquisition of this type of economistic knowledge. This knowledge deteriorates the use of peoples mind to an economic functional instrumentalism and undermines any kind of thinking devoted to govern people's life as citizens under living conditions, which are much more complex that serving competitiveness. There is no justification for restricting the life of European citizens to invest in knowledge and learning. Similarly one cannot justify restricting knowledge and learning to the rationale of economies and global competitiveness. The real life of the European citizen is much richer and more complex than simply being a learning human resource for knowledge-based economies.

4. The knowledge-based economy knowledge reduces the contents of knowledge in the life of European citizens as on a functional ingredient of an economic growth. It excludes societal and political aspects of the life of European citizens or worse: It subordinates even any societal and political aspects of life under the criteria of economic growth. The reduction of European citizens to an instrumental role in global economic competitiveness disregards the complex challenges of the real citizens. These challenges range from those of individuals within all kind of social entities or communities to the challenges of multinational European citizenship; not to mention those challenges of European citizens finding themselves as items on the policy agenda of the EU for other political and military global policy agendas, competing with the US about various global policy affairs.

5. The political activities focussing European policies on global economic competitiveness and directing knowledge to that economic instrumentalism also undermine the abilities and the knowledge of European *citizens* needed to make decisions about their life beyond the realms of employability. Citizens in the learning economy concept are not knowledgeable citizens, how much and hard they learn.

Rather the opposite is the case. Citizens in the learning economy do not have a political or social life or any individual attributes, nor do they have any knowledge about their political, social or individual life. They are people whose knowledge is untied and directed by political 'incentives' towards a life between keeping pace as a human resource in learning organisations and updating their employability in a learning society. These individuals deteriorate into objects of political campaigns, directed with 'economic incentives', they cannot refuse to accept.

Political strategies aiming at the construction of a European citizen as shear objects of political steering mechanisms functionalize citizens for global competition and obstruct their status, their rights and the knowledge they need as citizens to decide about their life themselves and according to their life agendas.

Notes

1. See also: OECD (Organization for Economic Cooperation and Development) (1996) *The Knowledge-Based Economy*. Paris: Organization for Economic Cooperation and Development.
2. As it will become apparent later, the difficulty to distinguish here between society and economy models when discussing the learning economy is due to the blurring differences between economy and society in the learning economy approach. In the learning economy theory the society is subordinated under the objectives of the learning economy.
3. As we shall see later, the way Lundvall/Borras are using those Polanyi categories has nothing much to do with the philosophical distinction of 'articulate and inarticulate intelligence" in his considerations about the 'tacit component of knowledge'. (Polanyi 1962, 70)
4. 'The point is that policy-makers are increasingly under the influence of economic theory and that the distance between new theoretical results and new policy ideas has been shrinking.' *(Lundval, B.-A, Borras., 1999, 42)*. In fact, as we will see later, the distance between the economy as an object of scientific reflections and policy making shrinks in the learning economy ideas to an extend that economic thinking vanishes in 'recipes for policies"(ibid, 16), the more they attempt to deny it.
5. See also: Kuhn, M. & Sultana, R. (eds) The Learning Society in Europe and Beyond, Lang, Forthcoming.
6. See in this volume Ronald Sultana, 'Concepts of Knowledge and Learning in Findings of FRP 4 and 5 Projects'.
7. See also Kuhn, M., Sultana, R. 'Homo Sapiens Europeus—Creating the European Learning Citizens', Peter Lang, forthcoming.
8. In fact, different from the theoretical radical totalitarism of learning economists, the practical policy reforms know to distinguish between a totalitarian ideology and the practical requirements of citizens. But this distinction is not the subject of this paper.
9. De Rick, 'Towards the conceptualization of a learning climate', 2003, unpublished paper presented on the EURONET workshop, Sterling October 2003.
10. See this volume, Chapter 3: Sultana, R., Concepts of Knowledge and Learning in Findings of FRP 4 and 5 Projects.

References

Archibugi, D. & Lundvall, B.A. (2001) *The Globalising Learning Economy: Major Socio-Economic Trends and European Innovation Policies*. Oxford: Oxford University Press.

Argyris, G. & Schoen, D. A. (1978) *Organizational Learning: A Theory of Action Perspective*. Reading Mass: Addison-Wesley.

Beck, U. (1992) *Risk Society: Towards a New Modernity*. London: Sage.

Burke, P. (2000) *A Social History of Knowledge*. Cambridge: Polity Press.

Castells, M. (1996) *The Information Age: The Rise of Network Society*. [Volume 1]. Oxford: Blackwell.

Cook, P. (2002) *Knowledge Economies. Clusters, Learning and Cooperative Advantage*. London: Routledge.

Cullenberg, S., Amariglio, J. & Ruccio, D. (eds) (2001) *Postmodernism, Economics and Knowledge*. London: Routledge.

Department for Trade and Industry (1998b) *Our Competitive Future: Building the Knowledge-Driven Economy: Analytical Background*. http://www.dti.gov.uk/comp/competitive/an_reprt.htm

Eatwell, J. et. All (eds) (1987) *The New Palgrave: a Dictionary of Economics* [Volume 2, p. 546]. London: Macmillan.

European Commission (2000) *Presidency Conclusions of the Lisbon European Council*. http://www.osce.org/docs/english/1990-1999/summits/lisbo96e.htm

European Commission. Sixth Framework Programme. http://fp6.cordis.lu/fp6/home.cfm

European Round Table of Industrialists (2001) 'Actions for Competitiveness through the Knowledge Economy in Europe' *European Business Journal*, Vol. 13 (4), pp. 183-7.

Gibbons, M., Limoges, C., Nowotny, H., Schwartzman, S., Scott, P. & Trow, M. (1994) *The New Production of Knowledge: The Dynamics of Science and Research in Contemporary Societies*. London: Sage Publications.

Habermas, J. (1996) *Legitimationsprobleme im Spätkapitalismus*. Frankfurt am Main: Suhrkamp.

Lukacs, G. (1962) *Die Zerstörung der Vernunft*. Neuwied: Luchterhand.

Lundvall, B.A & Johnson, B. (1994) 'The Learning Economy'. *Journal of Industry Studies*, Vol. 1 (2).

Lundvall, B.-A. & Borras, S. (1999) *The Globalizing learning economy: Implications for innovation policy, European Communities*. Luxembourg: Office for official publications of the European Commission.

Mannheim, K. (1980) *Strukturen des Denkens*. Frankfurt am Main.

Mannheim, K. (1972) *Ideology and Utopia: an Introduction into the Sociology of Knowledge*. London: Routledge.

Mannheim, K. (1952) *Essays on the Sociology of Knowledge*. London: Routledge & Kegan Paul

Neuweg, G. H. (2001) *Könnerschaft und Implizites Wissen: zur lehr-lerntheoretischen Bedeutung der Erkenntnis und Wissenstheorie Michael Polanyis*. Münster: Waxmann.

Nonaka, I. & Takeuchi, H. (1995) The *Knowledge Creating Company*. Oxford: Oxford University Press.

OECD (Organization for Economic Cooperation and Development) (1996) *The Knowledge-based Economy*. Paris: Organization for Economic Cooperation and Development.

Peters, M. (2003) Knowledge Networks, Innovation and Development: Education After Modernization. Paper presented on the EURONET workshop in Stirling October 2003.

Polanyi, M. (1958) *Personal Knowledge. Towards a postcritical philosophy*. Chicago: University of Chicago Press.

Rutherford, D. (1992) *Dictionary of Economics*. London: Routledge.

Stiglitz, J. (1999) 'Public Policy for a Knowledge Economy.' Remarks at the Department for Trade and Industry and Center for Economic Policy Research, London, Jan. 27 (http://www.worldbank.org/html/extdr/extme/jssp012799a.htm).

Stiglitz, J. (2002) *Globalization and Its Discontents*. London: Allen Lane.

Toffler, A. (1990) *The Third Wave*. New York: Bantam Books.

World Bank (1998/99) *Knowledge for Development: Including Selected World Development Indicators*. Oxford: Oxford University Press.

CHAPTER THREE

Concepts of Knowledge and Learning in Findings of FRP 4 and 5 Projects

Ronald G. Sultana

Introduction

This paper focuses on eleven selected FRP.4 and FRP.5 projects[1] where concepts of knowledge and learning feature centrally—either directly or indirectly—and where data or arguments contribute towards a conceptualisation of the Learning Society in an integrating Europe. These Framework projects will serve, in Seymour Papert's (1980) words, as 'subjects-to-think-with' in order to help critically engage the field of lifelong learning. In referring to Papert's methodological strategy, where one sharpens one's understanding by pitting being, thoughts and action against those of others, I am signalling that the present exercise is not based on a focused and detailed reading of the final project reports (over 2000 pages of text), as much as on a trawling through briefing papers that summarise the main findings[2] and which have helped me identify some key themes around which to organise this essay and which served as a springboard for some reflections. The purpose of this particular review, therefore, is to identify a number of declared or underlying concepts related to knowledge and learning, with a view to critically engaging the discourse on lifelong learning as this is being articulated in some of Europe's research community circles. The selection of themes is, needless to say, subjective, as are the interpretations of their significance.

Six broad aspects of knowledge/learning will be addressed in this context. First, the paper investigates the way that the different projects conceptualise the rationale for the construction of a Learning Society. The paper then considers the image of learning as a 'moral imperative', where European citizens are enjoined to commit themselves to further education and training as this is of benefit to themselves, to their country, and to the European project. A third point that is made is that 'learning', in most of the research projects under consideration, tends to be equated with 'competence' and 'skills', where 'performative knowledge' is privileged. Fourthly, many of the research projects share the view that learning is more likely to be successful when it is a social rather than individual activity. Closely linked to this view is, fifthly, a conviction that all citizens can learn if alternative educational contexts as well as alternative delivery (pedagogies) and assessment (accreditation) strategies are developed. Finally, the paper considers the manner in which the selected projects conceptualise the Learning Society, and their views regarding the gap between rhetoric and reality in implementing that ideal.

Each of these aspects of knowledge and learning are considered in turn in the sections that follow. The leitmotif running throughout the arguments made is that the discourse evolving around the debates on the Learning Society is marked by contradictions that are difficult to resolve, as they attempt to serve fundamentally irreconcilable humanistic, emancipatory, and technocratic interests.

Justifying the Learning Society

The notion of the 'Learning Society', together with the attendant concept and practice of 'lifelong education', has a long history that is anchored in the world view of several civilisations and cultural traditions, including those that emerged in China, India, classical Greece, and Renaissance Europe (Lê Thành Khôi, 1995). Over the past few decades, however, such notions have become part of the popular understanding of what education is about (Gelpi, 1985), with different, often conflicting discourses developing in order to justify attempts to bring about a Learning Society. As several commentators have observed (inter alia Ranson, 1998; Jarvis, 2001; Borg & Mayo, 2002), initially much of the discourse galvanised around the idea of education as a liberatory practice that enhanced participatory citizenship in a democracy. Drawing on the writings of Dewey, Gramsci, and Freire among others, the adult education field produced a series of key texts that promoted the idea of education beyond schooling, culminating in the highly influential UNESCO report by Faure and his colleagues in 1972, significantly entitled Learning to Be. Influenced by the deschooling movement, by radical critiques of the way education served the interests of capital and contributed to the reproduction of inequality, and by the left-leaning post-war climate, liberal humanist and even radical agendas were developed, alongside more utilitarian ones, with a view to ensuring that all citizens had access, throughout their life, to an education that was enabling and empowering socially, politically, and economically.[3]

It is important to stress this historical context, albeit briefly, both to avoid falling into the trap of thinking that the notion of a Learning Society is new (or uniquely 'western' for that matter), and more importantly, to be in a better position to compare and contrast current articulations with alternative ones. For the point that I will be making is that several of the research projects perused in the context of this review exercise tend to connect with an understanding of the Learning Society that is somewhat different from the humanist, liberal and radical notions that shaped the pedigree of the notion in the twentieth century. Rather, they tend to take for granted the economistic justification for lifelong learning (e.g. Sauquet) that has become commonplace in debates in this area, whether such debates take place in the international arena or are more focused on Europe and its strategy to become 'the most competitive and dynamic knowledge-based society in the world' (Lisbon European Council, 23-24 March, 2000).

This shift from an initial understanding of lifelong learning that was largely—though not solely—inspired by a vision of humanity that 'projected an expansive view of people with a range of subjectivities that extends beyond the production-consumption nexus' (Borg & Mayo 2002: 21), to a view of the Learning Society whose primary function is to guarantee the availability of suitable human resources necessary for the reproduction and accumulation of capital in a knowledge-based economy, deserves to be examined in some detail, if only because on this shift depend notions of learning and the learner that are the focus of this essay.

As I have argued elsewhere (Sultana 1995, 1996, 2002), the educational agenda of the European Union is increasingly being driven by neo-liberal concerns, with learning being seen as a commodity that must be harnessed to serve the aspirations of a Single Market. The target of establishing a free flow of capital, goods, persons and services is of course a strategic response by capital to develop more promising environments for success in the face of international competition, particularly from the USA and the Pacific Rim. While such an agenda is, in Europe, tempered by the Social Charter, it is undeniable that the EU's vision is informed by the assumptions of orthodox market economics, to the extent that, from the perspective of some of the representatives of the social democratic left, grave concerns arise as to the extent to which the European project will limit national economic-political scope for action in the maintenance of a welfare state. As part of integrated policy-making regimes, states find themselves increasingly entangled in an interlocking (asymmetric) network of bargained solutions (Muller & Wright, 1994; Habermas, 2001: 11), leading to a downward spiralling of social standards with 'harmonization' taking place according to the principle of the lowest common denominator (Haahr, 1992; Christiansen, 1992; Ross, 1992).

With reference to education generally, and to the notion of the Learning Society more specifically, an argument could be made about the coincidence of the Commission's agendas and the interests of international capital with a European base. It is well known, for instance, that the European Round Table of Industrialists (ERT)—established in 1983 and embracing as it does many of the largest, most successful and most influential companies in the region— wields an extraordinarily strong influence on the Commission (Ramsay, 1992). The lobbying power of ERT, and the impact this has on the field of education, is addressed at some length by Slowinski (1998). Representing 43 companies—twelve of which are listed in the top hundred corporations worldwide—with a combined turnover of _1350 billion and employing 4.2 million people worldwide, ERT meets twice annually, and presents reports to the EU on a regular basis in order to attempt to steer policy decisions. Certainly in the field of education, they do not seem to be failing: In March 1995 ERT published a report entitled Education for Europeans: Towards the Learning Society. Two years later, the EU released a White Paper entitled Teaching and Learning: Towards the Learning Society. In 1997, ERT published Investing in Knowledge: The Integration of Technology in European Education. This was echoed by a document put out by the European Commission that very same year, with the title Towards a Europe of Knowledge. The similarity of agendas goes beyond the title and is certainly more than skin-deep, indicating a tightly woven policy network that extends at all levels of education, higher levels included.[4]

This is not to say that the Commission's educational agenda is crassly or solely utilitarian; indeed some of the policies it has promoted have strong progressive moments, particularly in terms of its overall declared goals for social cohesion, for instance (see, inter alia Rohrs, 1992; Ryba, 1994). But it is precisely the complexity of the education discourse that emerges from the EU, and its ability to weave together contradictory elements (Hager, Kokosalakis, Cullen), that makes its consensualist appeal understandable. One way of articulating the tensions in the Commission's educational discourse is by drawing on the useful distinction that is made by Habermas (1976) between technocratic, hermeneutic and emancipatory rationalities. Habermas has argued that our life-world has become colonized by 'technocratic rationality', a positivist 'means-ends' mode of being, which in education would be translated into the consideration of learning as a boosting of the use value of human capital in order to meet production (and consumption) targets. Against technocratic rationality Habermas opposes other forms of 'being-in-the-world'—hermeneutic rationality highlights man's and woman's interpretative, meaning-making abilities, while emancipatory rationality signals humanity's mission to consider 'reality' as it is, in order to imagine a world as it could, and should be. The point made by several critical educators inspired by the analysis proposed by Habermas is that education has become dominated by the questionable values that operate in the sphere of production (Giroux, 1997; McLaren, 1997; Apple, 1995, 2001).

It is relevant to point out, in this context, that the presence of the technocratic rationality or economic imperative is strongly felt in a number of the Framework projects reviewed for the purpose of this exercise. As with several of the documents of the Commission that broach education, the development of a Learning Society is justified in terms of a human capital, rates-of-return approach (Hanushek, 1994) in that education pays, and VET pays even more (Smyth)—though this is not the case for long-term unemployed (Brandsma). Further and continuing education is to be encouraged since it pays dividends by improving labour market competitiveness at the individual, national, and supra-national (i.e. European) level. Learning is about enhancing the prospects for economic survival (Sauquet); learners need to be flexible (Svensson) and multi-skilled, constantly ready to re-invent themselves in order to respond to the needs of the labour market (Kokosalakis).

Other types of rationality compete—or co-exist—with this emphasis on education as an economic investment. Some of the projects, for instance, adopt what, within Habermas' typology, would be a hermeneutic rationality, where the citizen in a Learning Society engages in continuing education motivated by the desire for 'self-development', a process that is intensely 'cultural' in the anthropological meaning of that term, where culture is a tool for interaction in a community (Geertz, 1973, 1993). Emancipatory rationality leads the citizen to constantly draw on new knowledge in order to learn the virtues and skills of living in a democracy. Such an emancipatory agenda can have a European dimension, in the sense that a unity of values associated with participatory democracy is associated with European citizenship (Steedman).

Despite the fact that these three strands or rationalities are often present but are not necessarily reconcilable (Kokosalakis) leads to serious contradictions that are inherent in—and to—the lifelong learning discourse as this is being articulated in the current historical conjuncture. For, while the humanist, liberatory educational strands are driven, as we shall have occasion to note in some detail in a later section, by the conviction that most citizens can reach ever higher levels of cognitive competence through an immersion in a pedagogically sound paideia, the rationality underpinning prevailing economic arrangements constrains the creation of meaningful work in which such heightened competencies can be expressed. In the current context, it is easy to find oneself, as an educator, in the contradictory position of extolling the virtues of upgrading oneself in order to fill…downgrading jobs! In other words, a commitment to further education and training throughout life, when this is justified from within an economistic framework, requires the generation of work profiles that are meaningful, fulfilling, and which dignify one's being.

Now this is precisely the point that is made directly (Steedman) or indirectly (Brandsma, Smyth) by many of the Framework projects to justify the Learning Society: Namely that, increasingly, Europe is becoming a post-fordist, high ability society that requires its workers to be innovative, flexible, creative, and autonomous. Because of the upgrading of work demands, citizens should also upgrade themselves in order to be better able to communicate effectively, to work in teams and in groups, to know how to evaluate themselves and each other, and to identify and articulate work goals in a pro-active and intelligent manner (see Brown & Lauder, 1991). Little reference is made, however, to the preponderance of low-skilled, low-ability jobs that persist, despite all utopic forecastings, in enormous numbers in highly developed economies—and indeed to the fact that there may be a low-skills option to development (Brown et al., 2001). Various authors have pointed out the extent to which optimistic scenarios attempting to drum up support for painful restructuring do not correspond to empirical reality, and that what we have is not a skill crisis, but a job crisis (Livingstone, 1999; Avis et al., 1996; Wolf, 2002).

'Learning'—a new moral imperative?

In trawling through the eleven Framework research projects, one theme suggested itself quite powerfully, namely that in most projects, learning is presented as a 'moral imperative'. This, of course, reflects current preoccupations in Europe—and world-wide—with competitiveness in high ability societies. Such preoccupations are also echoed in mainstream policy documents, including those issued by the Commission, where improved economic performance is the key justification for lifelong learning. In this context, the citizen has a duty towards the state, towards Europe, and towards him/herself to invest in continued education and training in order to contribute to the wealth-generation process, to the development of 'high ability' economies, and to avoid becoming a burden to society (Sauquet, Heger). The 'work ethic' is here transposed into a different sphere: It is now the 'accumulation' of learning throughout life that regulates the heartbeat of the citizen of the 21st century.

This representation of the relationship between the citizen and learning has possibly attained such a taken-for-granted quality about it that it would require the tools of sociological method—and most notably a historical, anthropological, and critical imagination (Giddens, 1987)—in order to better appreciate its constructed and historically contingent nature. What I am here referring to as the 'learning ethic' stands in sharp contrast, for instance, with classical notions of a Learning Society, where members of the Greek polis aspired for a life of leisure to enjoy the pleasures of education and active citizenry (Hutchins, 1970).[5] It also stands in sharp contrast with Habermas' beautifully evocative characterisation of Europe as a 'learning society'—a society that has 'in the course of a rich Jewish and Greek, Roman and Christian heritage... learnt a sensitive attitude and a balanced response, both to the deplorable losses incurred by the disintegration of a traditional past and to the promise of future benefits from the 'creative destruction' of present productivity' (Habermas, 2001: 20). Contemporary 'mainstream' references to the Learning Society are poor by comparison to this 'normative self-understanding' described by Habermas, the 'painful learning process', the 'history of learning' that has led Europeans 'to construct new and ever more sophisticated forms of 'solidarity among strangers' (Habermas, 2001: 21). Much of what we read about the Learning Society tends to make virtue out of necessity, where the very term 'lifelong' has an ominous ring to it, particularly for those who associate learning with the 'hidden injuries' suffered in schools (Smyth). In this latter-day version of the Learning Society, citizens are exhorted to remain engaged in—and to take responsibility for their own—learning; i.e., to constantly evolve and re-shape themselves, right into their old age (Tikkanen, Cullen), in order to have use-value in the labour market. The fact that such 're-forming' is targeted not only at technical but also intra- and inter-personal qualities—such as social and communication 'skills' (see Steedman)—indicates how the far is the reach of the industrial agenda in the shaping of citizens. Learners are conceptualised as multi-skilled members of an unstable, ever-shifting society (Sauquet, Kokosalakis), integration into which depends on a Darwinian view of education, inasmuch as 'it is not the strongest of the species that survives, nor the most intelligent, but the one most responsive to change'. It is not at all incidental or insignificant that this excerpt from Darwin features on the first line of the first page of the World Bank 2002 publication, Constructing Knowledge Societies.

Of course, in one important sense, the concept of the 'Learning Society' is a pleonasm, in that for communities to survive, they have to be characterized by learning and adaptation to change—a point made by Donald Shon (1973) in his discussion of lifelong learning two decades ago. And the notion of continued learning and access to training opportunities renders some employment very attractive to some (upwardly mobile) workers (Svensson). Key educators and leading educational psychologists have shown that it is precisely this plasticity of human nature—what Bruner calls 'the will to learn' (1966)—that has ensured survival in the face of a changing environment. However, such considerations, when accepted uncritically, lead to the betrayal of the humanist values that have traditionally informed education. In contemporary conceptualisations, the learner becomes an 'object' of economic development. The 'needs' of the economy for skilled labour determine the mould in which the working citizen is required to fit, with knowledge becoming nothing more than a commodity, and therefore related to the field of 'having', and not of 'being'. This is not just an obtuse philosophical point. It has major implications for the type of further education and training that is offered to adults in the Learning Society, and whether it is strictly competency-based or whether it aims at the development of the person as a whole. It is all the more important given that the economy to which the citizen is enjoined to contribute to through a lifelong up-dating of skills is increasingly one which operates in a context where the wealth created through such educated labour is siphoned off to a few. There is well-nigh international consensus—even on the very part of such pro-marketeers as George Soros—that neo-liberalism increases the gap between the haves and the have-nots (Hobsbawm, 1998; Grass & Bourdieu, 2002: 66).

My argument is that the call for Lifelong Learning is appealing at one level, engaging as it does humanist notions of knowledge as a resource for self-development and empowerment. However, it is that very same appeal which works in an ideological manner to mask another, deeper level. Indeed, none of the Framework projects highlight the irony of the call to lifelong learning in a context shaped by extreme instability for workers (see Bauman, 1991), where privatisation and restructuring are undertaken to heighten capital accumulation and deepen the insecurity of labour, where contributions to social security and pensions are increasingly threatened not just by demographic deficits, but also by the vagaries and humours of the stock exchange, and where (as Cullen notes) the state seems to be increasingly disengaging itself from the economy, and intervening more and more in education and training (Kokosalakis, Cullen)—for which one cannot but read the formation of labour power according to the needs of industry. The point is not whether lifelong learning is an attractive ideal; rather, the point is to inquire: What sort of learning for what sort of life? In the context of an integrating Europe, where structural funds are becoming increasingly scarce, and where economic imbalances within and between established and in-coming members of the Union are bound to increase, one also needs to ask: What sort of learning, for what sort of life, for who? It is not outside of the logic of capital—or of European history, for that matter—to imagine a continent which has privileged sectors thriving at the expense of subordinate groups. Indeed, one cynic noted,

'If there ever was an all-European house, it had an upstairs and a downstairs... There was the industrialized West, and there was another, underdeveloped Europe to provide meals and servants—raw materials, food and cheap migrant labour... and Europe in 2018 will consist of a Western superstate whose floors are scrubbed by Romanians or Poles, and a periphery of beggarly Bantustans.' (Ascherson, 1988, p.12—cited by Slowinski, 1998)

The idea of having a qualified and trained workforce on the cheap—thanks to improved lifelong learning opportunities—is hardly palatable to anyone who is even remotely engaged with the idea of education as liberation, unless that idea is accompanied by effective economic and social measures that guarantee the resources that are required for dignified living. For 'moral imperatives' imply a relationship of reciprocity, with an obligation being counter-balanced by an entitlement. More and more, however, the notion of a Learning Society is premised on an imperative to learn that seems to be subject to the laws of diminishing returns for the citizen, and increasing returns for the captains of industry. This is particularly so as employers successfully export the financial burden associated with up-skilling and the learning enterprise onto the state, with their contribution in the so-called HRD area being either negligible, or so parsimonious that the state has to intervene and impose an obligation (Heger).

Performativity and knowledge

'Learning', in a good number of the research projects, tends to overlap very closely with the semantic fields covered by such words as 'competence' and 'skills'. While other aspects of 'knowing' are covered, the tendency is to privilege 'performative knowledge'—i.e. 'knowing how' (what one can do) rather than 'knowing that' (what one knows). There is a danger here of stripping knowledge from its social, moral and intellectual qualities, as a result of which the concern about the educational enterprise is exclusively with owning attributes rather than with being, in the sense developed by Faure and his colleagues in their 1972 report. This picks up earlier points made in this paper, and connects with classical, humanistic and emancipatory conceptualisations of education, where 'learning to do' is inseparable from the context in which knowledge and skills are to be applied. It also connects with the idea that all forms of education and training should contribute to the overarching ideals associated with the 'good life', and to the dispositional qualities and actions that constitute 'virtuous living'.

Competency-based forms of education and training tend to be preoccupied with breaking down knowledge into the smallest 'component parts', and to a focus on these parts rather than on the whole (Hyland, 1994)—a surprisingly

Fordist logic in what is often claimed to be a post-fordist age. As Smith (2002: 4) notes, 'the move from competence as a human virtue to a discrete thing that we possess is fundamental. In essence, it involves adopting a way of viewing the world that undermines the very qualities that many of us would argue make for liberatory education.' Much of justification for this approach is based on the need to facilitate assessment, comparability and transfer (Kokosalakis). It also smoothes progression between different skill levels (Steedman). And it is also true that competency approaches tend to demystify learning and enhance access by emphasising clearly articulated targets that encourage accountability of teachers, and not solely of learners. Indeed, such points are often made in defence of competency approaches as a way of ensuring equity in outcomes. The point however is that when technocratic rationality becomes the overriding logic in matters educational, the liberatory and empowering facets of the enterprise become pale shadows, only to be conjured up to fulfil an ideologically appeasing role.

The social nature of learning

It is one of the more positive qualities of the research projects focused on in this paper that they present learning as a group/social activity rather more than as being an attribute of the individual. This represents an important break from the overwhelmingly individualistic notions that tend to anchor most Commission documents in the field of education, notions that are, needless to say, intimately linked to a neo-liberal ideology that promotes privatisation and competitive individualism—and ultimately personal responsibility for 'self-learning' (Kokosalakis, Cullen). As Mayo & Borg note, in their critical analysis of the Commission's Memorandum on Lifelong Learning, 'In these stringent neo-liberal times, the notion of self-directive learning lends itself to a discourse that allows the State to abdicate its responsibilities in providing the quality education to which every citizen is entitled and shift them entirely onto the learners or larger entities such as NGOs' (2002: 10). What in this context we have called the 'moral imperative' to learn interpellates the individual in such a way as to place the onus directly on him or her to engage in the task of constructing a profile that matches labour market 'needs' and 'opportunities'.

In contrast is the more pedagogically and ideologically attractive scenario presented by several of the Framework projects, particularly when they focus on the activity of learning within work settings and organisations, and where learning is integrated as a valued part of the organisation (Sarcina, Tjepkema, Svensson, Brandsma). Considerations of organisational learning reinforce a Vygotskian understanding of 'ability' (Vygotsky, 1978, 1994; Wertsh, 1985), which stresses the fact that advancement in knowledge of all types can be made in the context of a supportive group. Vygotsky—and his colleagues Luria and Leontiev—had argued that the crux of learning was not the innate 'ability' of the student, but rather the skill of the teacher to provide an effective support as the learner moves from one form and level of understanding to the other. They were convinced that knowledge as well as intellectual potential was not so much a given attribute that an individual 'possessed', in the same way that one possesses capital. Rather, learning was an achievement that was socially achieved, and the level of knowledge and skill that a learner achieves is dependent on participation in collective activity. Simon (1986: 114) synthesises well the views of the Soviet school when she argues that 'what the child can do in co-operation today he [sic] can do alone tomorrow'. Therefore the only good kind of instruction is that which marches ahead of development and leads it, which is aimed not at the level the child has attained, as usually advised, but at 'ripening functions'.

Such notions have been relayed into mainstream educational psychology by such thinkers as Jerome Bruner, and more recently, his student Howard Gardner (1991, 1999). The former has recently argued that 'human mental activity is neither solo nor conducted unassisted, even when it goes on 'inside the head'' (Bruner, 1996: xi). It is this culturalist perspective that underpins several of the notions that many of the FP4 and 5 research papers work with. Among these notions or educational practices are references to 'collective intelligence' (Tjepkema), to 'relational capital' (Sauquet), to 'communities of practice' (Tjepkema), as well as to 'intergenerational' (Tikkanen), 'networked' (Cullen, Sauquet) and 'collaborative' learning (Sarcina, Steedman, Tjepkema), with motivation suffering in individualised learning environments (Brandsma). Not only are these notions central to any discussion of the process of knowledge integration, but they serve the purpose of taking us away from a preoccupation with measuring skills and ability, that is from a psychometric approach that, as we will see below, is linked to the social construction of ignorance for the purposes of selection and exclusion (Steedman). What drives the pedagogical relationship, therefore, is the search for the optimal ways in which learning can be facilitated, and for many, that optimum can be reached in interactional contexts.

This understanding of learning has several important implications. One of them has already been hinted at, namely that it signals a crucial shift away from élitist notions of continued learning for the few, to a conviction that all citizens can learn and achieve high levels of cognitive competence if only they are provided with the right pedagogical and resource environment. Indeed, some of the Framework projects speak of learning as an entitlement, whereby all citizens have the right to a guaranteed 'minimum learning platform' (Steedman), particularly given the situation whereby up to a third of students in some European countries are not equipped to participate in further education (Steedman). Another, related, implication of this culturalist approach to learning is that failure to learn is not necessarily a cognitive or attitudinal deficit ('learning gaps', as Heger refers to them), as it has often been made out be, but rather a result of a dysfunctional educative environment, one that somehow fails to connect with the materially-embedded learning styles (Bernstein, 2000) and cultural capital (Bourdieu & Passeron, 1990) of the student. In this regard, a number of Framework projects are careful to highlight the fact that age, class, gender and ethnicity mediate access (Sauquet, Smyth, Steedman, Tikkanen, Brandsma) to the learning entitlement referred to here, and that there is a 'segmented learning market' (Heger, Cullen) feeding an equally segmented labour market.

The projects are however somewhat less forthcoming when it comes to acknowledging—let alone highlighting—the contradictions that arise from presenting learning as a social achievement on the one hand, and the fact that the social context in which such a communal activity is to be achieved is overwhelmingly fragmentary. As Bauman (2001: 3) has argued, in a world where market ideologies have become dominant and infuse all areas of life, we have increasingly lost a sense of working together to direct our lives. Echoing the concern expressed earlier about the engineering of insecurity, Bauman pursues the theme of fragmentation by noting that:

> 'Insecurity affects us all, immersed as we all are in a fluid and unpredictable world of deregulation, flexibility, competitiveness and endemic uncertainty, but each one of us suffers anxiety on our own, as a private problem, an outcome of personal failings and a challenge to our provide savoir-faire and agility. We are called, as Ulrich Beck has acidly observed, to seek biographical solutions to more systematic contradictions; we look for individual salvation from shared troubles. That strategy is unlikely to bring the results we are after, since it leaves the roots of insecurity intact; moreover it is precisely this falling back on our individual wits and resources that injects the world with the insecurity we wish to escape.' (Bauman, 2001: 144)[6]

Alternative routes to learning

Closely linked to the notion that all citizens can learn, is the view—one that comes across particularly strongly in several of the Framework projects, and which reflects the thinking expressed in the Commission's Memorandum—that the institutional contexts and social practices associated with regular schooling fail a large number of people. These, it is argued, can reconnect with learning if alternative educational contexts as well as alternative delivery (pedagogies) and assessment (accreditation) strategies are developed (Tjepkema, Steedman, Kokosalakis, Smyth, Svensson).

Such a focus on alternative routes to knowledge and skill acquisition is central to current debates about initial and continuing education, and is very promising in that it recognizes and values the serendipitous nature of learning. One rather idealistic way of expressing this notion, and linking it with the one discussed in the previous section, is to say that 'students flower in different ways, but all have it in them to bloom'. Many, of course, have wilted in mainstream school environments and in formal education settings (Smyth), where a 'one size fits all' mentality tends to prevail. The emphasis in several of the projects that are trying to prefigure the Learning Society is on flexibility—flexibility of entry into learning, of scheduling provision, of funding—emphasising, therefore, a demand-led, not a supply-led service (Kokosalakis). Such an approach breaks down a number of boundaries associated with traditional formalised learning (Husén, 1974, 1986; Kress, 2000), among them being:

- 'The boundary of *time*, with education being extended beyond organised or institutionally controlled time, thanks to increasing opportunities for learning made available by community-based initiatives, as well as by information and communication technologies' (Sauquet, Tikkanen).
- 'The boundary of *place*, with providers operating in contexts that are normally associated with leisure or work, implying that they move to the site of the clientele, rather than the other way around' (Cullen).
- 'The boundary of *institutions*, with universities, colleges, and HRD specialists collaborating with companies (Tjepkema, Kokosalakis) in facilitating organisational learning, thus developing 'learning alliances' (Svensson) in 'networked public spaces''(Cullen, Sauquet).
- 'The boundary of *audience*, breaking down the marshalling of age-specific groups around learning tasks' (Tikkanen).
- 'The boundary around *knowledge*, with the blurring of borders between the knowledge sanctioned in educational institutions and the knowledge of the everyday, between the 'sacred' and the 'profane', between programmed and incidental learning or tacit knowledge' (Steedman, Tjepkema).

Such flexibility and blurring of boundaries are presented by the Framework projects as a part of an attractive set of progressive alternatives that democratize access and facilitate re-entry routes into learning (Steedman, Sarcina, Kokosalakis, Tikkanen). I agree. I would like, however, to make one important caveat. The problem with non-formal, alternative learning routes, and 'non-dedicated learning environments' is that, by definition, they tend to be unorganised, or at least unsystematic. As such, informal and non-formal learning strategies do not lend themselves easily to assessment (Steedman), or to accountability and guarantees, and that, as with the idea of the 'individual learning account' which perhaps best encapsulates such flexible pedagogical practices, the condition for success is the notion of shared responsibility, whereby different partners, including the state and employers, make their contribution. As Borg & Mayo (2002: 18) note, 'There is always the danger that the notion of shared responsibility, currently being practiced in the UK, the Netherlands, and Sweden, could one day follow the health and pensions' track and become an individual rather than a shared responsibility.' To this I would add another concern. When Framework projects echo the Commission's desire to establish a broader delivery platform, with social partners pooling their respective resources so that alternative sites—and principally the workplace— are re-organised for the purpose of learning (Steedman, Tjepkema), issues as to which educational agendas will prevail cannot, and must not be elided.

Rhetoric and reality

Finally, some of the projects end up questioning the extent to which the ideal of the Learning Society, attractive though it may well be for a whole host of (contradictory) reasons, is more present discursively than in reality (Tjepkema, Kokosalakis). Such questioning raises important issues regarding how far the whole enterprise of learning that citizens are being enjoined to take on is, in fact, not only an objectively attainable one (i.e. is it possible), but also a subjectively appealing one (i.e. is it desirable). In other words, are citizens keen to be party to the construction of the Learning Society? Does this resonate with their needs, given our earlier discussion of constant learning and adaptability a species-specific phenomenon? Such doubts are important, because they strike at the very heart of the representation of the 'learning citizen'.

The doubts expressed within the context of the Framework projects tend to fall within the realm of examining the objective conditions that must be fulfilled if a knowledge-based society is indeed to come about. The implementation gap is thus explained with reference to such environmental factors as: The capacity of SMEs to provide required resources (Sarcina), an ageing workforce that is less disposed to learning (Tikkanen), and the availability of time to integrate knowledge (Svensson, Tjepkema).

This kind of logic echoes the preoccupation of the industrial class itself, which, through its mouthpiece the ERT—and specifically the latter's Working Group on Competitiveness—castigated EU member states for failing to deliver on their Lisbon promises, claiming that 'the overall cost of doing business in Europe remains too high', to the detriment of the goal of making Europe 'a global competitor in the new knowledge-based economy' (ERT, 2002: 3, 4).

Drawing its legitimacy from the fact that 'Entrepreneurs are creators of wealth and of jobs', and empowered by the fact that 'the Lisbon agenda established a balance between economic and social issues, tilted in favour of entrepreneurship' (ibid, 3), the ERT expresses impatience with the European Council penchant for 'identifying problems rather than solving them' (ibid, 5), and points to ten key priority areas for implementation. Unsurprisingly, these include further liberalization, drastic reductions in regulation, and the elimination of tax obstacles to cross-border business activities. More directly relevant to our argument, another key priority area is education, given the 'growing awareness of [its] importance...for economic growth, employment and competitiveness' (ibid, 11). The ERT notes the increased take-up of new technologies in schools, but expresses major concern about the fact that 'there seems little focus on the parallel development of the culture and attitudes that would foster a more positive approach to lifelong learning, innovation and entrepreneurship' (ibid, 11).

The affinity with the Framework projects is not in terms of ideology, as much as in the attribution of the failure of progress in the long march towards the Learning Society to environmental factors—in this case, the failure of governments to create appropriate incentives and conditions to re-shape 'culture and attitudes'. An alternative to this stance is to ask a more fundamental question, one that has driven the argument right through this paper: Why should citizens want to engage in lifelong learning that is defined in these economistic terms—especially when the realities of the everyday needs and burdens of citizens (such as parenting, loving, etc) are hardly taken into account (Svensson). For, in my view, the failure of progress in achieving the so-called 'knowledge-based society' is not to be necessarily read as a deficit on the part of schools, governments, or citizens, but rather as a reaction against—and resistance to—the further colonisation of our world by technocratic rationality (Cullen), and to the reduction of what Masschelein (2001: 2), drawing inspiration from Hannah Arendt, refers to as the 'logic of bare life.' As educators, let us by all means strive to encourage learning in all its guises, within and outside the traditional narrow confines of space and time, if such education empowers persons to become subjects, and not objects of history. But let us also be more aware of the structural features that drive the LLL rhetoric in corporate Europe, where the agendas vehicled by that rhetoric are, despite their progressive moments, nevertheless beneficial to some very powerful social groups. In this sense, the very form of knowledge/learning, and how this articulates with societal structures of power where private and public interests seem to converge, deserves to be an object of more focused analysis than that afforded by the Framework projects.

Notes

1. The eleven projects are the following: 'Innovations in education and training' (co-ordinator: J. Cullen); 'Lifelong learning for older workers' (T. Tikkanen); 'Learning environments within companies' (L. Svensson); 'Lifelong learning: implications for universities' (N. Kokosalakis); 'Integrated funding models for lifelong learning' (R.-J. Heger); 'Lifelong learning: the role of human resource development within organisations' (S. Tjepkema); 'School to work transitions in Europe' (E. Smyth); 'Training the long-term unemployed' (J. Brandsma); 'Small business training and competitiveness' (A. Sauquet); 'Organisational learning: the role of SME clusters' (R. Sarcina); 'Low skills: a problem for Europe' (H. Steedman).

2. These briefing papers are available on the 'New Perspectives for Learning' site, http://www.pjb.co.uk/npl/ – Similarly helpful were longer summaries of some of the full project reports by Michael Medlock.

3. Critical humanistic approaches to education are predicated on three main tenets. According to Aloni (1999), the first is 'philosophical, consisting of a conception of [the human] as an autonomous and rational being and a fundamental respect for all humans by virtue of being endowed with freedom of will, rational thinking, moral conscience, imaginative and creative powers.' The second tenet is socio-political, 'consisting of a universal ethics of human equality, reciprocity, and solidarity and a political order of pluralistic, just and humane democracy.' The third tenet is 'pedagogical, consisting in the commitment to assist all individuals to realize and perfect their potentialities and 'to enjoy', in the words of Mortimer Adler, 'as fully as possible all the goods that make a human life as good as it can be.'

4. Details regarding the European Round Table of Industrialists, as well as relevant documents issued by ERT, can be found on the following web site: http://www.ert.be

5. True enough, such pleasures could only be enjoyed at the expense of exporting labour onto slaves—but one could argue that machines and technology have replaced slaves in today's world. It is interesting to note that, while the claim is often made that citizens nowadays have more leisure time to enjoy, learning is in fact hampered because there is not enough quality time available, in sites such as the work place, for reflection and integration of knowledge and skills into personal competence (Svensson). It is also interesting to note that while earlier critiques of capitalism focused on the imposition of 'time discipline', and the way this led to a bifurcation between the worlds of 'work' and of 'leisure' (Clarke & Critcher, 1985), now leisure is increasingly defined as learning time, with 'learning' being directly connected to the skills requirements of the labour market. In other words, the needs of capital for further accumulation in the face of competition colonize the surplus time that was once (potentially) the citizen's respite from the logic of capital.

6. As cited in Smith (2002: 3).

References

Aloni, N. (1999) 'Humanistic education'. In *Encyclopedia of Philosophy of Education.* http://www.vusst.hr/ENCYCLOPAEDIA/humanistic_education.htm

Apple, M.W. (1995) *Education and Power.* New York: Routledge.

Apple, M.W. (2001) *Educating the 'Right' Way: Markets, Standards, God, and Inequality.* New York: Routledge.

Ascherson, N. (1988) 'Below stairs in Europe's house.' *The Observer,* December 11, p.12.

Avis, J., Bloomer, M., Esland, G. & Gleeson, D. (1996) *Knowledge and Nationhood: Education, Politics and Work.* London: Cassell.

Bauman, Z. (2001) *Seeking Safety in an Insecure World.* Cambridge: Polity Press.

Bernstein, B. (2000) *Pedagogy, Symbolic Control and Identity: Theory, Research, Critique.* Lanham, Maryland: Rowman & Littlefield Publishers Inc. [revised edition]

Borg, G. & Mayo, P. (2002) 'The EU Memorandum on lifelong learning. Diluted old wine in new bottles?' Paper presented at the 2002 BAICE Conference, Lifelong Learning and the Building of Human and Social Capital. University of Nottingham, 6-8 September 2002.

Bourdieu, P. & Passeron, J.C. (1990) *Reproduction in Education, Society and Culture.* London: Sage. [2nd edition]

Brown, P. & H. Lauder (1991) 'Education, economy and social change'. *International Journal of Sociology of Education*, Vol. 1, pp. 3–23.

Brown, P., Green, A. & Lauder, H. (eds) (2001) *High Skills: Globalization, Competitiveness and Skill Formation.* Oxford: Oxford University Press.

Bruner, J. (1966) *Toward a Theory of Instruction.* Cambridge, Mass.: Harvard University Press.

Bruner, J. (1996) *The Culture of Education.* Cambridge, Mass.: Harvard University Press.

Christiansen, J.F. (1992) 'The Danish 'no' to Maastricht.' *New Left Review*, No. 195, pp. 97-101.

Clarke, J. & Critcher, C. (1985) *The Devil Makes Work: Leisure in Capitalist Britain.* London: Macmillan.

Edwards, R. (1997) *Changing Places? Flexibility, Lifelong Learning and a Learning Society.* London: Routledge.

European Round Table of Industrialists (1995) *Education for Europeans: Towards the Learning Society.* http://www.ert.be

European Round Table of Industrialists (1997) *Investing in Knowledge: The Integration of Technology in European Education.* http://www.ert.be

European Round Table of Industrialists (2002) 'Will European Governments in Barcelona keep their Lisbon promises?' *ERT to the Barcelona European Council of March 2002* (message dated February 2002). http://www.ert.be/pdf/ERT%20Message%20to%20Barcelona.pdf

Faure, E. et al. (1972) *Learning to Be.* Paris: UNESCO.

Gardner, H. (1991) *The Unschooled Mind: How Children Think and How Schools Should Teach.* New York: Basic Books.

Gardner, H. (1999) *Intelligence Reframed. Multiple Intelligences for the 21st Century.* New York: Basic Books.

Geertz, C. (1973) *The Interpretation of Cultures.* New York: Basic Books. [1993 edition]

Gelpi, E. (1985) *Lifelong Education and International Relations.* London: Croom Helm.

Giddens, A. (1987) *Sociology: A Brief but Critical Introduction.* New York: Harcourt Brace Jovanovich. [2nd edition]

Giroux, H.A. (1997) *Pedagogy and the Politics of Hope: Theory, Culture, and Schooling: A Critical Reader.* Boulder, Colo.: Westview Press.

Grass, G. & Bourdieu, P. (2002) 'The 'progressive' restoration: a Franco-German dialogue'. *New Left Review*, No. 14 (March-April), pp. 63-77.

Haahr, J.H. (1992) 'European integration and the Left in Britain and Denmark.' *Journal of Common Market Studies*, Vol. 30(1), pp. 77–100.

Habermas, J. (1976) *Knowledge and Human Interests.* London: Heinemann.

Habermas, J. (2001) 'Why Europe needs a constitution.' *New Left Review*, No. 11 (Sept.-Oct.), pp. 5-26.

Hanushek, E.A. (1994) 'The economic returns of educational investment.' In E.A Hanushek *Making Schools Work: Improving Performance and Controlling Costs.* Washington, DC: Brookings Institute.

Hobsbawm, E. (1998) 'The death of neo-liberalism'. *Marxism Today*, November-December. http://csf.coloradu.edu/forums/ipe/jan99/0154.html

Husén, T. (1974) *The Learning Society*. London: Methuen.

Husén, T. (1986) *The Learning Society Revisited*. Oxford: Pergamon.

Hutchins, R.M. (1970) *The Learning Society*. Harmondsworth: Penguin.

Hyland, T. (1994) *Competence, Education and NVQs. Dissenting Perspectives*. London: Cassell.

Jarvis, P. (ed.) (2001) *The Age of Learning. Education and the Knowledge Society*. London: Kogan Page.

Kress, G. (2000) 'A curriculum for the future'. *Cambridge Journal of Education*, Vol. 30(1), pp. 133-145.

Lê Thành Khôi (1995) *Éducation et Civilisations: Sociétes d'Hier*. Paris: UNESCO & Nathan.

Livingstone, D.W. (1999) 'Beyond human capital theory: The underemployment problem.' *International Journal of Contemporary Sociology*, Vol. 36(2), pp. 163-192.

Masschelein, J. (2001) 'The discourse of the learning society and the loss of childhood.' Journal of Philosophy of Education, Vol. 35(1), pp. 1-20.

McLaren, P. (1997) *Revolutionary Multiculturalism: Pedagogies of Dissent for the New Millennium*. Boulder, Colo.: Westview Press.

Muller, W.C. & Wright, V. (1994) 'Reshaping the state in Western Europe: The limits to retreat.' *West European Politics*, Vol. 17(3), pp. 1-11.

Papert, S. (1980) *Mindstorms: Children, Computersand Powerful ideas*. New York: Basic Books.

Ramsay, H. (1992) 'Whose champions? Multinationals, labour and industry policy in the European Community after 1992.' *Capital and Class*, Vol. 48, pp. 17-39.

Ranson, S. (ed.) (1998) *Inside the Learning Society*. London: Cassell.

Rohrs, H. (1992) 'A United Europe as a challenge to education'. *European Journal of Intercultural Studies*, Vol. 3(1), pp. 59-70.

Ross, G. (1992) 'Confronting the new Europe.' *New Left Review*, No. 191, pp. 49-68.

Ryba, R. (1994) ''Unity in Diversity': The enigma of the European dimension in education.' Paper presented at the 16th C.E.S.E. conference, Copenhagen.

Schön, D. (1973) *Beyond the Stable State. Public and Private Learning in a Changing Society*. Harmondsworth: Penguin.

Simon, J. (1986) 'Psychology in the service of education: the work of A.R. Luria, 1902-1977.' *Education with Production*, Vol. 4(2).

Slowinski, J. (1998) 'SOCRATES invades central Europe.' *Education Policy Analysis Archives*, Vol. 6(9). http://www.olam.ed.asu.edu/epaa/v6n9.html

Smith, M. K. (2002) 'Community'. In *The Encyclopedia of Informal Education*. http://www.infed.org/community/community.htm

Sultana, R.G. (1995) 'A uniting Europe, a dividing education? Supranationalism, Euro-centrism and the curriculum.' *International Studies in Sociology of Education*, Vol. 5(2), pp. 115-144.

Sultana, R.G. (1996) 'The European Union and its educational agenda: a wolf in sheep's clothing?' In K. Watson, S. Modgil & C. Modgil (eds) *Educational Dilemmas: Debates and Diversity* [Volume 3]. London: Cassell, pp. 66-74.

Sultana, R.G. (2002) 'Quality education and training for tomorrow's Europe: A contrapuntal reading of European Commission documents.' In A. Nóvoa & M. Lawn (eds) *Fabricating Europe: The Formation of an Education Space*. Dordrecht: Kluwer, pp. 109-130.

Vygotsky, L.S. (1978) *Mind in Society*. Cambridge, Mass.: Harvard University Press.

Vygotsky, L.S. (1994) *The Vygotsky Reader*. Oxford: Blackwell.

Wertsh, J. (1985) *Vygotsky and the Social Formation of Mind*. Cambridge, Mass.: Harvard University Press.

Wolf, A. (2002) *Does Education Matter? Myths about Education and Economic Growth*. London: Penguin.

World Bank (2002) *Constructing Knowledge Societies: New Challenges for Tertiary Education*. Washington DC: World Bank.

CHAPTER FOUR

Intellectual Technologies in the Constitution of Learning Societies

Richard Edwards

Introduction

There are a number of issues that intrigue me in current EU policy debates on lifelong learning and a learning society. The first is why learning is identified so centrally as a focus for policy. Education and training have always been important aspects of policy in the post-Second World War period, but it is now given even greater significance. Many of the responses to social and economic conditions are laid at the door of education and training as a first port of call. However, despite the logic built into the discourses of continuous change associated with constructs such as the knowledge economy and information society, this seems to over-emphasise the role of education generally and qualifications specifically in addressing social, economic and civic challenges. Second and perhaps more significantly, it is not simply education and training which are part of the policy embrace, but learning itself, as illustrated by discourses of lifelong learning, learning organisations and learning societies. Learning and learners become the focus of policy as much as, if not more than, structures of provision, wherein the individual is often positioned as responsible for their own condition, with less concern for the wider structures of inequality built into the labour marker and social relations in general. The message at times seems to be one of consuming your way out of exclusion through learning and qualifications, when, of course, opportunities are structurally patterned. Thus, while access to skills and qualifications might be increased, they may not be widened (Green 2002), and despite or because of the specific discourses of lifelong learning in play, opportunity may be circumscribed. This is something to which research can contribute as much as challenge.

For some policies of lifelong learning are part of a revised welfare statism (e.g. Field 2000) in which there is an attempt to mobilise civil society and a greater emphasis on individualised responses to social and economic conditions. The argument is that the practices of governing are now less concerned with providing services for populations than in mobilising those concerned to help themselves. This is a view also shared in part by Griffin (2002) who argues that welfare state policies to provide education are being displaced by consumerist strategies where the state enables rather than provides. However, unlike Field, Griffin positions these reconfigurations in governing as part of a neo-liberal assault on the welfare state. For Griffin, the policy discourse of lifelong learning precisely signifies this shift, displacing, as it does, welfare state concerns for the provision of adult education. Despite their differences, both Field and Griffin are reflecting on the changing forms as well as contents of policy and policy-making.

This is an area that is being explored more widely in the social sciences. The shift in forms of governing—emphasising the mobilising of civil society and the support for active citizenship—has also been a central issue for those writers who draw upon Foucault's (1991) work to examine changing forms of governance in advanced liberal democratic states (e.g. Rose 1999, Dean 1999). In these writings, there is a focus on the specific strategies and techniques of governing, those 'actions at a distance'—including lifelong learning - through which there is an ordering of social practices (Miller and Rose 1993). In this paper, I want to explore the role of research in relation to EU policy on lifelong learning as part of the strategies and techniques of contemporary governing, wherein research is positioned as one of the intellectual technologies of governance. Here the subjects drawn upon to represent lifelong learning and learning societies are 'an 'intellectual technology', a way of making visible and intelligible certain features of persons, their conducts, and their relations with one another' (Rose 1998: 10-11). In particular, I want to explore the subject that is both drawn upon to do research and the subject who is positioned to be worked upon and through by policy. What I want to suggest is that the research-policy discourse positions the subject in specific ways and provide the tools through which those subjects are worked upon and encouraged to work upon themselves to make them more productive—economically and socially. Here the learning subject is positioned in particular ways—autonomous, flexible, enterprising—within a moral economy designed to populate and order a learning society of a particular sort. This is signified in pedagogies that focus on the development of autonomy, self-direction, core and transferable skills, learning to learn, etc. A learning subject is one who adopts a learning approach to life as part of their care of their selves. Lifelong learning becomes one of the intellectual technologies through which social, economic and political practices are re-ordered.

Within this type of analysis, policy and research are explored for the mobilisations of certain subjects/disciplines to both represent what is occurring and put forward directions for policy. Certain populations are constituted as objects to be researched and acted upon e.g. 'youth', 'women', 'small and medium enterprises' (New Perspectives for Learning 2001). These are taken to be pre-existing in a social reality to be explored rather than constituted through discursive practices. However, as Miller and Rose (1993: 80) point out in relation to the economy, 'before one can seek to manage a domain such as an economy it is first necessary to conceptualise a set of processes and relations as an economy which is amenable to management'. In other words, while objects of research and policy are 'an effect of stable arrays or networks of relations' (Law 2002: 91), they are treated as naturalistic objects, pre-existing in the social world. I am therefore following Pels, et al (2002: 11) in the view that 'objects need symbolic framings, storylines and human spokespersons in order to acquire social lives; social relationships and practices in turn need to be materially grounded in order to gain spatial and temporal endurance'. In other words, they need ordering, part of which is provided through the circulation of policy and research discourses: 'different modes of ordering produce certain forms of organisation. They produce certain material arrangements. They produce certain subject positions. And they produce certain forms of knowledge' (Law 2001: 3). What I am suggesting is that the symbolic work is not being addressed in EU lifelong learning policy research; the performative aspects of research and policy are thereby left reflexively unquestioned: 'every category creates a boundary (or, more dramatically, a wound) and hence a space for a specular/textual performance that can be claimed as territory whether 'real' or 'imagined'' (Schostak 2002: 153).

Research projects provide a range of intellectual technologies through which there is an attempt to represent and order phenomena. 'The government of a population, a national economy, an enterprise... or even oneself becomes possible only through discursive mechanisms that represent the domain to be governed as an intelligible field with its limits, characteristics whose component parts are linked together in some more or less systematic manner' (Miller and Rose 1993: 80). More widely, one can view the attention to education, training and learning as part of the strategies for the 'administration of life' (Munro 2000), in which more explicit calculations are attempted through which to establish the efficiency and effectiveness of learning. As I have indicated, in relation to representations of a learning society, economics, psychology sociology are to the fore as the subjects drawn upon. In the process, certain types of subjectivity are mobilised. Here I am using subjects in the double sense to be found in Foucault (1979)—both bodies of knowledge and subjectivities. The reason for this is that if we act on the basis of something being the case, it has effects on what becomes the case. What bodies of knowledge are mobilised in discourses of lifelong learning and a learning society? What bodies—i.e. material artefacts—are mobilised in discourses of lifelong learning? How is lifelong learning constituted as a domain to be mobilised? How are bodies mobilised? The mobilising of subjects is part of the way in which power is exercised in society, where power is taken to both enable and constrain and to circulate in the social rather than be held by certain groups or organisations (Foucault 1980).

Research is as much embedded in these processes as it comments upon them, providing resources that attempt to represent and order social practices. Here learning, knowledge production and the exercise of power are integral to one another and are embodied in the multiple meanings of 'subject' and 'discipline'. 'Power and knowledge directly imply one another: That there is no power relation without the correlative constitution of a field of knowledge, nor any knowledge that does not presuppose and constitute at the same time power relations' (Foucault 1979: 27). Here power/knowledge becomes literally embodied in the technologies adopted, including those of policy.

What concerns me the assumptions and effects are built into research and policy discourses of lifelong learning and a learning society; the lack of reflexivity in the policy focused research in this area; and the methodological insecurity of the research. Underpinning this is a concern with the forms of lifelong learning being developed through research which appears to take for granted certain populations as a focus and certain processes e.g. flexibility, as desirable and desires outcomes. Part of the reason for these concerns are the locations of research in particular fields of study/intellectual technologies e.g. economics, psychology, sociology, politics, within which an unreflexive stance is either adopted through choice and disciplinary affiliation or through contractual compliance to funders. The outcome may be a research base for EU policy in this area, contributing to the spread of technologies of lifelong learning, but the social, economic and political practices being ordered— organised and commanded—in the process may leave much to be desired.

Such an analysis then is not simply conceptual. While the above sketches a theoretical position, it is one that is concerned with understanding concrete practices, including those of research-policy. Its points to questions about the desirability of different conceptions of a lifelong learning, which are questions of value, where these are taken to be variable, context-dependent and pragmatic (Flyvbjerg 2001), as the concepts we use and the assumptions we have inform our actions. To adopt certain technologies of lifelong learning therefore is to always already be an actor in the world, to be part of some network or other. It therefore pays to reflexively examine the discourses of lifelong learning and a learning society as a form of social action in the world, their symbolic and substantive contribution to policy. Discourse, like social structure, is 'not a noun but a verb' (Law 1992: 385). What then are the research discourses of lifelong learning and a learning society?

EU Framework Projects

There is neither the time nor space to engage in a detailed analysis of each of the projects that has been conducted. Also I do not consider it entirely legitimate to try and engage in any 'authoritative' deconstruction of the work undertaken. Such critical work is readily available. Here I am more interested in posing questions as part of a dialogue about these research projects, the subjects upon which they draw and the subjectivities they construct through their own intellectual technologies. To encourage reflexivity is not to talk about the lack of reflexivity in research, but to dialogue with those involved in research-policy practices, as I am myself engaging certain intellectual technologies in my own musings.

Let us first consider the six 'tools' or 'areas of action' identified to support the EU lifelong learning initiative (New Perspective for Learning 2001: 1):

– Building partnerships,
– learning requirements in the knowledge-based society,
– investment in learning,
– making learning more accessible,
– developing a culture of learning,
– quality assurance for learning.

If we doubt the role of research as intellectual technologies, we are reminded by the policy discourse of tools and areas of actions. These are domains to be acted upon in support of lifelong learning, which are themselves tools for lifelong learning, which research is there to support. The narrative structures of these tools/areas of action are largely technicist, as evidenced through the controversial discourse of effectiveness and its fellow traveller, efficiency. Implicit to this discourse are assumptions about for instance:

– EU citizens either being in of having to anticipate a 'knowledge-based society',
– partnership being inherently worthwhile,
– learning being something that one can make more accessible,
– people not learning unless there is a culture of learning,
– the possibility and desirability of learning being quality assured.

We can question each of the above from a variety of positions. For instance, the notion of a knowledge-based society is itself an intellectual technology through which to help re-order EU societies from manufacturing to service economies, in which information rather than knowledge plays a crucial role. Partnerships may bring benefits in some areas, but not in others, for instance where there is concern for keeping alive the diverse languages and cultures within the EU. Learning is an individual and collective endeavour in which people engage either explicitly or implicitly throughout their lives. It is therefore not learning that is made more accessible but education and training opportunities. Similarly, it cannot be a case of either a culture or learning or not so much as one of the natures of the culture and what learning is valued i.e. given weight within the formal structures of education and training.

What I am pointing to here is a conceptual ambiguity in the policy tools of the EU, in which learning is brought to the fore in the discourse of policy, but the substantive issues remain embedded in the policy action areas of education and training. This is reflected in the research projects themselves which overwhelmingly focus on the formal contexts of education and training and to a lesser extent non-formal provision in the workplace. Other contexts of learning are largely overlooked. In John Field's term, there is an attempt to govern the ungovernable. Therefore the slippage is back to the governable, which is perfectly understandable. But then perhaps, we should drop the discourse of lifelong learning and revert to slightly older concerns for lifelong education and training.

If we now move on to individual projects, we can explore who is to be governed and how. Looking at the list of projects, it should be said that they appear to signify a number of snapshots at particular areas and issues rather than be informed by any strategic sense of either policy imperatives or research. Indeed one wonders if some of these projects add much to the existing knowledge base, and maybe even replicate existing national and regional studies. And whether they have purchase in relation to national policy, which   is taking different forms across the EU (Green 2002) is an open question. However, these are additional matters, not altogether relevant here.

The who

Research and policy construct the objects which become the subjects of investigation. They are mobilised through research and policy as key to lifelong learning. They are both constructed through the intellectual technologies of research and worked on and through by policy. There are organisations, issues and populations that are identified in the individual projects. Unsurprisingly, the organisations identified are 'school', 'public sector education', 'universities', 'small and medium businesses'. This indicates the policy concern with the provision of education and training that I mentioned earlier. Issues include 'active citizenship' (Holford and Edirisingha 2000), 'computer-supported collaborative learning', 'organisational learning', 'early literacy' and 'low skills'. These are areas in which policy leavers are sought to either address identified problems e.g. low skills, or promote particular practices e.g. organisational learning.

More importantly for this paper, the populations identified in the projects include 'unemployed youths', 'the long term unemployed', 'the low skilled', 'adults', 'non-traditional adults'. Generalised categories are thereby constituted as the populations to be acted upon in the development of a learning society. What are the subjects drawn upon and the subjectivities constituted in the process? Here I sketch four possibilities.

There can be little doubting the economic imperative and discourse underpinning much of the policy discourse of lifelong learning. This is signified through a focus on unemployed youths and the low skilled and the somewhat patronising assumption of 'coping' with an ageing workforce. What technologies are in play in the economic mobilising of the subject? In a certain economic discourse the subject is the individual learner who accumulates, forgets and abandons skills throughout their lives as a way of entering into, sustaining their position within and progressing through the labour market. In the accumulation of skills, the subject becomes more productive and individually competitive within the labour market as well as contributing to the competitiveness of the economy as a whole. Even though they are reliant on being mobilised within a certain network to govern their conduct in this way, they are represented as individualised, severed from their relations, as part of the dispositional autonomy, enterprise and flexibility that is sought form them. The subject is therefore represented as an accumulation of skills, and/or an accumulator of skills, disembodied and disembedded from specific economic, social and cultural contexts. Rose (1998: 154) summarises this well: 'enterprise here designates an array of rules for the conduct of one's everyday existence: Energy, initiative ambition, calculation and personal responsibility. The enterprising self will make an enterprise of its life, seek to maximise its own human capital, project itself a future, and seek to shape itself in order to become that which it wishes to be. The enterprising self is thus both an active self and a calculating self, a self that calculates about itself and that acts upon itself in order to better itself'. The subject is individualised and thereby constituted as responsible for their own position in the social formation. The intellectual technology for this discourse is economics and, in particular, human capital theory, wherein competitiveness is precisely tied to the development of productivity through increased knowledge and skills, usually measured through the proxy variable of qualifications.

Other intellectual technologies are also in play. The intellectual technology derived from a certain branch of psychology aims 'to promote individual self-fulfilment through greater participation in all forms of learning' (Coffield 2000:10). This is a discourse which is mobilised strongly among liberal educators and those who tend to support the notion of learning for its own sake and learning as an outcome of intrinsic motivation. The subject is one who is capable of growth and whose potential can be developed through learning. There is a sense in which the subject of development is one that embraces knowledge, skills and emotions, but there is also a clear decontextualisation of the learner in such discourses. Class, gender and ethnicity tend to be constructed as personal characteristics rather than orderings of identity. At the heart of these discourses is a paradox, as self-fulfilment can itself be argued to be extrinsic to motivation and therefore instrumental rather than intrinsic to learning. The discourse tends to position the subject as someone whose development only results in the good at both individual and societal levels. The notion that self-fulfilment and learning can result in negative outcomes—however defined—or that learning cannot overcome negative behaviour and emotions is marginalized in such discourses. The intellectual technology for such discourses is that of humanistic psychology, with its concern for the development and growth of the whole person, and associated therapies of client centredness and pedagogies of student centredness.

A third discourse constructs a social rather than individualised view of learning and emphasises collaboration rather than competition. Here lifelong learning is ordered around a moral purpose, as a response to the social exclusion experienced by those who gained least from initial education (Ranson 1998). The subject is contextualised within certain social relations and networks that, for some, structure and, for others, pattern their learning opportunities. They are contextualised if not always embodied. The subject is therefore a social subject; one's whose social position affects their learning, their learning opportunities and the opportunity structures available to them. The intellectual technologies for this strand of discourse are those arising out of certain branches of sociology, embracing social anthropology as method and social capital as a theoretical framework. Yet it is not necessary that the social capital argument results in a moral purpose to address social inclusion, as to generate social capital in specific contexts may well inevitably entail excluding some. While social capital might be used to explain social exclusion, where capital and exclusion are themselves the attempts to represent and order social life in particular ways, it does not automatically lead to a value position that exclusion should be addressed and overcome.

Related to the intellectual technology of sociology is that of politics and the concern to mobilise a population of 'active citizens', wherein there is often an elision between the active and the good citizen. Constructing a European space is a political as well as economic, social and psychological challenge for EU policy. One might assume a citizen is simply a matter of domicile and nationality. This is formalistic rather than substantial. It takes citizenship to be a transcendental category rather than a lived experience, embodied and embedded. It also does not reflect the complex relationships between domicile and identity that exist. Delanty (2000) argues that citizenship entail rights, responsibilities, participation and identity. One problem for the EU is that it is a legal entity with which populations do not identify and in whose processes they rarely participate. There is a cultural gap, often expressed as a democratic deficit, between the EU and the populations it embraces. Yet to mobilise active citizens might imply consensus where there may be dissensus and it is significant in such discourses that notions of social cohesion are to the fore. Even within the recognition of diversity, there is a sense in which something has to provide the glue to hold things together. It is also notable that the technologies through which to engage active citizenship spread beyond the realm of the formal to the non-formal and informal, as questions of identity and participation are not mobilised through education and training alone (Holford and Edirisingha 2000).

The above are schematic and over-generalise, but they are intended as heuristic devices through which to consider the subjects mobilised in policy related research in this area in the EU. What subject are mobilised? By whom? Why? With what effects? All of these are important conversations in which to engage.

The how

I wish to say less about the how at this point in time. Subjects are to be mobilised through practices that promote innovation, flexibility and mobility. These are applied as much in relation to organisations as they are to populations. Innovation, flexibility and mobility are mobilised as the norms through which to develop a learning society and characteristics of such a society. Governing therefore has less to do with a rational process of social reform and more to do with fashioning conduct based on certain norms and values, wherein populations are represented as active subjects and not passive objects. Characteristics such as flexibility, autonomy, self-direction and learning become ontological conditions for successful societal participation. Here 'the self is to be a subjective being, it is to aspire to autonomy, it is to strive for personal fulfilment in its earthly life, it is to interpret its reality and destiny as a matter of individual responsibility, it is to find meaning in existence by shaping its life through acts of choice' (Rose 1998: 151). Central to choice is the capacity to learn and, as this is an ongoing process, there is the necessity for learning to be lifelong. Insofar as learning is positioned as a principle of the 'good life', a range of technologies are deployed through which human beings are positioned as learners. Thus almost every aspect of human life becomes available for research and surveillance, as something from which they can learn in any context—the home, workplace, online, etc. This work is supported by 'experts of organisational life, engineering human relations through architecture, timetabling, supervisory systems, payment schemes, curricula, and the like' (Rose 1998: 154). The social order is positioned as a learning order and different populations are targeted to be worked upon to enhance their capacity to learn to choose and choose to learn in order that they are mobile and flexible.

Attempting to order people's values and norms therefore becomes a key dimension of change processes, within which there is a certain Darwinian logic. Adapt through innovations, flexibility and mobility, or... Thus national and international competitiveness have been 'recoded, at least in part, in terms of the psychological, dispositional and aspirational capacities of those that make up the labour force... Personal employment and macro-economic health is to be ensured by encouraging individuals to 'capitalise' themselves, to invest in the management, presentation, promotion and enhancement of their own economic capital as a capacity of their selves and as a lifelong project' (Rose 1999: 162). Populations are positioned less as active subjects in the constitution of social, economic, and political practices, and more as needing to adapt to change processes over which they are positioned as having little or no control or choice. Change is ontologically gerrymandered i.e. social practices are positioned as natural.

I do not wish to pursue this further here or now, but it is a further aspect of the reflexive conversations to be had about EU policy-related research in support of lifelong learning and a learning society.

Research as intellectual technologies?

'The new citizen is required to engage in a ceaseless work of training and retraining, skilling and reskilling, enhancement of credentials and preparation for a life of ceaseless job seeking: Life is to become a continuous economic capitalisation of the self' (Rose 1999: 161). This is an over-generalisation, but in providing the intellectual technologies for policy through research we need to engage in reflexive questions about our own knowledge production practices, their assumptions and effects in the processes of governing. In other words, we need to engage in an ecological reflexivity.

Each intellectual technology struggles to represent and order a particular subject as a population in a learning society, networking them in different ways and emphasising different characteristics. When engaging in conversation about lifelong learning, the positioning of subjects in crucial, as are who and what are named as populations. Who is authorised to converse? Who converses authoritatively? How is the conversation governed? Upon what exclusions and inclusions is it based? All are important questions when challenged with the reflexive issues arising from the embedded and embodied nature of social science. In the above I have somewhat nomadically wandered in the attempt to make some meaning out of the current interest in discourses of lifelong learning and learning societies, the intellectual technologies through which they are mobilised, the subjects thus mobilised, and the difference and diversity once one focuses on learners and learning. The above is a sounding board for conversing about the assumptions within particular projects from which I have extracted some of the who's and how's of EU research.

Lifelong learning can be seen in certain positions to be powerful in contemporary orderings and the forms of governing at a distance outlined above. Whether the populations thus ordered e.g. the excluded, the long terms unemployed non-traditional adults, active citizens, feel their interests to be represented in such orderings in open to question and the assertion and development of alternative intellectual technologies.

References

Coffield, F. (2000) 'Introduction: A critical analysis of the concept of a learning society'. In F. Coffield (ed) *Differing Visions of a Learning Society*. Bristol: Policy Press.

Dean, M (1999) *Governmentality: Power and Rule in Modern Society*. London: Sage.

Delanty. G. (2000) *Citizenship in a Global Age: Society, Culture, Politics*. Buckingham: Open University Press.

Field, J. (2000) 'Governing the ungovernable: Why lifelong learning policies promise so much yet deliver so little.' *Educational Management and Administration*, Vol. 28, (3), pp. 249-261.

Flyvbjerg, B. (2001) *Making Social Science Matter*. Cambridge: Cambridge University Press.

Foucault, M. (1979) *Discipline and Punish: The Birth of the Prison*. Harmondsworth: Penguin.

Foucault, M. (1980) *Power/Knowledge*. Brighton: Harvester.

Foucault, M. (1991) 'Governmentality'. In G. Burchell, C. Gordon and P. Miller (eds) *The Foucault Effect: Studies in Governmentality*. London: Harvester.

Green, A. (2002) 'The many faces of lifelong learning: Recent education policy trends in Europe'. *Journal of Education Policy*, Vol. 17 (6), pp. 611-626.

Holford, J. & Edirisingha, P. (2000) *Citizenship and Governance Education in Europe: A Critical Review of the Literature*. Guildford: Scholl of education studies, University of Surrey.

Griffin, C. (2002) 'Lifelong learning and welfare reform.' In R. Edwards, N. Miller, N. Small & A. Tait (eds) *Supporting Lifelong Learning*, [Volume 3: Making Policy Work]. London: Routledge.

Law, J. (1992) 'Notes on the theory of the actor-network: Ordering, strategy and heterogeneity'. *Systems Practice*, Vol. 5(4), pp. 379-393.

Law, J. (2001) *Ordering and obduracy*. Centre for Science Studies and the Department of Sociology, Lancaster University. http://www.comp.lancs.ac.uk/sociology/soc068jl.html

Law, J. (2002) 'Objects and spaces', *Theory, Culture & Society*, Vol. 19 (5/6), pp 91-105.

Miller, P and Rose, N. (1993) 'Governing economic life'. In M. Gane and T. Johnson (eds) *Foucault's New Domains*. London: Routledge.

Munro, I. (2000) 'Non-disciplinary power and the network society'. *Organization*, Vol. 7 (4), pp. 679-695.

New Perspective for Learning: Insights from European Union funded Research on Education and Training (2001) Issue 2, December.

Pels, D., Hetherington, K. & Vandenberghe, F. (2002) 'The status of the object: Performances, mediations, and techniques'. *Theory, Culture & Society*, Vol. 19 (5/6), pp. 1-21.

Ranson, S. (eds) (1998) *Inside the Learning Society*. London: Cassell.

Rose, N. (1998) *Inventing Ourselves: Psychology, Power and Personhood*. Cambridge: Policy Press.

Rose, N. (1999) *Powers of Freedom: Reframing Political Thought*. Cambridge: Cambridge University Press.

Shostak, J. (2002) *Understanding, Designing and Conducting Qualitative Research in Education*. Buckingham: Open University Press.

2

Learning in
Working Contexts

CHAPTER FIVE

Knowledge, Learning and Competencies in Organisations: Lessons from Projects under 4th and 5th Framework Programmes

MASSIMO TOMASSINI

Introduction: Knowledge, learning and competencies in the knowledge-based economy/society[1]

New conditions for knowledge development occur in the *learning economy*, where the traditional demarcations between the economic and the social dimensions, as well as those between learning, knowing and organising, are becoming increasingly blurred. The economic performance of firms, regions and countries (and in many ways also those of individuals) is in fact linked to their capability to learn and adapt to new conditions. At the same time learning depends on the accumulation and competent use of *tacit knowledge*, produced within specific organisational contexts, and on a dynamic arrangement for continuously integrating such contextual knowledge with data, information and other kinds of codified knowledge (Lundvall and Borras, 1999).

The organisational dimension, from this viewpoint, is crucial in the learning economy. It appears as a relational dimension whose dynamics are strictly intertwined with collective forms of knowledge creation, use and diffusion. Knowledge and organisation are in a mutual relationship of continuous co-creation.

Concerning such a relationship, important interpretations should be underlined, for instance: (i) The need for fostering continuous interactions between explicit and tacit knowledge in innovative companies (Nonaka and Takeuchi, 1995); (ii) the nature of *organisational learning* as generated in a continuum between practice, learning and organising (Gherardi and Nicolini, 2000); (iii) the important function of *communities of practice* (Wenger, 1998; Wenger et al., 2002) for assuring learning and cooperation in informal organisational and inter-organisational settings.

Moreover, in a world in which information and knowledge exchanges are continuously multiplied, the organisational dimension must be necessarily understood also in terms of *inter-organisational dimension*. The decline of traditional ways of working in large organisations and the multiplication of new socio-economic forms of production and organisation, all more or less structured according to *network* patterns, have created new forms of knowledge and learning. Inter-organisational systems—notably those related to networking of SMEs (clusters, industrial districts, etc.) are crucial sources of knowledge creation and development. Factors such as *proximity*, *trust* and *collective interpretation* allow for the creation of social and cognitive resources for continuous acquisition of *local* competitive advantage. (Lazaric and Lorenz, 1998; Lawson and Lorenz, 1999).

The changing role of knowledge and the increasing importance of the organisational dimension in the learning economy/society generate new needs for competencies and new ways of understanding their social meaning, in some ways diverging from more traditional approaches.

While the latter assign higher priority to negotiation and certified recognition of competencies, even through new technological devices, new exigencies require continuous competence development often along fuzzy or ill-defined paths. *Competence* as *knowledge-in-action* (Schoen, 1983) is in fact highly dynamic and context-related. Competencies of a significant majority of employees hinge upon disciplinary bodies of knowledge and problem-solving patterns that are continuously evolving. Moreover, the 'situatedness' of competencies in specific organisational patterns of learning and practice, the strict link between working and socialising, the collective/communitarian nature of many competencies, the correlation between individual/group abilities and organisational strategic capabilities determine the ineffectiveness of pre-defined patterns and require new forms of competence identification, assessment and development (Consoli Benadusi, 2000).

E&T systems all over Europe are generally late in catching up with the above trends, while a culture of learning at a European scale ought to be created as a background for the development of personal/social competencies and the growth of informal knowledge and social capital (Gavigan et al., 1999). The need for something that can be defined as *enlarged lifelong learning* seems to emerge in relation to several policy hypotheses in this field (Tomassini, 2002). New coherent lifelong learning policies cannot be identified only at the level of *formal education* resources; even the generic recognition of channels of *non-formal education* and *informal learning* for individuals (Ocde-Ceri, 2001) seems inadequate in relation to the emerging complex forms of knowledge and competencies. New types of relationships are needed between the worlds of education and of organisations and higher levels of *reflexivity* ought to be developed within E&T systems as well as in other institutions and forms of social life (Giddens, 1991). Emerging exigencies in this field seem to require investments in new ideas and practical approaches concerning the real links between work, learning and education.

Analysis of ten projects under 4th and 5th Framework Programme

Several of the above assumptions and concerns are shared by the research projects analysed in this paper. According to the specific goals assigned to this analysis, ten already completed European projects have been selected that directly dealt with processes of knowledge creation, use and exchange inside organisations and networks and therefore took into account important phenomena linked to learning at work and to competencies development in different organisational contexts.

The projects, carried out in various periods between 1997 and 2002, seem to have several starting points and conclusions in common, even in terms of policy indications, although they have non-homogeneous characteristics in terms of width and depth. Such non-homogeneity is largely due to the fact that the projects belong to two different categories: 'thematic networks' (devoted to create links and exchanges between experts and to exploit results of already carried out research activities) and 'RTD projects' (research projects mainly aimed at developing field inquiries), the latter dealing with recent relevant experiences in large companies and in SMEs, which provided the contexts for rather extensive case studies.

Considering the whole set of projects, the range of participating countries (Table 1) and industries involved (Table 2) is broad. Within projects, which also had empirical analysis objects, a total of about 140 case studies have been carried out (Table 3), approximately three quarters of which are about large companies while one quarter is about SMEs.

Aims and structure of the paper

The analysis of main contents of the projects has been carried out having in mind the 'valorisation' and diffusion goals explicitly assigned to the initiative within which this paper has been developed. On the other side the need for

TABLE 1: 4th and 5th FRP projects dealing with knowledge, learning and competencies

Title	Acronym21	Co-ordinator	Type	Partners
Work process knowledge in technological and organisational development	Whole	UK	Thematic network	B, D, DN, E, FIN, F, I, P, S, UK
Ways of organizational learning in the chemical industry and their impact on vocational education and training	OrgLearn*	D	Research project	B, D, I, UK
The role of HRD within organizations in creating opportunities for life-long learning: concepts and practices in seven European countries	Hrd & Lll*	NL	Research project	B, FIN, F, G, I, NL, UK
Innovations in Information Society Sectors— Implications for Women's Work, Expertise and Opportunities in European Workplaces	Servemploi	IRL	Research project	E, D, DN, I, S
In-company Training and Learning. Learning Environments of Knowledge Intensive Company Units in Five European Countries	Latio	S	Research project	DN, IRL, NL, S, UK
Co-ordination Competencies and Knowledge in the European Autombile System	Co-Keas	F	Thematic	D, E, F, I, NL, UK
Developing Learning Organisation Model in SME Clusters	Delos	I	Research project	A, E, I, NL, UK
Small Business Training and Competitiveness: Building Case Studies in Different European training Cultural Contexts	Smes-training	E	Research project	A, E, I, N
Work Experience as an Innovative Education and Training Strategy for the 21° Century	Work Experience *	UK	Thematic network	DN, E, H, IRL, S, UK
Forum for European Research on Vocational Education and Training ('The Learning Organisation' sub-group)	Fervet/Lo*	D	Thematic network	D, FIN, G, I, E, UK, P, NL

TABLE 2: Industries involved

Whole	Financial services, Health services, Electric utilities, Chemical, Car industry, Machine tool, Clothing
OrgLearn	Chemical production
Hrd & Lll	Insurance, Meteorology, Financial services, Retail (hyper-market), Hotel and tourism, Consultancy, Postal services, Cleaning, Road transportation, Domestic appliance manufacturing, Chemical, Sales electronic devices, Food, Cosmetics, Aero-engines, Paper machinery, Construction, Metal, Brewery, ICT products and services, Telecommunication, Bar-code manufacturing, Mineral extraction and production
Servemploi	Financial services, Retail
Latio	Telecommunication, ICT products and services, Building, Air transportation, Electric utilities, Chemical, Pharmaceutical, Metal, Brewery, Ornamental (flowers and plant),
CoKeas	Automotive
Delos	Machine tool, Automobile auxiliary industry, Toys, Materials and metals, Bio-medical, Newsagent
Smes-training	Consultancy, Cleaning service, Health service, Domestic appliance manufacturing, Chemical production, Machine tool, Food industry, Materials and metals, Paper machinery manufacturing, Bio-medical, Brewery, ICT products and services, Telecommunication, Mineral extraction and production, Wine production

TABLE 3: Case studies within research projects

OrgLearn	Learning practices in 15 plants in 4 large companies
Hrd & Lll	Hrd policies in 28 large companies
Servemploi	Employment and competencies policies in 30 large companies
Latio	Learning environments within 22 large companies
Delos	Learning processes within 12 SMEs clusters
SMEs Training	Training policies in 22 SMEs

linking this specific analytic exercise with broader European policy and research perspectives on knowledge learning and competencies has also been taken into account.

The analytical framework through which projects are examined takes into account both theoretical and practical issues in order to highlight aspects that could enrich the European perspectives and suggest possible actions for the implementation of European programmes especially in the socio-economic research area more closely related to learning and E&T themes. Considering the 'theoretical issues' it seems possible to answer questions concerning the background that underpins the vision of the *knowledge-based society*. Relevant questions to be answered can be, for instance, those concerning the nature of learning in the knowledge/learning society and economy, the kind of learning that actually takes place in organisations, the meaning of the *learning organisation* in the evolving social and economic context. The concern for the 'practical issues' should help to provide suggestions regarding the ways in which learning development could be supported. Relevant questions from this viewpoint are for instance related to the development of team learning, to the evolving characteristics of competencies in real working place, to the central theme of *flexibility*. In terms of consequences on the E&T systems several questions should be answered such as those about the changes that are occurring within organisational settings and, more than this, those about the impacts of the new ways of learning, closely related to practice and socialisation at work, and also on traditional educational settings and their constituencies (including young people).

As a whole the analytical exercise on 4th and 5th Framework Projects tends to provide some materials for creating a new picture of knowledge, learning and competencies related to evolutionary organisational trends that could stimulate new action lines for European decision-making and new choices concerning already established programmes.

The following section 2 is devoted to a short review of European policy and research perspectives. Section 3 concerns some theoretical concepts elaborated within the projects. Section 4 is dedicated to the outcomes of the field research projects: At this level the focus is not on empirical results as such, but on organisational dynamics and practices that the projects have shed some light on and that are relevant for real developments of knowledge, learning and competencies in organisational settings. Section 5 is about the ways in which the problem of the transformation of E&T functions and activities is tackled within different projects. In section 6 some recommendations are provided to European policy-makers, especially as far as further research developments are concerned.

Emerging European perspectives

Policy perspectives for the knowledge-based economy

Projects reviewed in this paper deal with themes that are crucial for the socio-economic development of Europe according to the frameworks provided by the *Targeted Socio-Economic Research* programme—within the wider 4th Framework Programme—and the *Improving the Human Potential and the Socio-economic Knowledge Base* programme—within the 5th Framework Programme. Both these programmes have been directed towards competitiveness and scientific and technological development from one side and to societal themes on the other side, in which 'knowledge' and 'learning'— assumed in a plurality of meanings—play key roles.

In the recently launched 6th Framework Programme this double orientation is even more developed as a specific emphasis has been put on innovative views regarding the social side of economic development. As stated in one of the programmatic documents, *Citizenship and Governance in a Knowledge-based Society* ('Priority 7' of the 6th FRP, European Commission, 2002), there is a clear need for a closer understanding of changes in work in the knowledge-based society, of the relationships between these changes and the use of knowledge and of skills, and of their implications for quality of life. In lieu of the traditional views of work as a production factor and of organisation as an abstract setting for value-producing practices, this perspective stresses that there are 'different ways of achieving flexibility' and that 'new forms of work organisation (e.g. network organisations or employees' self-organisation)' should be analysed. It also stresses the need for the 'development of skills and occupational identities' and the 'social dialogue', in relation to aspects such as the 'quality of life' within and outside the work environment.

This kind of interests clearly reflects, as previously noted, policy concerns, which in the last ten years, have been largely influenced by ideas such as 'social cohesion', social dialogue and lifelong learning (Greco et al., 2003). These have been translated into strategic assumptions in which economic development—which in the European approach is mostly seen as a combination of R&D investments and firms competitive capabilities—should always be paralleled with social development and with goals related to the simultaneous development of work, learning, education and training.

In *Making a European Area of Lifelong Learning a Reality* (European Commission, 2001) one can find important statements about the facilitation of access to learning opportunities in different contexts—including firms and other organisations. The document encourages social partners 'to promote learning at all levels and especially at the enterprise level'. The well-known *Memorandum on Lifelong Learning* (European Commission, 2000) defined lifelong learning as 'all purposeful learning activities undertaken on an on-going basis with the aim of improving knowledge, skills and competence' and recognises that 'putting lifelong learning into practice demands that everyone work together effectively—both as individuals and in organisations'.

These approaches are explicitly linked to the well-known statements issued by the *Lisbon European Council* (2000) affirming that 'Europe must become the most dynamic and competitive knowledge-based economy in the world capable of sustainable growth with more and better jobs and greater social cohesion' and that one of the ways for attaining such an ambitious goal concerns the 'complementarity between lifelong learning and adaptability through flexible management of working time and job rotation'. During the Nineties the close links between changes in work, organisation, learning and the need for new forms of education and training have been underlined by policy-makers in both areas.

In the E&T area these links have been remarked upon by documents such as: *Teaching and Learning: Towards the Learning Society* (1995), *Towards a Europe of Knowledge* (1997), *Education and Active Citizenship* (1998) in which the stress is increasingly on the shift from teaching to learning and on the establishment of links between citizenship and employability.

In the work and industrial relations area such links have been explored in the *Partnership for a New Organisation of Work Green Paper* (1997), and by the *Growth, Competitiveness and Employment White Book* (1994), which also stressed the links between technological innovation, firm's competitiveness and organisational innovation. More recently, important aspects concerning the development of working conditions have been dealt with in the *Promoting a European Framework for Corporate Responsibility Green Paper* (European Commission, 2001) and in the related *Best Workplaces in the EU Special Award* initiative (European Commission, 2003). In both—the latter representing a sort of practical extension of the former—a strong emphasis is put on organisational innovation in view of reaching better quality at work and on the need for improving good practices in the area of human resource development.

European research on knowledge-based economy

Substantial scientific backing of the above political orientations can be found in important socio-economic research projects carried out in the final years of the Nineties. These projects provided theoretical indications and empirical evidence of the relationships between learning, work and organisations. In particular, the stream of research projects presented in the *Globalising Learning Economy; Implications for Innovation Policy* report (Lundvall and Borras, 1999) and in the book *The Globalising Learning Economy: Major Socio-Economic Trends and European Innovation Policy* (Archibugi and Lundvall, 2000) created a relevant background for the new European perspective.

Within the *learning economy* approach—in which the capabilities to learn and adapt to new conditions are seen as increasingly determining the performance of individuals, firms, regions and countries (Lundvall and Borras, 1999)—the need has been underlined for the simultaneous innovation of organisational settings and learning opportunities. Such innovation is closely linked to the differences and interdependencies between codified knowledge and tacit knowledge: 'tacitness' is in fact seen as the real source of competitive advantage that can be reached and enhanced through continuous learning particularly at the organisational level. The best placed organisations, in this approach, are considered those able to implement suitable learning conditions in relation to issues such as: Developing professional skills in areas of larger competitive advantage; establishing synergies within the creative potentials of groups and teams; keeping the organisation flexible and coherent with the strategic inputs; establishing relationships, informal alliances and networks with clients, providers and other enterprises. A European model of the *learning organisation* has been suggested, based on the above characteristics and tested through specific experiences like, for instance, the Danish LOK project involving businesses, institutions (like local governments, schools and universities, R&D centres), social partners and academic (Lundvall, 2002).

Further developments of this approach, also supported by empirical outcomes, showed that establishing the firm as a learning organisation can have positive impacts on a wide range of performance variables (Lundvall and Archibugi, 2001). The strategic relevance of such an approach is even reinforced by the limited extent to which these kinds of organisational characteristics are actually diffused within the European productive fabric: Empirical outcomes, taken in particular from a large inquiry comparing the innovative behaviours of firms, show that only a small minority of firms (10-15 %) have introduced the major traits of the 'learning organisation' and that 'there is an enormous unexploited reserve of economic competitiveness, especially in manufacturing and business service sectors in Europe' (Coriat, 2001).

In this perspective the emerging European model of knowledge and learning development has been seen as largely based on strategies of *integrated competence building* activated at different levels: At the firm—micro—level where flexibility should be reinforced by extensive inter-firm mobility; at the inter-firm—meso—level, where competencies can grow through diffused forms of *co-operation, alliance and networking* among firms; at the overall—macro—level, where synergies should be reached between different policies (social, educational, industrial, etc..). In particular such policies should be aimed at maintaining the balance in terms of *social capital reproduction* (through the maintenance of a protected labour market for un-skilled and socially at risk people), environment preservation and political stability (Lundvall and Archibugi, 2001).

Such indications confirm in many ways the importance of the *regional dimension* of learning: 'territory and proximity play a central role in the genesis of tacit knowledge and in the capacity to exploit it. The region is increasingly the level at which innovation is produced through regional networks of innovators, local clusters and the cross-fertilising effects of research institutions' (Lundvall and Borras, 1999: 39). On the other side the need for new strategies of *integrated competence building* implies the parallel need to engage all concerned actors in *lifelong learning* initiatives. Several institutional changes and innovation policies are requested from this viewpoint, fostering increased co-operation between private firms and the public sector, and providing support and incentives for regional institutions involved in development policies (especially for industrial districts and SMEs clusters).

But in many ways *lifelong learning* is not only an area of local and/or national specific interventions: It appears as a general approach underpinning substantial changes in education and training (E&T) systems, in their relationships with productive systems and in new ways of understanding the integration of explicit and tacit knowledge. In this perspective E&T systems are increasingly required to establish closer links with other places in which processes of knowledge and competencies creation and development occur. For different reasons—and for better or worse—phenomenon of 'institutional convergence' (Conceicao and Heitor, 2001) is actually taking place between formal education institutions – in particular universities—and other institutions—in particular enterprises. E&T systems should reflect on these trends and develop new methods for integrating explicit and tacit knowledge flows. As it has been clearly stated: '…it seems essential to place renewed emphasis on education and, to a certain extent, to reinvent its social and economic role. Educational institutions must rethink their relationships with the individuals, families and communities… presenting themselves as vital providers of opportunities to develop formal learning processes while at the same time encouraging a way of life that promotes learning through social interaction' (Conceicao and Heitor, 2001: 93).

Theoretical underpinnings of the projects

How can the projects presented in section 1 be placed in the thematic streams that have briefly depicted? Which ways do they contribute to the development of new policy orientations towards the learning economy/society? A first area of contribution can be identified at the theoretical level. Although theories and concepts used in the set of projects analysed here are varied and substantially non-homogeneous, the projects as a whole provide some interesting inputs in relation to terms that are currently used in the European discourse but frequently lack sufficient depth.

Important theoretical suggestions have in particular been provided concerning the ways in which knowledge is reproduced in organisations and learning processes are managed. However, beyond differences in terminology, different theoretical orientations can be identified. In the majority of cases the basic research assumptions have referred to the need to integrate individuals' knowledge and learning into the larger organisational dimension. In other cases such an integration has been taken for granted: Knowledge and learning have been assumed as 'situated' in the organisational context and the analytic focus has been put on social relations and multiple ways of looking at reality within the contexts.

Individuals and organisations

An example of the first kind of approach can be seen in the *Whole* project, which suggests an extensive use of the *work process knowledge* concept. The term is a translation of *Arbeitsprozesswissen*, coined by W. Kruse in the Eighties; in its original meaning it designates the kind of knowledge that employees should posses for understanding the interdependencies among different roles and activities within complex labour processes. In *Whole* the emphasis is not on *labour* but on *work*, involving at the same time labour and *production* processes. In flexible computerised workplaces *work processes knowledge* is assumed to be useful for different kinds of activities and needs, like the ones of coping with the demands of functional flexibility, supervising complex computer-controlled engineering systems, operating as nodes within distributed decision systems (Boreham, 2002).

Work processes knowledge is fundamentally 'practical knowledge' but cannot be confused with mere 'know-how' or 'procedural knowledge'; it includes a dimension of theoretical understanding integrated with experiential know-how gained through collective as well as individual experience in specific workplace cultures. Members of organisations in this perspective are also members of communities of practice; they 'create and share knowledge in the practice of their work, and record their individual perceptions in the structures that constitute their culture' (Boreham, 2002: 5). In this kind of approach the practical, theoretical and social dimensions of knowledge are kept together: Work processes knowledge is 'tacit but not elusive', it is embedded in people's ways of doing things but it must be made explicit and exchangeable within organisational policies and devices.

Individual experience—as seen within both *Whole* and *Orgalearn* projects—is at the basis of *work processes knowledge*: It 'contains ideas, concepts, thoughts and emotions' and 'supports *work processes knowledge* by integrating aesthetic, practical and rational action' (Fischer, 2002). From this viewpoint the stress is on learning as an individual experience that the organisation allows and reproduces according social and cultural patterns. The main focus of this kind of projects is on individual processes of learning and on the complex paths of integration between the individual and the organisational dimensions, assuming the former as the origin of the latter. 'Organisational knowledge is more complex than individual knowledge and 'distributed' information, but has its origin in the movement of representations of individual knowledge' (Sauquet, 1999).

Especially when using the concepts of *organisational learning* and the *learning organisation* such integration between individual and organisation has been assumed as the most crucial factor, following the approaches of Argyris and Schoen (1978, 1996) and Senge (1990, 1994). In particular several projects recalled the distinction between two types of learning, at the basis of the Argyris's approach, i.e. between 'single loop learning', linked to small adjustments in an organisation's actions in reaction to different kinds of problems, and 'double loop learning', taking place when small adjustments are not enough and radical changes are needed as far as the same organisation's 'governing variables'—basic assumptions and rules—are concerned. This is, for instance, the main reference of the *Hrd-Lll* project whose main focus is the 'learning organisation', assumed as the one that 'responds to (and anticipates) changes in its environments by learning on a strategic level... and, to do so, makes use of the learning of all employees' (Tjiepkema et al., 2002: 10). From this viewpoint, a qualitatively enhanced role of employees at all hierarchical levels is the main feature of the *learning oriented organisation*—the conceptual variant put forward as specific of this project—whose main tasks are those of: (i) Creating on-the-job as well as off-the-job facilities for employee learning, and (ii) stimulating employees not only to attain new knowledge and skills, but also to acquire skills in the field of learning and problem-solving and thus develop their capacity for future learning" (Tjiepkema et al., 2002: 12). An active role of the individual employee in learning is crucial in this perspective, based on the capacity: (i) To acquire or create new knowledge for the organisation (e.g. by learning from daily work experience, studying new technological advancements or learning about work practices used by other companies); (ii) to disseminate this knowledge to others within the organisation; (iii) to apply the new knowledge in improved or renewed work practices, products and services.

Intrinsic organisational processes

Social and institutional views of learning processes in organisations are of course not absent among those put forward in the set of analysed projects. For instance—within the Whole project—Pauwels and Van Ruysseveldt (2002) adapt to organisational learning the scheme of institutionalisation process, articulated into three stages: Externalising, objectifying, internalising. 'In organisations externalisation occurs when personal knowledge is transferred to others. This can happen through formal and informal channels, by personal contacts or by use of communication technology. This knowledge can be objectified by the organisation in the form of rules, procedures, structures, etc. and can thus function as a kind of organisational memory. This does not mean that this organisational memory is static. Objectified knowledge is also liable to change. Through internalisation, an employee reabsorbs this organisational knowledge, in order to become, and remain, a member of the organisation' (Pauwels and Van Ruysseveldt, 2002: 9).[3] In the OrgaLearn project, the analysis of work-teams in a chemical company—an innovative research-led organization in which the free exchange of knowledge is a vital part of the work and where the knowledge base is as collective as it is individual—suggested that a significant part of work process knowledge is contained in the interactions between the members of the group, as well as inside the heads of the employees (Mariani, 2002).

In other contributions the 'mentalistic' side of individual learning is replaced by developmental cognitive perspectives focusing on the organization of highly integrated elements of human cognition. According to such perspectives it is possible to understand the development of learning in work settings as the interplay of four types of entities: 'representations and concepts' (related to objects, their properties and relations); 'activity organizers' (schemes of different levels: Rules, procedures, methods, etc.); 'instruments' (artifacts and their utilization schemes) and 'situations' (classes of situations). 'So a particular activity observed in a single situation can be described as a particular interaction between these more structured entities, made specific by the context and by the subjective manner in which the activity is undertaken' (Samurcay and Vidal-Gomel, 2002).

An attempt to integrate the individual and the situated (cultural and institutional) dimensions of learning has been made by the *Latio* project in which learning phenomena are seen in terms not of *learning organization* but of *learning environment*, conditioned in specific cases by different kinds of contexts: National institutional contexts, organisational contexts, working contexts and distance communication contexts. Moreover learning environments are seen as multiple realities put in place from different perspectives, in particular the management and the educational perspective. In both perspectives learning can be considered as a relational issue 'in that knowledge, skills, competencies, all what is learned is seen as qualities of human relationships to the world' surrounding the learner (Svennson et al., 2002). But in the educational perspective learning development (through teaching) is mostly aimed at creating new opportunities, at defining 'curricula' (accepting the Deweyian definition whereby curriculum is 'the study of how to have a world"), at formally recognising the learning acquisitions. In the management perspective, on the other side, learning is something to include either in 'strategic' ways of managing human resources or in actions oriented towards broader forms of 'development', mostly leveraged through 'competence development systems' (Svennson et al., 2002).

Competencies development

The development of competencies has been of course one of the major issues in all analysed projects. Following the *Whole* project—competencies are considered as resources for work activity, produced by a constructive activity, based, among other things, on experience (Rambardel and Duvenci-Langa, 2002). Here competencies are assumed as being determined, besides by experience, by external knowledge and collective or social competencies which the subject at work can access through the mediation of other workers or artefacts, by the kind of situations encountered and by intrinsic subjective attitudes towards learning.

Within the same project interesting links are identified between competence and both work process knowledge and the experiential sources of learning. *Vocational competence* is seen, through a quite similar although not identical meaning, as *operational knowledge* including 'conceptual knowledge about the world to be acted on' and the ability to operate in systems of actors. (Rogalski et al., 2002). From this viewpoint competencies are knowledge resources incorporating potentials for action, and therefore involving: (i) Operational knowledge which is actually available or may be mobilised;

(ii) schemes of action for different classes of situations; (iii) individual and collective properties enabling operators to adapt to situational pressures.

Competencies can be in fact either individual or collective. The latter can take a double meaning: They can simply refer to the activities of individuals engaged in a collective inquiry but they can also mean that a team—a set of operators engaged in a common task—may be considered as an entity: A *virtual operator* in charge of the task itself. In individual terms, competencies are seen as resources at the subject's disposal which s/he develops within her/his productive activity in line with the tasks and nature of the situations faced, particularly regarding relations to others and oneself. This way the 'psychological subject' is assumed to be able to determine the properties of competencies, but these are also partly determined by the nature of the work situations, with which they must be functionally appropriate (Rabardel and Duvenci-Langa, 2002). The recognition of competencies of single operators can be thus integrated in the recognition of 'core competencies' of the 'activity fields' in which the operators take place.

Beside the sociological and psychological interpretations of competencies, these can also be considered in economic terms. Within the *Hrd/ll* project, according to the results of interviews in a case study, competencies are defined as bodies of knowledge and skills, which are critical in the process of value generation and which have to be constantly monitored and developed, 'understanding how tacit knowledge at different levels can be transformed in explicit and explicit manageable knowledge, closely related to the company value chain' (Tomassini and Cavrini, 2002).

Competencies development in wider contexts

Such an economic interpretation allows further connections between competencies as individual—or group—resources and competencies as firm capabilities. The latter was the way of tackling the issue within the *CoCKEAS* project where, following the well established literature, 'core competencies' are assumed to correspond to firms' specific technological and organisational capabilities. These capabilities are the products of a firm's history and organisational learning, and have many points in common with the tacit and non-transferable knowledge embedded in the firm's routines. In this perspective competencies also represent co-ordination resources both at the intra-organisational and at the inter-organisational level. Internal co-ordination appears to be based on complementarity of competence resources in knowledge sharing between various departments of a firm, while a crucial external strategic issue is the one of exchanging knowledge with other organisations in which complementary competencies are embedded (Lung, 2002).

Other projects within the analysed set develop concepts linked to knowledge, learning and competencies from inter-organisational perspectives. In particular the *Delos* project tried to interpret the dynamics of SME's clusters (industrial districts, networks or less articulated aggregations of enterprises on a local basis) in terms borrowed from the 'learning organisation' approaches. The formation of clusters is seen not exclusively as the result of economic-productive aggregations, but also in terms of information flows, pooling of tacit and explicit knowledge, competencies handling and exchange. Different actors (local institutions, business association, schools, universities, research centres etc.) are involved in such dynamics, playing the role of 'learning agents'.

Four main learning processes are seen as in action in such clusters, dealing with (i) 'learning by doing and experience', concerning the ways in which firms – also with the support of learning agents – accumulate their own know-how over time, learn by doing and innovate their routines (technological, managerial, organisational…); (ii) 'knowledge sharing', at both the intra-firm level (through the implementation of communications systems, inter-functional working groups etc…) and the inter-firms level (knowledge alliances, networks, institutionalisation of informal links, etc…); (iii) 'acquiring relevant external knowledge', through the scanning of specific firm environments, through relationships with clients and suppliers, through inter-firm co-operation in the acquisition of relevant knowledge from different sources (patents, marketing, R&D, organisational consulting, etc…); (iv) 'developing knowledge and competencies': the ways individual firms systematically identify, reward and train the competencies they need and the learning agents actively support firms in the development of competencies at the local level through common training programmes, placement programmes, labour market regulations, etc. (Sarcina, 1998).

Development practices

Important project results looked at practices that take place in organisations for the development of knowledge, learning and competencies. Empirical research operations carried out within different projects showed that several relevant development activities are implemented in organisations of different nature and several types of organisational devices and arrangements are activated that allow simultaneous gains in terms of both learning and effectiveness of productive processes.

The learning organisation in practice

In firms that tend to implement the 'learning organisation' metaphor in their own realities, the development practices take place in a systemic logic. In the conclusions of a first round of the OrgaLearn project regarding large chemical plants, Boreham and colleagues suggested five different criteria that substantially identify the learning organisation: (i) 'organisational work routines are being evaluated and improved': Different initiatives (like the adoption of a systematic management approach, the use of innovative methodologies for the design of procedures and competencies, and information exchanges between different sites) are undertaken in order to focus on work routines and on the ways to improve them; (ii) 'formal and informal learning processes are being evaluated and improved': In particular, informal learning, especially in groups and teams, is evaluated and reinforced as a vital part of the organisation's culture; (iii) 'transformations occur in the culture of the organisation': Culture change—especially regarding issues such as collaboration, communication and safety—is considered as a major objective. Both operators and the management are aware of the need for abandoning old practices (what, in another approach, is called 'unlearning'); (iv) 'knowledge is being created within the organisation, at different levels (not only by the managers/scientists) and it is being shared within the organisation': major improvements in plant design can be reached involving operators at different levels in understanding and formalising their own usual working routines and practices; (v) 'learning from the environment is encouraged and systematically evaluated': In this case 'environment' means in particular organisations of the same kind, encountering the same range of problems and being interested in reciprocal benchmarking (Boreham et al., 2002).

In this perspective, the *learning organisation* seems to be neither an abstract ideological construct—as suggested by much of the management literature—nor a simple synonym of the 'flexible organisation', where learning means fast—and maybe unreflective—adaptation to new operational conditions and sudden changes in the use of labour resources. The 'learning organisation', on the contrary, appears as a very practice-oriented construct emphasising aspects such as: valorisation of experience, systematic implementation of reflective practices, fostering of self-organising procedures and cultural attitudes, active management drives towards 'animating' and help in learning/unlearning opportunities. Such an orientation seems to be confirmed through a brief review of development practices presented within analysed projects.

In the *OrgaLearn* project, different cases of operators' direct interventions on standard operating procedures have been reported on. In different plants, operators are enabled in writing plant-specific operations manuals containing knowledge that is needed for running the plant, complying with safety regulations and for trouble-shooting. While usually these manuals were prepared by engineers and technicians with specific responsibilities in the plant installations, the new regulations allow normal shift workers to produce such complex documents based on their own day-to-day experience of the production process. Such manual writing takes place in small groups, composed of one or more experienced worker, one newcomer and a moderator; from time to time specific process stages are interactively analysed in a period of three to four weeks. The analysis is then converted into a chapter of the plant handbook, which also includes answers to possible questions about trouble-shooting and safety. Important learning effects arise from discussions within the 'manual team' based more on experiential knowledge than on technical knowledge (Fischer and Roben, 2002), and from the opportunities to include suggestions for improvement, management ideas and incidents reports in the plant standard operation procedures (Pauwels and Van Ruysseveldt, 2002). Links are in some cases established between such manual writing methodologies and internal competence development systems: The manual teams are in these cases considered as 'learning cells' and their results are incorporated into the organisational memory also at the training level - as new courses are planned in relation to learning needs emerging from experience sharing and collective problem-solving (Boreham and Morgan, 2002). Moreover, more individual-centred initiatives seem to have significant impacts on organisational learning, such as the incentive for the maintenance and exchange of 'grey booklets' in which operators can store several day-to-day observations about the process (Pauwels and Van Ruysseveldt, 2002).

In other cases within *OrgaLearn* relevant development practices are those named as 'systematic approach' or 'site exchange'. The former is an initiative aimed at encouraging staff to work independently in teams, to solve problems encountered in the workplace, and to learn from the process. The initiative regards the formation of problem-solving groups that can decide on and implement action whenever a problem is identified (e.g. a recurrent fault in a piece of equipment) or when an incident occurs (e.g. a complaint from a contractor) with the help of an expert facilitator. In collective problem-solving the groups follow a specific methodology articulated in different steps, such as: setting goals and agreeing success criteria, gathering the information needed to solve the problem, taking action, reviewing the degree of success achieved. 'Site exchange' is a form of benchmarking of best practices in different plants. It also provides inputs for the assessment of group and individual performances carried out through the 'tasks and targets' system. The benchmarking procedures are based on site appraisal meetings and subsequent information aimed at all employees through different communication channels. Also in this case inputs are provided for in-company training courses commissioned on the basis of learning needs identified in appraisal meetings (Boreham and Morgan, 2002).

'Internal and external mobility' are other mechanisms considered important for implementing forms of organisational learning based on sharing and renewing work practices. In a semi-autonomous R&D plant attached to a big chemical manufacturing plant, rotations are intensively used, and rewarded, according to three main different typologies: among roles and teams within the same unit, among units of the same department, among departments (laboratories, plants, etc.) and between divisions (R&D and manufacturing). Such a rotation system allows operators to acquire both a general 'work-process-knowledge' and the knowledge related to the specific working styles of different communities inside the larger organisation. Relevant knowledge flows are also activated through *external mobility* involving temporary workers holding university degrees hired with a specific contract—for a 12-month period—which implies their rotation on brief term activity programmes and their participation in different training actions (Mariani, 2002b).

Competence management systems

A specific relevant position within organisational development practices is played by *competence management systems*. They tend to constitute frameworks for competence recognition; handling of career paths, recruitment and mobility policies, training needs assessment and several other important purposes. Some of the reasons for the diffusion of such systems have been clearly described within one of the case studies of the *Latio* project. Through a competence management system firm's management can: (i) Be kept informed about accessibility of knowledge embedded in skills all over the firm; (ii) handle skills requirements in relation to changes in external environments; (iii) find useful information in order to check the alignment between new processes and existing competencies within restructuring or re-engineering processes; (iv) design HR strategies (including training strategies) fitting for access to new market segments; (v) channel the efforts to enhance flexibility in relation not only to technical skill needs, but also to broader development goals, e.g. interpersonal skills, leadership abilities, innovation, etc. (Svensson et al., 2002).

Findings from the projects suggest that competence development is largely diffused in European firms, but that aims and methods vary considerably in different contexts. In many cases, competence policies are developed in terms of a common language that everybody can understand within the organisation and adapt to specific exigencies. Competence policies and instruments can contribute to organisation governance providing both parameters for measuring the (economic) value of performances, and shared (cultural) value inputs generated by the different the communities of practice that inhabit the organization.

The results of different case studies show that a rich mix of models of such policies and systems is in place in organisations of different kinds, supporting management strategies which range from more or less up-dated 'command and control' models to real learning oriented models.

Through the above results concerning different competence development systems, an interesting landscape of increasing quality of work is depicted within the set of analysed research projects. The background message emerging from research carried out under 4th and 5th Framework Programme is generally positive: the exigencies linked to both continuous reinforcement of employees patrimonies of competencies (and, evidently, to value on the labour market) and to firms interest for resources development and up-dating are both valorised through competence-related policies and tools. However, some limitations are underlined concerning the risk that relatively stable sets of competencies could introduces rigidities in learning development activities often requiring more open transformation horizons (Svensson et al., 2002).

Cases of competence under-development

More radically, a relevant negative exception in the landscape of competence development seems to be constituted by the systematic quality downgrading of lower status service jobs discovered by the *Servemploi* project in industries, namely retail and financial services, mostly employing women. The project drew a rather pessimistic picture of the opportunities for knowledge and skills development available to junior female employees. It also underlined the point that current visions of the knowledge society and the knowledge-based economy do not acknowledge the existence of such problems and do not recognise the crucial role of inequalities related to social class and gender.

The project suggested that junior female employees often have no access at all to codified knowledge (or 'know-what') related to the products and services they sell and to the tools and techniques needed in their own jobs. In *Servemploi* women's access to apprenticeships and other types of formalised on-the-job training (even though never really diffused), is seen as slowly being displaced by techniques that depend far more strongly upon more informal, employee-led, one-to-one learning. Work shadowing and learning-by-doing are two of the main methods by which women learn their skills and acquire their expertise (Webster et al., 2001).

Under these premises, the *Servemploi* case studies suggested that junior female employees in customer-facing services often have no access to at all to codified knowledge (or 'know-what'), i.e. knowledge of the products and services they sell, and knowledge of the tools and techniques needed to do their jobs. In place of these forms of knowledge, such women are most likely to be involved only 'in the relational and communications skills necessary for the direct delivery of the service to the customer'. Although with some partial exceptions—in countries where formal training is still institutionally valued—the project underlines that: (i) Training activities for women are becoming individualised process but in a negative sense as the social nature of skilling is denied within such processes; (ii) competencies acquired through such training cannot be clearly accredited and recognised at the formal level; (iii) junior staff used as trainers of colleagues are not rewarded for performing such tasks.

Transformations in E&T functions and activities

All analysed projects devoted some attention to E&T and as a whole provided interesting inputs for reflections about the evolutionary dynamics of knowledge, learning and competencies in organisations. Such inputs can be systematised within three main areas: Changes in in-company training functions and activities, changes requested to overall E&T systems; transfer of experiential contents from organisations to overall E&T systems.

Changes in in-company training functions and activities

Important change phenomena can be found in in-company HRD and training departments, and even in line management, all subject to significant restructuring in relation to the increased role of learning within organisations. In many cases organisations analysed by projects created internal lifelong learning systems based on the reshaping of traditional E&T practices in order to connect activities concerning codified knowledge with activities trying to facilitate learning, to harness tacit knowledge and to interact with organisational change. In these cases the new meanings and value of learning generates the re-positioning of formal in-company training activities: the traditional training department still exists in many situations (especially large firms), but it is increasingly dependent from the HRD department. In the latter, particularly in those that have been labelled as 'learning-oriented organisations' (Tijepkema et al., 2002), activities are deliberately focused on the broader field of learning instead of on training ('which is but one form of learning').

The strategic aim is 'facilitating learning' instead of 'delivering training'. Even definitions are frequently changed in this perspective, for instance the 'training department' becomes the 'centre for organisational learning and change' or the 'learning and development centre'. In parallel the HRD departmental structure is softened: the HRD seems to generally increase its decentralization and closeness to local management needs: Some HRD officers are placed in the line organisation while the direct responsibilities of line managers for staff development are accrued and explicitly recognised. From one side the HRD function keeps the initiative for general policies concerning human resource usually interrelated with wider strategic directions from the top management about technological innovation, organisational development, use of knowledge resources. On the other sideline managers are in charge of direct relationships with staff as far as individual and group development needs are concerned in strict relation with day-to-day organisational practices (Tijepkema et al., 2002).

This trend has been shown by different research findings. The *Latio* project in particular identified a specific LTD (learning, training and development) space and recognised that in different companies an integration of learning, training and development practices is occurring, especially linked to growing responsibilities attributed to the line in human resource development and to increased mentoring activities. However, at the same time such integration entails risks of failure when only already defined competencies are supported and innovative learning is insufficiently taken into account. 'The often tight time limits for delivery of results were to a certain extent experienced as a challenge and stimulated learning but to a far too large extent they prevented reflection over and integration of what is learned into the competence of the employee and of the organisation' (Svensson et al., 2002).

Changes requested in VET

The above transformations of learning inside organisations of course also have consequences as far as relationships between productive systems and E&T systems are concerned. Several analysed projects underlined the need for deep transformations in E&T regarding contents, methods, strategies and partnerships with other relevant social subjects inside the world of organisations. In general, it seems possible to identify a passage from 'linear' conceptions of the E&T mission and activities—linked either to scientific-disciplinary paths or to the support of specific labour market requests—to more 'interactive' conceptions in which E&T systems have been seen as co-evolving with productive-organisational systems. The traditional 'linear' conceptions underline the *impacts* on E&T of what is occurring within organisations (in particular in terms of up-dating of the E&T 'outputs'); the 'interactive' conceptions on the other side assume that autonomous transformations take place in both fields linked to the need for both formalised E&T programmes and tacit knowledge development interventions within work and organisational processes. A number of projects dealt with such an issue with different approaches. One of the conclusions of the *Latio* project, for instance, was that 'governments and educational institutions should support organisation specific and internal training activities and forms of co-operation other than participation in regular courses, but with possibility of certification. One important part of such a support within the EU is improving transparency and the free flow of information' (Svensson et al., 2002). From this viewpoint, broad scope normative devices could allow local negotiated interventions to open up a variety of solutions directly linked to contextual needs.

From another viewpoint, more structured and training-centred interventions have been advocated within the framework of a *co-production* of vocational curricula from enterprises and public bodies allowing a combination of vocational school training and experiential work-based learning (Fisher, 2000). In this way, formal vocational education can contribute to the development of work-process knowledge, which in this kind of approach can be consciously developed through formalised tools (Boreham and Lammont, 2001). Such a co-production has been put in practice, for instance, within the collaboration between companies and technical schools for setting up of the 'car mechatronics' EOP (European Occupational Profile)—through which previously separated curricula have been restructured and their tasks and competencies have been unified.

In order to reach such a goal the collaboration between schools and companies has been first of all based on a shared model of the work process and subsequently in the identification of training needs in a flexible perspective. In such a perspective, vocational education and training schemes are functionalised not to separated activities, but to the overall work process knowledge determined simultaneously by the technological set-ups, by social processes involving customers' needs and preferences, and by safety-consciousness and environmentally-aware exigencies. 'In other words the technical knowledge and skills are taught in the wider socio-economic context of *society and work...* In this way work process knowledge can act as the organising principle for bridging theory and practice, and for creating a theoretically-informed but essentially practical approach to knowledge and skills...' (Boreham and Lammont, 2001: 103).

More institutional and policy-oriented recommendations are put forward in the *Smes-training* project, such as those of: (i) Fostering training programmes that are experience-based and tailored to the particular needs of firms to improve employees' capacity to learn from real world experience; (ii) encouraging more specific training programmes for new employees to learn new skills and transfer existing ones; (iii) promoting training programmes between universities and innovative SMEs aimed at reinforcing distinctive competencies for products and markets; (iv) promoting varieties of training courses to maximise network opportunities.

Changes requested in overall education systems: the 'connectivity' model

The results presented so far show that significant lifelong learning phenomena occur in the work place, and involve a plurality of socio-cultural factors and reshape the traditional meanings of *education, training, development* in relation to the central role of *experience*.

Such a central role has also been taken into account in new interpretations and hypotheses concerning E&T beyond the strict 'vocational' dimension, which are continuously being put in question by real characteristics of organisational dynamics. Within *Whole*, Alves distinguished three different, although closely intertwined, elements of work process knowledge. They are related to (i) individual identity and social life (including attitudes and values learned in the socialisation process); (ii) practical experience of daily working life in organisations (regarding the ways in which learning experiences are constructed); (iii) the formal process of learning and competence development (Gaio Alves, 2001). From this interesting perspective, the acquisition of competencies is made possible by the matching of the *personal dimension* of competence with the *professional dimension*—trying to combine the development of individual capacities with traits needed to participate in the labour market. University education, as also shown by empirical research, should reinforce its capacity to keep together two such dimensions, and largely requires attention to work process knowledge and work process-based co-structuring of work and theory.

The *Work Experience* project provided further and extremely interesting clues in this direction. It allows us to understand the complexities of the objectives that should be designed not only for VET policies, but also for general education policies addressed to young people who are still outside working situations and therefore require updated frameworks facilitating their transitions (Guile and Griffith, 2001; Maruhenda and Griffith, 2002). Guile and Griffith argued that most models of work experience in general education and in VET have, in effect, either played down the influence of context upon learning or have approached this issue in a very mechanistic way. In particular traditional ways of conceiving experience, which underpin many current educational approaches, underestimate or ignore the needs for 'negotiating' learning during work experience and for receiving support in relating formal and informal learning given the uneven distribution of knowledge in work roles (Guile and Griffith, 2002).

The project depicted five different models, from the traditional *adaptive* model (based on the idea of 'launching' young people into work situations) to the more recent *connectivity* model aimed at the fostering cognitive and social abilities that are relevant to work experience. Traditional models, from this viewpoint, do not take into account that general education and VET should support not only a 'vertical' development axis but also a 'horizontal' one. The former—that cognitive development theories usually refer to and formal education is aimed at—is in fact 'intellectual development', consisting of individual progress through a hierarchy of knowledge and abstraction and de-contextualisation skills. 'Horizontal development', on the other side—arising from recent developments in socio-cultural theory— 'refers to the process of change and development which occurs within an individual as s/he moves from one context (e.g., school) to another (e.g., a workplace)'. It regards 'changes in an individual's sense of identity as a result of the experience of working in a school, factory or community centre' and requires the capacity to develop new mediating concepts to cope with the demands of working effectively in different organisational settings (Engestroem, 1995; Guile and Griffith, 2002).

Therefore, this approach suggests that there is a need for new curriculum frameworks, which at the same could develop time knowledge, skills and identity. The *connectivity* model is based on a reflexive theory of learning that emphasises the influence of the organisational context upon student learning and development, the situated nature of learning and the need for developing 'boundary crossing' skills. Learners should be supported in 'taking explicit account of the learning which occurs within and between the different contexts of education and work' and in understanding workplaces as composed by interconnected 'activity systems' and populated by different 'communities of practice'[4]. One important orientation of education and training activities for young people should regard, for instance, the personal social behavioural skills that support personal and organisational learning and that are directly linked to work experience. 'Horizontal development' is something that goes far beyond key-skills development and it is not simply concerned with problem-based know-how (Guile and Griffith, 2002). Access to work experience has to be prepared, in this perspective, by E&T policies fostering reflexivity and the use of multiple mediating artefacts aimed at facilitating young people's understanding of how knowledge can be used to achieve economic transformation and to support social cohesion.

Towards organisational citizenship

The results of 4th and 5th FRP projects taken into account so far, seem to add some significant traits to the emerging European perspective, briefly outlined in section 2, on knowledge, learning and competencies in organisations. They allow the policy relevance of such results in relation to values, principles and guidelines expressed in different European policy statements, also quoted in section 2, and in particular to those of the current socio-economic strand of the 6th Framework Programme.

Overall projects findings

The projects results seem to enrich the European perspectives insofar as they (i) produced relevant conceptual frameworks for interpreting work and learning dynamics, (ii) shed light on current learning and development practices in organisations and networks of organisations, (iii) underline the needs for new strategies of involvement of E&T systems as active partners in organisational/ productive dynamics.

The projects as a whole—although highly differentiated in terms of background and objectives—seem to depict an evolutionary reality of knowledge, learning and competencies. This cannot be understood in terms of restrictive views of 'workplace learning'—often seen as a sort of lower order learning when compared to learning produced by formal education institutions. On the contrary, organisations in general—except not insignificant cases of de-skilling—appear to be powerful places of knowledge creation, use and circulation, where continuous developments of competencies at all levels are required.

At the conceptual level, many of the research projects were based on updated assumptions whereby knowledge used in productive processes is created and held by individuals but, at the same time, produced by the same organisational contexts in which individuals live and work. Learning, in its turn, is considered a relational issue dependent on the interactions of social actors—and of their perspectives—within multifaceted learning environments. Competencies are assumed to be individual or collective abilities that have to be put into practice in order to perform specific activities and to face situations arising within such activities.

Empirical research showed several practices in which resources linked to knowledge, learning and competencies are developed in different organisations. Such practices imply continuous stimulation of participation and reflexivity in operating and managing production processes. Competencies are managed through different kinds of systems which positively satisfy—

although some relevant exceptions have been identified—social and organisational needs related not only to performance assessment, but also to the establishment of shared reflexivity frameworks regarding learning, innovation, interpersonal relationships, leadership and other crucial aspects of organisational life.

Education and training have a crucial role to play within such evolutionary tendencies, but deep changes are needed, especially in the 'lifelong learning' perspective. Traditional in-company training activities tend to be increasingly linked to HR development practices, managed through alliances between different organisational functions and designed coherently with experiential paths. This also has consequences outside organisations, in wider social contexts where new generations have to be prepared to acquire formal knowledge, use knowledge and valorise experience in work activities.

Beyond flexibility: organisational citizenship

As a whole, the projects' results show that knowledge, learning and competencies are continuously developed in European organisations—although with some relevant exceptions—and that the patterns of this development necessarily entail qualitatively relevant changes in policy perspectives. Several current functionalistic assumptions in the European debate are overcome which consider knowledge only from its economic value and assume the 'learning organisation' is a synonym for the 'flexible' or 'adaptable to change' organisation. On the contrary, concepts and practices revealed by the set of analysed projects show that in many organisations, knowledge and learning resources are frequently dealt with in forms that tend to transcend the mere economic dimension of organisational development and workplace learning. What is occurring in the largest majority of the selected cases seems to represent the emergence of a new dimension within firms' cultures and practices. Knowledge and learning are not only high value resources, but also the pillars of a new organisational citizenship whose main actors are workers, professionals, managers, entrepreneurs continuously creating, using and exchanging knowledge in their own specific work contexts.

The idea of *organisational citizenship* here is borrowed from different sources within organisational thought. In a consolidated notion of organisational citizenship, this is expressed through constructive and cooperative behaviours and performances which are neither prescribed nor contractually compensated by formal reward systems, but freely occur in terms of mutual help and task achievement within organisations (Bateman and Organ, 1983; Organ and Konovsky, 1989; Organ, 1997). Thus organisational citizenship appears linked to characteristics such as altruism (helping others), conscientiousness (regarding task accomplishment), sportsmanship (stressing the positive aspects of the organization instead of the negative), civic virtue and courtesy (helping in preventing problems from occurring) (Organ, 1988).

In a more critical approach, organisational citizenship represents first of all a social *practice*, i.e. 'a way of life pursued by people—inside and outside organizations—who share a historical context in which they contest the meaning of social or legal norms and struggle to define collective and individual identity' (Gherardi, 2000: 115; Gherardi, 2003). From this viewpoint organisational citizenship appears as a metaphor through which it is possible to understand different aspects within organisational cultures and to shed light on different paradoxes and ambiguities, including—in particular, within Gherardi's approach—those related to women's participation in organisational life, i.e., to *gender citizenship*. This way citizenship is assumed less in the current 'liberal-individualistic' meaning (whereby being a citizen in a democratic country is a right of status, acquired through birth or legal acquisition) and more in its 'classic civic-republican' meaning which implies an active participation in civic life. 'In the former case, individuals born need do nothing to become citizens because they are so by right, while in the latter case individuals prove themselves to be citizens by what they do. Action sustained by a mental attitude constitutes, in this latter case, citizenship, and it maintains a community whose members assume joint responsibility for its continuity and identity' (Gherardi, 2000: 116; Gherardi, 2003). Different models of organisational citizenship can be identified within the latter dynamic perspective, all having in common the idea that citizenship is a matter of interpretation and discourse-based construction of meanings inside specific communities of practice.

Within management studies the theme of the organisational citizenship has been recently developed in terms of *corporate citizenship* understood as an evolution of the current meaning of citizenship—'an essentially passive legal status involving only minimal civic obligations and relying on a distant and entrenched governing elite'—in many ways applicable both to modern societies and to organisations' (Manville and Ober, 2003: 48). The new meaning of citizenship, related to emerging needs within companies, is connected by Manville and Ober to the classical Greek concept of 'politeia': A 'system which is not imposed but rather grows organically from needs, beliefs and actions of people'. 'Politeia' in this sense is 'as much a spirit of governance as a set of rules or laws'. According to this model—very much in line with the same theoretical foundations of what the scientific community in this field refers to as 'organisational learning'[5]—the functioning of an organisational 'politeia' is characterised by the existence of 'participatory structures', 'communal values', and 'practices of engagement'.

'Participatory structures' alludes to flat organisations, minimal hierarchies, engagement of employees-citizens in governance and jurisprudence, transparent procedural rules for policy-making. 'Communal values' is first of all referred to—for ancient Athenians as well as for knowledge workers today—as *motivation*, coming from higher level purposes and from 'a sense of shared ownership in the community destiny'. The individual and the community dimension are crucial at this regard. The shared belief of engagement in the life of the community can be considered as 'educational' in the broadest sense, being linked to the chances for every individual 'to become better, to grow wiser and to fully develop his talents'. 'Practices of engagement' regards the practical dimension in which structures and values have to take place, or, in other terms the *cultural dimension* as it determines 'how work gets done'. In this perspective the authors speak about practices of democracy as linked not only to a 'doing citizenship' but also to a 'learning citizenship' (Manville and Ober, 2003: 52).

Of course the above is a model largely based on large corporations where citizenship can be developed according *active* connotations, but is also intrinsically linked to *status* factors, referring to belonging to a specific big and powerful organisational reality. However, within the learning economy many examples of specific *practices* of organisational citizenship can be unquestionably identified in the wider world of organisations. Included in this wider world are public administrations, service organisations in different sectors, third sector structures and even small autonomous activities networked within broader economic-organisational realities.

The learning economy fosters, in many ways the emergence of new forms of citizenship. These have been defined both as 'organisational', 'in the sense that individuals may become citizens not only of states but also of other organisations', and 'marginal', 'as it can be held temporarily, may be multiple, and even partial, i.e. restricted to some functions only' (Frey, 2000: 1).

In these kinds of views 'organisational citizenship' responds to paramount social and economic exigencies in the learning economy and represents a suitable horizon for new policies capable of overcoming traditional oppositions —like those between citizen and employee, life and work, consumption and production, learning and innovation.

Organisational citizenship as a new perspective for lifelong learning

This is why the 'organisational citizenship' perspective seems highly coherent with the previously mentioned 'citizenship and governance' approach of the European Commission (2002), especially where the latter refers to the need for understanding new tendencies in work settings and new ways for the development of lifelong learning. The 'organisational citizenship' perspective can support choices beyond linear and functionalistic views and requires the adoption of more complex interpretation models.

The images of organisations linked to that of the big industrial company— even like the one at the basis of the 'corporate citizenship' view—have to be replaced with images that are more dynamic. These could capture the vast multiplicity of organisational configurations, assuring the conditions for the production of goods and services and the reproduction of social life in our hyper-complex societies.

In many ways the 'organisational/learning citizen' is a reflexive member of different organisations and communities of practice involved in the dynamics of change: S/he does not inhabit a single 'politeia' in her life course—or even in a given moment—but a number of 'cities' (organizations) and 'alliances between cities' (networks) each one having a specific 'politeia'.

Also, the current idea of work as reproduced through 'jobs', defined in relation to pre-codified tasks and performances belonging to clearly distinguished families and based on established competence bases, has to be largely integrated with other ways of looking at work activities within the 'learning society'. This requires continuous updating technical skills and a plurality of work competencies (including those of social, discursive, learning, ethical nature) that cannot be formalised and are even difficult to be fully understood outside the implementation contexts. Such competencies are generally crucial in a 'risk society' (Beck, 1996) where the conditions for citizenship are not at all taken for granted and must be continuously produced by social actors through reflective practices and self-improvement behaviours.[6]

As far as E&T systems are concerned, new ways of interpreting their functions are needed in the light of the *Memorandum,* where lifelong learning is considered 'not just one aspect of education and training', but as 'the guiding principle for provision and participation across the full continuum of learning contexts' (European Commission, 2000). This requires more attention to the specifically organisational characteristics of lifelong learning contexts (Tosey and Nugent, 2000) and in many ways requires the deepening of the basic approach of the Memorandum. The Memorandum itself considers lifelong learning mostly in terms of extensions of 'formal education' schemes to specific audiences, and seems to adopt a rather individualistic vision of 'non formal education' and 'informal learning' which should be integrated into 'formal education'.

Research in the 'citizenship and governance' perspective has a very important role to play in the implementation of ideas linked to 'organisational citizenship', to the support of 'learning to learn capabilities', and to the design of new educational curricula in the logic of the 'connectivity model'. Several research policy indications in these regards can be developed in relation to three intertwining—*micro, meso*, and *macro*—levels. At the three levels, the fundamental objectives seem to be the ones that enhance *reflective practices* of different kinds. At the micro level, *reflexivity*, as already seen, is a very basic component of development practices assuring at the same time productivity, participation and learning in specific organisations. It is also the background for new education and training practices within the 'connectivity model'. However, reflexivity is also crucial as a governance approach at the local (meso) level where different actors have to reach shared visions and to implement common problem-solving methods. It appears as a basic value to be developed at the European level (macro) as well, where new forms of citizenship and governance are to be fostered and new tools and experiences coherent with this purpose are to be circulated. In many ways these tendencies are related to internal needs of our 'late modernity' characterised by the reflective dimension. It both allows us to describe social life and to enter it, in order to transform it, not as a mechanical process, and not necessarily in controlled ways, but as individuals, groups and organisations that take it as a constant component of their action frameworks (Giddens, 1991).

The orientation of research policies towards practices—as also stated in the recent citizenship and governance approach—seems to largely coincide, in this perspective, with an orientation towards *reflective practices*. The main research questions deal not only with (i) the ways in which knowledge and learning are practically developed and competencies are continuously enhanced, but also with (ii) the ways in which it would be possible to increase the scale and scope of positive actions and of the tools supporting them.

The micro level: action methodologies for the development of organisational citizenship

At the micro level, research should be aimed at understanding both current *organisational citizenship* phenomena and at fostering new forms of their development through reflective practices. This could mean, for instance (i) to deepen the analyses so far carried out within organisations about participative design of 'competencies management systems', allowing new criteria for participation, motivation and engagement, or (ii) to launch inquiries about newly established 'development centres' aimed at creating development paths for individuals based on training, self-assessment of learning results, exchange of experience among peers within communities of practice, or (iii) to analyse the use of 'situated curricula' within E&T activities, aimed at transferring learning contents derived from organisational experiences into educational practices. Moreover, it would be interesting to analyse cases concerning experiences of use of *action methodologies*, the wide family of tools and techniques which includes (i) *action research* (participative research processes carried on by social actors in a given context with the help of professional researchers); (ii) *action learning* (problem-solving activities based on real-time working-through of organisational issues); (ii) *action science* (a method aimed at improving inter-personal and organisational effectiveness through the discovery of hidden beliefs and defences) and several others.[7]

Besides analysing cases of successful implementations of action methodologies, it is very important to encourage new forms of social research based on these reflexivity-based tools. This is because they tend to valorise the 'insider knowledge' of members of organisations, and trigger the creation of new visions and context interpretations. The main subjects of such research lines could be employees, HRD practitioners, middle managers, shop stewards, and of course teachers/trainers and other E&T operators involved in co-operation experiences with productive organisations.

The meso level: inter-organisational and inter-institutional co-operation

The meso level in this perspective is mainly the level of *inter-organisational and inter-institutional co-operation,* including for instance, networking of SMEs, partnerships between E&T institutions on a local scale, multilevel governance of knowledge and competences (e.g. through specific programmes) in a territorial context, etc… At this level reflexivity can support the development of new forms of local (inter-organisational) citizenship through active involvement of local policy-makers, employers' representatives and trade unionists. Relevant research lines could be for instance identified in relation to (i) the innovative role of VET institutions in different local contexts where the traditional skills formation functions are accompanied by other functions related to technological intermediation and development consultancy; (ii) the need for joint inquiries between E&T systems and productive organisations aimed at discovering new patterns of 'connectivity'.

Also at this level action methodologies can play a significant role in processes of 'perspective making/perspective taking' in which different actors have to communicate their own specific—often highly specialised—viewpoint and to reciprocally take the viewpoint of the others: Methods based on joint inquiry can help such mutual knowledge within practices that strictly link reflection, generation of new visions, testing and then implementation of new courses of action.

Different forms of interactions should be implemented in order to facilitate the comparison of different interests and development hypotheses having implications for E&T programmes design. The 'research' side of these interactions should be valorised as they can lead to specific shared outcomes and not only to confrontations of institutional viewpoints. In many ways, this approach, linking research and relations between social actors, could be a new key to the so-called *integrated policies* (in the E&T, work, industrial and scientific research fields), to be designed through guided interactions of relevant social subjects at the meso level.

The macro level: supporting new research approaches and the emergence of an interactive social science

The macro level is the one of *socio-economic research policy design.* At this level the references to reflexivity and to action methodologies are coherent with the *interactive social science* approach. This is an emerging innovative way of looking at both social research activities and institutional procedures for designing and financing research programmes. 'Interactive social science' is in fact 'a style of activity where researchers, funding agencies and 'user groups' interact throughout the entire research process, including the definition of the research agenda, project selection, project execution and the application of research insights' (Scott et. Al., 1999, quoted in Caswill and Shove, 2000).

Trying to apply the ISS perspective, at least partly, to the EC activity model should imply significant changes as far as the *policy relevance* of European research is concerned. As showed in recent field research on European project-leaders, the policy relevance is a contested terrain, given the gap between official statements and current practices. From one side it is declared that 'research must contribute to provide the policy decision-making process with a sound knowledge of the challenges facing Europe, of their main consequences and of possible policy options to tackle them' (Council of Europe, 1998). On the other side researchers report that the results of their efforts are frequently disregarded, the adoption of solutions provided is accidental and temporary, the use of research findings is subordinated to already established political agendas (Greco et al., 2003).

Implementing the *interactive social science* approach—at least suggesting the adoption of it as an experimental part of the *networks of excellence* activities—could be a politically significant step towards a new role for the Commission—closer to the exigencies of European citizens and open to bottom-up indications coming from socio-economic realities.

Micro, meso and *macro*, in this perspective, appear not as ordered layers of a top-down construction, but as interrelated steps of new forms of citizenship and governance based on (social) knowledge creation and on competence development at different levels. Even the recently suggested creation of a *European High Level Council on Innovation and Competence Building* (Archibugi and Lundvall, 2001) could take the form not of a rigid institution, but of an agile structure supporting the activities of networks of different nature and scope all over Europe.

Concluding remarks

The results of the research studies that this article has dealt with (carried out within the Fourth and Fifth Framework Programme of the European Commission) show how knowledge, learning and competencies are fundamental issues for organisational development and how, at the same time, they cannot be reduced to homogeneous categories.

In particular, different practices have been observed within enterprises that concern relevant lifelong learning needs related to the integration of explicit and tacit knowledge, the improvement of learning within production processes and the management of competencies

Although the metaphor of the *learning organisation* is increasingly less apt to synthetically express such needs, as it did in previous phases of organisational thought, it can still represent phenomena that are important for both people and organisations. Included here are the valorisation of experience, the implementation of reflective practices and the promotion of self-organising attitudes and procedures.

However, new keys must be provided for policy-making in order to interpret the ever complex articulation of the organisational dimension in which crucial lifelong learning events take place involving individual and trans-individual developments.

In this chapter, one such key has been identified within a renewed concept of *organisational citizenship*-understood as a social practice regarding participation and dynamic identity related to social action. Such a concept can be effectively linked to the one of *reflexive meta-competence*. This should characterise typical behaviours of our late modernity (even within organisational contexts) insofar as it underlines the situated and 'emergent' nature of acting and learning. In this perspective, organisational citizenship is not about static forms of belonging to specific organisations but, on the contrary, it is related to needs of continuous learning development based on active participation within a plurality of organisations and communities of practice (including those, for instance, supporting micro-enterprises and autonomous multi-client work activities).

E&T systems should increasingly take into account such exigencies and involve themselves in new forms of lifelong learning development, characterised less by a central role of E&T institutions as such, and more by the convergence on shared objectives of different stakeholders in lifelong learning processes.

New research experiences—more on the practical-participative side than on the merely academic one, within the logic of reflective practices and action *methodologies*—should experiment with opportunities and problems of such a convergence at different levels: *Micro* (intra-organisational), *meso* (inter-organisational and inter-institutional) and *macro* (i.e. at the level of policy design).

Notes

1. This paper is mostly based on the analysis of available projects documentation (books, published and unpublished articles, web documents – especially those provided on the www.cordis.lu website). Important inputs have also been collected through the workshops organised within the 'Towards the learning economy" project, in particular the workshop specifically dedicated to 'domain 1" (Barcelona, 15 and 16 February 2002).

2. (*): acronyms attributed here for easing quotations. The other acronyms are the original ones.

3. This way of looking at organisational learning processes as institutionalisation process has many things in common with the Nonaka's *spiral of knowledge* representing the continuous conversion of explicit knowledge into tacit knowledge in forms defined as *socialisation, externalisation, combination, internalisation* (1994, 1995). Nonaka is a largely quoted author within the set of analysed research projects but its theoretical constructs are mostly integrated with those stemming from more traditional areas of organisational learning, without specific analyses of differences and contradictions that in fact exist between 'knowledge-creation" and 'learning" (Tomassini, 2003).

4. Both 'activity systems" theory and 'communities of practice" theory underline the *situated* nature of work and learning. In the former, subjects at work and objects of work are involved in dynamics related to rules, community, division of labour, mediating artefacts (Engestroem, 1999). In the latter, the stress is on characteristics such as common enterprise, mutual learning, shared repertories (Wenger, 1998).

5. '…organisations are political systems. They are political both in the ancient sense of *polis* (that is they are governments) and in the more contemporary sense of an interplay of contending interests and associated powers" (Argyris and Schoen, 1978: 328)

6. From another viewpoint the perspective adopted here has several commonalities with the 'active citizenship" approach, in which lifelong learning is seen as part of policies and governing techniques aimed at promoting cultural norms and values coherent with the ideas of learning as an endless process, while the learner is seen as guided by principles of self-reliance and entrepreneurship (Edwards, 2002)

7. Important contributions exploring the complex world of *action methodologies* (or *action technologies*, or *reflexivity methods*) can be found in: Reason and Bradbury (2000), Raelin (1999), Dickens and Watkins (1999), Greenwood and Levine (1998), Chisholm and Elden (1993).

References

Archibugi, D. & Lundvall, B.A. (2001) *The Globalising Learning Economy: Major Socio-Economic Trends and European Innovation Policies*. Oxford: Oxford University Press.

Argyris, G. & Schoen, D. A. (1978) *Organizational Learning: A Theory of Action Perspective*. Reading Mass: Addison-Wesley.

Bateman, T. S. & Organ, D. (1983) 'Job Satisfaction and the Good Soldier: The relationship between affect and employee 'citizenship''. *Academy of Management Journal*, No. 26, pp. 587-595.

Beck, U. (1996) 'Reflexive Modernisierung'. In U. Beck, A. Giddens, S. Lash (eds.) *Reflexive Modernisation*. It. ed.: *Modernizzazione riflessiva*, Trieste: Asterios.

Benadusi, L. & Consoli F. (1999) 'L'emergere della metodologia delle competenze nel pensiero teorico e pratico manageriale'. *Osservatorio ISFOL*, Vol. 20 (5-6), pp. 30-89.

Boreham, N. & Lammont, N. (2001) *Work process knowledge in technological and organisational development. The 'Whole' project.* Web document.

Boreham, N. (2002) 'Work process knowledge in technological and organisational development'. In N. Boreham, R. Samurcay & N. Fischer (eds) *Work Process Knowledge*. London and New York: Routledge.

Boreham, N. & Morgan, C. (2001) 'Cases of Organisational Learning in Company U (United Kingdom)'. In M. Fischer, P. Röben (eds) *Ways of Organisational Learning in the Chemical Industry and their Impact on Vocational Education and Training. A Literature Review.* Bremen: Unpublished paper for the 'OrgaLearn' project.

Boreham, N., Fischer, M., Huys, R., Mariani, M., Morgan, C., Parlangeli, O., Röben, P. & Van Ruysseveldt, J. (2001) 'Criteria for organisational learning in a learning company'. In M. Fischer, P. Röben (eds) *Ways of Organisational Learning in the Chemical Industry and their Impact on Vocational Education and Training. A Literature Review.* Bremen: Unpublished paper for the 'OrgaLearn' project.

Caswill, C. & Shove, E. (2000) 'Introducing interactive social science'. *Science and Public Policy*, June, pp. 154-157.

Chisholm, R. & Elden, M. (1993) 'Emerging varieties of action research: Introduction to special issue'. *Human Relations*, Vol. 46 (2), pp. 121-142.

Conceição, P. & Heitor, M. (2001) 'Universities in the Learning Economy: Balancing Institutional Integrity with Organizational Diversity'. In D. Archibugi, B.A. Lundvall (2001) *The Globalising Learning Economy: Major Socio-Economic Trends and European Innovation Policies*. Oxford: Oxford University Press.

Coriat, B. (2001) 'Organizational Innovation in European Firms: A Critical Overview of the Survey Evidence'. In D. Archibugi, B.A. Lundvall (2001) *The Globalising Learning Economy: Major Socio-Economic Trends and European Innovation Policies*. Oxford: Oxford University Press.

Dickens, L. & Watkins, K. (1999) 'Action research: Rethinking Lewin'. *Management Learning*, Vol. 30 (2), pp. 127-140.

Edwards, R. (2002) Mobilising lifelong learning: governmentality in educational practices. University of Stirling: Unpublished paper.

Engestroem, Y. (1995) *Training for Change*. London: ILO publications.

Engestroem, Y., Miettinen, R. & Punamäki R.L. (eds) (1999) *Perspectives on Activity Theory*. Cambridge: Cambridge University Press.

Engestroem, Y. (1999) 'Activity theory and individual and social transformation'. In: Y. Engestroem, R. Miettinen, R.L. Punamäki (eds) *Perspectives on Activity Theory*. Cambridge: Cambridge University Press.

European Commission (1994) *White Book: Competitiveness and Employment*. Web document.

European Commission (1995) *White paper. Teaching and Learning: Towards the Learning Society.* Web document.

European Commission (1997) *Green Paper: Partnership for a New Organisation of Work.* Luxembourg: Office for Official Publications of the European Communities.

European Commission (1997) *Towards a Europe of Knowledge-Commission Outlines Action on Education and Training.* Web document.

European Commission (1998) *Education and Active Citizenship in the European Union.* Luxembourg: Office for Official Publications of the European Communities.

European Commission (2000) *A Memorandum on Lifelong Learning.* Web document.

European Commission (2000) *Presidency Conclusions of the Lisbon European Council.* Web document.

European Commission (2001) *Green Paper: Promoting a European Framework for Corporate Social Responsibility.* Luxembourg: Office for Official Publications of the European Communities.

European Commission (2001) *Partnership for a new Organization of Work-Green Paper.* Web document.

European Commission (2001) *Making a European Area of Lifelong Learning a Reality.* Web document.

European Commission (2002) *FP 6 Integrating Programme. Priority 7: Citizens and Governance in a Knowledge-Based Society.* Web document.

European Commission (2003) *Best Workplaces in the EU & Three Special Awards 2003.* Web document.

Fischer, M. (2000) *Work process knowledge as a reference point for professional learning.* Unpublished paper.

Fischer, M. (2002) 'Work experience as an element of work process knowledge'. In N. Boreham, R. Samurcay and N. Fischer (eds) *Work Process Knowledge.* London and New York: Routledge.

Fischer, M. & Röben, P. (eds) (2001) *Ways of Organisational Learning in the Chemical Industry and their Impact on Vocational Education and Training. A Literature Review.* Bremen: Unpublished paper for the 'OrgaLearn' project.

Fischer, M. & Röben, P. (2002) *Cases of Organisational Learning in European Chemical Companys. An Empirical Study.* ITB-Arbeitspapiere 35, Bremen: Unpublished report.

Frey, B. (2000) *Citizenship in a Globalised World.* University of Zurich. Web document.

Gaio Alves, M. (2001) *The construction of 'Work Process Knowledge': the Contribution of Initial Education and the University.* Unpublished paper.

Gavigan, J., Ottitsch, M. & Maharoum S. (1999) *Knowledge and Learning. Towards a Learning Europe (Eur 19034 En).* Brussels: European Commission.

Gherardi, S. (2003) 'Gender Citizenship in Organizations'. In P. Jeffcut (ed.) *The Foundations of Management Knowledge.* Routledge: London.

Gherardi, S. (2000) 'Cittadinanza Organizzativa, Cittadinanza di Genere e Discorsi Civici dentro e fuori dalle Organizzazioni'. *Sociologia del Lavoro*, No. 80, pp. 111-128.

Gherardi, S. & Nicolini, D. (2000) 'The Organizational Learning of Safety in Communities of Practice'. *Journal of Management Inquiry*, Vol. 9 (1), pp. 7-18.

Giddens, A. (1991) *Modernity and Self-Identity: Self and Society in the Late Modern Age.* London: Polity.

Greco, L., Landri, P., Tomassini, M. & Wickham, J. (2003) *Reinterpreting the applied/policy relevant dimension of the European socio-economic research: a preliminary analysis.* Dublin-Rome: Unpublished paper for the 'European Dimension' project.

Greenwood, D. & Levin, M. (1998) *Introduction to Action Research: Social Research for Social Change.* Thousand Oaks: Sage.

Guile, D. & Griffith, T. (2002) *Learning through Work Experience*. University of London: Unpublished paper.

Holford, J., Jarvis, P. & Griffin, C. (1999) *International Perspective on Lifelong Learning*. London: Kogan Page.

Lawson, C. & Lorenz, E. (1999) 'Collettive learning and knowledge development in the evolution of regional cluster of high technology SMEs in Europe'. *Regional Studies*, Vol. 33 (4), pp. 305-317.

Lazaric, N. & Lorenz, E. (eds) (1997) *The Economics of Trust and Learning*. London: Elgar.

Lundvall, B-A. & Borras, S. (1999) *The Globalising Learning Economy: Implications for Innovation Policy*. Luxemburg: Office for Official Publications of the European Communities.

Lundvall, B-A. & Archibugi D. (2001) 'Introduction: Europe and the Learning Economy'. In D. Archibugi, B.A. Lundvall (2001) *The Globalising Learning Economy: Major Socio-Economic Trends and European Innovation Policies*. Oxford: Oxford University Press.

Lundvall, B-A. (2002) *Innovation, Growth and Social Cohesion. The Danish Model (New Horizons in the Economic of Innovation)*. Oxford: Oxford University Press.

Lung, Y. (ed.) (2002) *Coordinating Competencies and Knowledge in the European Automobile System, CoCKEAS final report*. Web document.

Manville, B. & Ober, J. (2003) 'Beyond Empowerment: Building a Company of Citizens'. *Harvard Business Review*, January 2003, pp. 48-53.

Mariani, M., (2002a) *Work Process Knowledge in a Chemical Company*. Unpublished paper for OrgaLearn project.

Mariani, M., (2002b) 'Cases of organisational learning in the company I (Italy)'. In M. Fischer, P. Röben (2002) *Cases of Organisational Learning in European Chemical Companys. An empirical study*. ITB-Arbeitspapiere 35, Bremen: Unpublished report.

Montedoro, C. (ed.) (2002). *Le Dimensioni Metacurricolari dell'Agire Formativo*. Milan: Franco Angeli.

Nonaka, I. (1994) 'A Dynamic Theory of Organizational Knowledge Creation'. *Organization Science*, Vol. 3, pp. 14-37.

Nonaka, J. & Takeuchi, H. (1995) *The Knowledge Creating Company*. New York: Oxford Press.

Nyahn, B., Cressey, P., Kelleher, M. & Poell R. (eds) (2003) *Facing up to the Learning Organization Challenge. Selected European Writings*. Luxembourg: Office for Official Publications of the European Communities.

Organ, D.W. (1988) *Organizational Citizenship Behaviour: The Good Soldier Syndrome*. Lexington: Lexington Books.

Organ, D. W. (1997) 'Organizational citizenship behavior: It is construct cleanup time'. *Human Performance*, Vol. 10 (2), pp. 85-97.

Organ, D. W. & Konovsky M. A (1989) 'Cognitive versus affective determinants of organizational citizenship behaviour'. *Journal of Applied Psychology*, Vol. 74, pp. 157-164.

Pauwels, F. & Van Ruysseveldt, J. (2002) 'Cases of organisational learning in the company B (Belgium)'. In M. Fischer, P. Röben (2002) *Cases of Organisational Learning in European Chemical Companys. An empirical study*. ITB-Arbeitspapiere 35, Bremen: unpublished report.

Rabardel, P. & Duvenci-Langa, S. (2002) 'Technological change and the construction of competence'. In N. Boreham, R. Samurcay and N. Fischer (eds) *Work Process Knowledge*. London and New York: Routledge.

Raelin, J. A.. (1999a) *Work-based Learning. The New Frontier of Management Development*. Upper Saddle River: Prentice Hall.

Reason, P. & Bradbury, H. (2001) *Handbook of Action Research: Participative Inquiry and Practice*. Thousand Oaks: Sage Publications.

Rogalski, J., Plat, M. & Antolin-Glenn, P. (2002) 'Training for collective competence in rare and unpredictable situations'. In N. Boreham, R. Samurcay and N. Fischer (eds) *Work Process Knowledge*. London and New York: Routledge.

Samurçay, R. & Vidal-Gomel, C. (2002) 'The contribution of work process knowledge to competence in electrical maintenance'. In N. Boreham, R. Samurcay and N. Fischer (eds) *Work Process Knowledge*. London and New York: Routledge.

Sarcina, R. (ed.) (1998) *DELOS Project: Developing learning organisation model in SME clusters. Final report of project*. Unpublished document.

Sauquet, A. (ed.) (2002) *Small Business Training and Competitiveness: Building Case Studies in Different European Cultural Contexts, TSER Project*. Web document.

Schoen, D.A. (1983) *The Reflective Practitioner. How Professionals Think in Action*. New York, Basic Books.

Scott, A., Skea, J., Robinson, J. & Shove E. (1999) Designing 'interactive' environmental research for wider social relevance. *ESRC Global Environmental Change Programme*, Special Briefing n. 4, May.

Senge, P.M. (1990) *The Fifth Discipline: The Art and Practice of the Practice of the Learning Organisation*. New York: Doubleday Currency.

Svensson, L. et al. (2002) *Learning Environments of Knowledge Intensive Company Units in Five European Countries*. Final report.

Tjepkema, S., Stewart, J., Sambrook, S., Mulder, M., Horst Ter, H. & Scheerens J. (eds) (2002) *HRD and Learning Organisations in Seven European Countries*. London: Routledge.

Tiepkema, S., Ter Horst, H. & Mulder, M. (2002) 'Learning organisations and HRD'. In S. Tjepkema, J. Stewart, S. Sambrook, M. Mulder, H. Horst ter, J. Scheerens *HRD and Learning Organisations in Seven European Countries*. London: Routledge.

Tomassini, M. (2001) *Knowledge and Competencies in the Learning Economy: Issues and Challenges for E&T Systems*. Rome: ISFOL. Unpublished paper.

Tomassini, M. (2002a) *The Learning Organisation in the Learning Economy*. Rome: ISFOL. Unpublished paper.

Tomassini, M. & Cavrini A., (2002b) 'Cases from Italy'. In S. Tjepkema, J. Stewart, S. Sambrook, M. Mulder, H. Horst Ter, J. Scheerens (eds) *HRD and Learning Organisations in Seven European Countries*. London: Routledge.

Tomassini, M. (2002) 'I sistemi educativi e formativi nella learning economy: presupposti e ipotesi per lo sviluppo di metodologie basate sulla riflessività'. In C. Montedoro (ed.) *Le Dimensioni Metacurricolari dell'Agire Frmativo*. Milan: Franco Angeli.

Tomassini, M. (2003) 'Learning organization and human resource development in the knowledge economy'. In B. Nyahn, P. Cressey, M. Kelleher, R. Poell R.. (eds) *Facing up to the Learning Organization Challenge. Selected European Writings*. Luxembourg: Office for Official Publications of the European Communities.

Tosey, P. & Nugent, J. (1999) 'Beyond the Threshold: Organizational Learning at the Edge'. In J. Holford, P. Jarvis, C. Griffin *International Perspective on Lifelong Learning*. London: Kogan Page.

Webster, J., Wickham, J. & Collins G. (2001) *Innovations in Information Society Sectors— Implication for Women's Work, Expertise and Opportunities in European Workplaces*. Dublin: Employment Research Centre at Trinity College. Web document.

Wenger, E. (1998) *Communities of Practice. Learning, Meaning and Identity*. Oxford: Oxford University Press.

Wenger, E., McDermott, R. & Snyder, W. (2002) *Cultivating Communities of Practice*. Boston: Harvard Business School Press.

CHAPTER SIX

The Knowledge Economy, Work Process Knowledge and the Learning Citizen—Central but Vulnerable

NICK BOREHAM

The European policy context

As all European researchers know, at the start of the new millennium the European Council set itself 'a new strategic goal for the next decade: To become the most competitive and dynamic Knowledge-based economy in the world...' (Communiqué of the Lisbon European Council, 23/24 March 2000, p. 2). The fact that the European Council felt confident to make such a bold declaration reflects a broad consensus among policy makers that knowledge is the most important factor of production. This point of view is articulated most clearly in the OECD's (1996) report *The Knowledge-Based Economy*, which argues that the global economy is being driven by the increasing codification of knowledge and its transmission through communications and computer networks. Lundvall (2001) has extended this argument by introducing the term 'learning economy' to emphasize that what really matters is not access to a pool of knowledge, but creating new knowledge and forgetting the out-of-date. When the OECD report states that 'education will be the centre of the knowledge-based economy, and learning the tool of individual and organizational advancement' (p.14), it forges a crucial link between economic and educational policy making. Learning and work are now fused in a significant and radical way, in that learning has become the new work, or at least, a significant part of it.

Within the European Union, the integration of working and learning is one of the building blocks of the so-called European route to the modernization of industry. The way forward was mapped out at the Essen meeting of the

European Council in 1994, which declared the need for 'a more flexible organization of work in a way which fulfils both the wishes of employees and the requirements of competition' (European Communities 1997, p.3). The kinds of work organization the Council envisages as the foundation of the future European knowledge economy are those which adapt swiftly to changing market conditions, discontinue outdated working practices, invent new ones, engage in continuous improvement and—as Tomassini explains in Chapter 4—tend towards the characteristics of the learning organization (Senge, 1990). A complete transformation of work in Europe remains a distant and sometimes contested goal, but empirical studies such as the regular reviews of industrial working practices carried out by the European Commission reveal that many industrial sectors are indeed replacing bureaucratic work systems and fixed procedures by more flexible systems of continuous improvement (European Foundation for the Improvement of Living and Working Conditions, 2002). The new ways of working involve *inter alia* the reduction of vertical and horizontal demarcations, the replacement of functional departments by multi-functional business units and the delegation of responsibility to self-managing teams. The common thread running through structural changes of these kinds is their potential for facilitating individual and organizational learning by involving all employees in the pursuit of innovation and competitiveness (Boreham, 2002b).

Work process knowledge

As the reviews of EU funded research in the present volume show, contemporary discussions of the knowledge needed for the new work systems envisaged by European policy makers rely on a limited range of concepts, especially *tacit knowledge* (which is opposed to *codified* or *explicit knowledge*) and *knowing how* (which is opposed to *knowing that*). Tacit knowledge is cited by both OECD (1996) and Lundvall (2001) as the driving force behind the knowledge (or learning) economy. Certainly, the concept of *tacit knowledge* is useful for highlighting the fact that a considerable amount of work-related knowledge is embedded in working practices in ways that make it difficult to articulate. And although less reference is made to *knowing how* in current debates, this concept is also useful for acknowledging the way experience is crystallized in working practices. Fischer (2002), for example, has pointed out that when skilled manufacturing work is automated, the supervisors of the new systems still require the sensory skills they learned through manual work in order to monitor automated operations such as cutting and drilling.

Nevertheless, despite their value in particular situations, the concepts of *tacit knowledge* and *knowing how* have limitations when it comes to designing the kinds of vocational curricula needed for a knowledge economy. Their main drawback is that their binary structure makes the contestable assumption that the knowledge used for work is *either* tacit *or* codified, and *either* knowledge how *or* knowledge that. Setting up a binary opposition between tacit and codified knowledge encourages the belief that employees' tacit knowledge can be mined, extracted, translated into codified knowledge and distributed throughout the organization. This is proposed, for example, in Nonaka and Takeuchi's (1995) *The Knowledge Creating Company*, a work which has influenced several of the EU projects analyzed in the present volume. But arguably, 'knowing' is a unitary process which involves both tacit and codified knowledge, which interact in ultimately inseparable ways (see Boreham, 1992, 1994). The binary opposition between *knowing how* and *knowing that* is equally problematic, for it reflects a Cartesian dualism of the mental and the physical, a way of looking at the world which reinforces the separation of school and workplace in the formation of vocational competence. 'Knowing that', conceived as an internal mental event, is domain-independent in the sense that it is abstracted from its material context. If we view knowledge in this way, it becomes easy to fall into what Knorr Cetina and Preda (2001) call an 'exteriorized' theory of how knowledge relates to practice. By exteriorized they mean that knowledge, as a factor of production, operates externally to the work process—comparable, for example, to the financial capital which can be injected into a firm by an external agency such as a bank. However, if we aspire to create a learning economy built out of learning organizations, one in which knowledge is generated in the work process itself, this is surely an inappropriate frame from which to approach the challenges of vocational education and training.

In place of these binary terms, then, an alternative way of conceptualizing work-related knowledge is needed which integrates the *tacit* with the *codified* and the *how* with the *that*. In fact, what is needed is a conceptualization of work-based knowing as a socio-cultural activity—one in which 'knowledge' and 'learning' are constitutive of the work process itself. The concept of *work process knowledge* was developed by a 10-country research network which was established in 1994 and is still active. The network was funded from 1998-2000 by the European Union within its Framework IV Targeted Socio-Economic Research programme to carry out a project entitled *Work Process Knowledge in Technological and Organizational Development* (the WHOLE project, Boreham and Lammont 2000). The concept of work process knowledge, the focus of this network, is far more sensitive to the knowledge requirements of modernized work than the binary terms we have been discussing. The definition of work process knowledge was not arrived at *a priori* but was derived from a large number of empirical studies of flexible and/ or informated work, which between them covered 10 European countries. The studies covered 22 industries spanning the full range of manufacturing and service sectors of the European economy (Table 1) (see Boreham & Lammont, 2000, and Boreham *et al.*, 2002, for detailed project reports).

TABLE 1: Industries Studied by the WHOLE Network to Explore Work Process Knowledge

---

MANUFACTURING

Continuous process manufacturing: paper making, steel manufacture, chemicals, power generation

Assembly: mineral water bottling, automobile manufacturing

Small batch manufacturing: mechanical engineering, clothing, machine tools, medical equipment

SERVICES

Material services: air traffic control, marine navigation, military flying, hotel industry, electrical maintenance, telecommunications sales, automobile service and repairs

Human services: fire service, health service, education

Information services: industrial design, financial services, industrial laboratory work

---

References to 'process knowledge' can be traced to the 1920s, and the term *Arbeitsprozeßwissen* (meaning labour process knowledge) was introduced in Germany in the context of total quality management by Kruse (1986). However, *work process knowledge* in the sense used in this chapter has a rather different meaning. It was defined by Boreham *et al.* (1995) in terms of four attributes:

(1) Contrary to what is implied by the Taylorist principle of narrow jobs, each underpinned by the minimal level of knowledge required for that job alone, work process knowledge implies a systems-level understanding of how the work process is configured in the organization as a whole (including the business process, the production process and the labour process). This breadth of view is required by several aspects of the changes that are taking place in contemporary European work systems, including flexibilization, the emphasis

on cross-boundary working and the inter-connectivity of sites and functions that may result from automation.

(2) Work process knowledge is used directly in the performance of work—such knowledge is 'active' as opposed to 'inert' with regard to the work in question. This part of the definition restricts work process knowledge to the sub-set of all possible knowledge, namely that which is useful for work. (The sum total of human knowledge includes much that is valued as an end in itself, but we are not concerned with that at the present, only with work-related knowledge). Thus what counts as work process knowledge depends on the nature of the work in question, as one item of information might underpin work in one context and not in another.

(3) Work process knowledge is constructed by employees while they are engaging in work, particularly when they are solving problems. Typically, solving a problem will involve creating insights or understandings that enable effective action to be taken, and work process knowledge is formed in this way. The concept of work process knowledge is thus dynamic, in the sense that this way of knowing is embedded in the interactions that occur when people are engaged in work.

(4) In place of the binary opposition between *knowing how* and *knowing that* and the binary opposition between *tacit* and *codified* knowledge, the concept of work process knowledge is holistic, in the sense that it is a synthesis of different ways of knowing. Following from point (3) above, when solving a problem in the workplace, employees often call upon diverse intellectual resources and synthesize them into a new idea. The synthesis typically occurs in a dialectical process which resolves contradictions between explicit or codified forms of work-related knowledge on the one hand, and the more experiential ways of knowing that arise from engagement in work itself on the other.

Numerous case studies of work process knowledge can be found in the reports of the WHOLE project (Boreham & Lammont, 2000; Boreham *et al.*, 2002) and a reading of these reports is necessary fully to clarify the meaning of the term. For the purposes of the present chapter, however, the meaning of work process knowledge will be explained by referring to one of these studies—Mariani's (2002) investigation of an Italian knowledge-creating chemical company. In response to increasing international competition in the field of plastics manufacturing, this company changed its focus from the production of plastics to research and development. Previously, research and development into new plastics constituted 20% and production 80% of the company's activity, but these proportions were reversed and the core business became researching new types of plastic, developing the technology to produce them and licensing the resulting processes to other companies. Many of the latter were located in second and third world countries, where labour costs were low. These companies had been squeezing the Italian company out of its markets, but with its new policy of capitalizing its knowledge assets, it soon recovered competitive advantage.

The research and development which became the company's new core activity was located in its laboratories and pilot chemical plant, the latter being small-sized production facilities which experimented with technological processes for manufacturing the new substances discovered in the laboratories. New production processes developed in these plants were licensed to other companies, together with the patents for the new substances. However, in order to develop as many new processes as possible, the pilot plants had to be reconfigured for a new production process many times each month. This meant that the employees operating these plants had to work much more flexibly than is usually the case in continuous process manufacturing. Not only were they continually stepping into new work roles as new technologies were tried out, but all grades of worker were involved in evaluating the new processes while operating the pilot plant—learning was now an essential part of their work. Work process knowledge comes into the picture once it is appreciated that, in order to perform successfully in these roles, they needed to understand the work process as a whole: as one experienced employee commented, 'It should never be allowed to happen that an individual cannot interpret a certain output because he or she does not know what happened at a previous stage in the process' (Mariani, 2002, p. 24). In recognition of this, the induction of new workers now placed more emphasis on understanding the production process as a whole and less on training them for specific roles. Detailed studies by Mariani revealed that much of the knowledge used by these workers also met the other criteria of work process knowledge. In particular, extensive use was made of meetings and other ways of structuring conversations in order to promote continuous dialogue among employees ranging over all aspects of the production process. It was by participating in this dialogue that employees solved the problems of running the pilot plant innovatively, synthesizing scientific and experiential perspectives on the production process.

Work process knowledge as a conceptual tool for exploring the learning needs of the knowledge economy

The concept of work process knowledge has proved valuable for addressing a wide range of the problems encountered in building a European knowledge economy. These include attempts to introduce total quality management, new forms of work based on socio-technical system thinking, developing employees' capacity for supervising the kinds of complex, dynamic production system created by automation, integrating academic study with work experience in intermediate-level vocational training and dealing with the crisis in the graduate labour market provoked by the loss of 'graduate' jobs. In all these cases, a broad knowledge of work processes at a systems level enables individuals to cope with the challenges of a changing work environment. Moreover, the concept of work process knowledge is a useful tool for designing training and development to support them in this.

Total quality management

Total quality management is being sought in modernized workplaces all over Europe. However, total quality management depends on the ability of employees to understand the interrelatedness of the different parts of the organization's work process. Employees need to understand, for example, that a problem which manifests itself in one department might be caused by events in another department, and might then have repercussions in a third. It was Kruse (1986) who identified the need for this kind of understanding and called it *labour process knowledge*. Labour process knowledge, an early form of the concept of work process knowledge, includes:

– An expanded understanding of work roles in parts of the organization other than the employee's own, and
– participation in a workplace culture which provides a service to colleagues in support of an overall high quality of service to the customer.

Many public and private sector enterprises try to achieve total quality by standardising operating procedures and controlling their employees' behaviour by imposing detailed rules and regulations on them. However, this top-down approach is inconsistent with the aim of creating the flexible and adaptive organizations envisaged by the OECD (1996), Lundvall (2001) and the European Communities (1997). Two of the WHOLE researchers, Norros and Nuutinen (2002), have pointed out that this kind of standardization undermines the very essence of work, which in their view is based on the acceptance of personal responsibility for one's actions. They argue that the complexity and uncertainty of modern work processes requires a capacity for judgment on the part of employees at all levels, together with a capacity to meet unique situational demands which are impossible to predict when writing rules and regulations. Arguing the case that quality can be achieved through a more discretionary and participatory approach to work, Norros and Nuutinen identify work process knowledge as an essential prerequisite for enabling employees to meet unforeseeable demands by exercising judgement. More generally, they locate the need for work process knowledge in the fact that 'the coming of the information society and the increase of knowledge intensive work bring with them a dissolution of the boundaries of time and place' (ibid, 26).

Socio-technical systems

Socio-technical systems theory developed in the Tavistock Institute in London in the 1950s, and was subsequently taken forward by American, Scandinavian and Flemish researchers. Initially, the socio-technical systems approach was defined as the use of autonomous work groups to humanize manual work. Later, the emphasis was placed on using these groups to increase productivity, based on the belief that autonomous work groups can respond more quickly to new demands than employees working within traditional hierarchical structures.

An example of the use of autonomous (or nearly autonomous) groups in manufacturing is the 'production island', a strategy for improving flexibility by bringing several different functional departments into a single unit. Boundaries between the departments are dissolved, the new unit is staffed by multi-skilled (or at least multi-tasked) employees, and work is designed along socio-technical principles. The organization of manufacturing work within production islands depends on integrating indirect work (e.g. production planning) with direct work (e.g. machining). Consequently, an individual employee's knowledge of his or her direct work (e.g. knowledge of specific persons, machinery, material and tools in the workplace) has to be integrated with the more abstract knowledge required to understand the process of planning production runs, as skilled workers in the production island are now expected to make decisions about the scheduling of pro-duction events. The knowledge requirements for working in production islands were explored in a survey of German skilled workers and apprentices by Fischer (1995), who found that work process knowledge was an essential requirement for this kind of work. In addition to their specialist vocational qualifications, employees needed to understand how the work process was configured in the organization as a whole in order to achieve the degree of flexibility expected of production islands. What makes this finding especially interesting is that their work process knowledge had been acquired informally—typically, when spontaneous and close co-operation with other departments became necessary in order to resolve problematic situations, such as breakdowns in production.

Supervision of complex dynamic environments

One kind of work that has attracted a great deal of research attention throughout Europe is the supervision and control of complex self-regulating systems (either human-made, such as nuclear power plants, or natural systems such as forest fires, which can equally well be regarded as self-regulating systems). The main role of the supervisor of these systems is to intervene when the system is evolving in an unwanted direction and return it to a more desirable state, but this obviously depends on being able to understand the way the system is behaving. There are many examples of this kind of work, including co-ordinating hospital emergency departments (Boreham *et al.*, 2000), operating advanced air traffic control systems (Millot & Mandiau, 1995) and fighting forest fires (Rogalski *et al.*, 2002).

Human-system co-operation in regulating complex, dynamic systems was studied by a research network entitled *Cognitive Approaches to Dynamic Environment Supervision* (CADES), which was sponsored by the French national research organization Centre Nationale de la Recherche Scientifique (Hoc *et al.*, 1995). One of the findings to emerge from this network was that, in order to supervise and intervene successfully in complex, dynamic systems, supervisors need 'a broadening of the conventional knowledge base' (Boreham, 1995, p. 103). The model of system supervision which dominates in industry and occupational psychology today assumes a narrow knowledge base, typically the symptoms and causes of specific faults in the system for which the supervisor is responsible (see, for example, Leach *et al.*, 2003). However, analysis of the supervisory function in complex dynamic systems by CADES researchers indicated that supervisors need to think more broadly—in terms of 'whole systems interacting with their environments' (Boreham, *loc. cit*). The effective control of complex, dynamic systems generally requires the supervisor to consider previous developments and possible future events. It also requires him or her to consider interactions with other systems that are geographically distant but connected to the system being supervised. Understanding the whole system and its interconnections, rather than the traditional narrow focus on what is going on at the operator's own work station, is the essence of work process knowledge.

Integrating academic study with work experience

As the foregoing paragraphs illustrate, work process knowledge is an important consideration when analyzing the demands of work in complex, dynamic environments. The concept of work process knowledge is also proving useful in vocational curriculum development in many European countries, including

Germany and the Netherlands. One of the most significant findings of the WHOLE project in this connection is that employees often draw on theoretical knowledge but do not seem to be 'applying' it directly. The interpretation of this within work process knowledge theory, as suggested above, is that the employees' theoretical understanding is synthesized with their personal knowledge of the work situation to create new understandings. It is these that constitute the work process knowledge which guides their activity.

The process of creating knowledge in the context of work by synthesizing theoretical and experiential ways of knowing has significant implications for the design of vocational education and training, which can be illustrated by the curriculum development approach known as *the work-process co-production of vocational curricula* (Bernard, 2000). This is an experimental approach to the design of vocational curricula, currently being developed in Germany, which integrates work-based learning with academic study. The aim is to ensure that the intermediate-level employees for whom the curriculum is intended are given an adequate (and relevant) theoretical understanding of the work process, including specific scientific knowledge, while they are learning experientially through authentic participation in the workplace. The principles upon which this approach is based can be summarized as follows:

1. A partnership is forged between the formal vocational training system (e.g. a vocational school or technical college) and the company which employs the trainees.
2. Work process knowledge is used as the conceptual framework for selecting theoretical content and practical experience relevant to the work role.
3. Theory teaching is co-ordinated with experiential learning in the workplace.
4. Trainees' capacity to construct their own work process knowledge *in* and *through* work is a major objective of the curriculum (Fischer & Rauner, 2002; Boreham, 2004a).

Space does not permit an extensive discussion of this approach to curriculum development. Nevertheless, the role played by work process knowledge can be appreciated by considering the *working and learning tasks* which are a major component of the curriculum These are production tasks specially designed to integrate learning and working on the shop floor, and they provide an environment in which trainees bring both theoretical and experiential learning to bear on authentic work problems (Dehnbostel & Molzberger, 2004). Combining theoretical and experiential knowledge in the context of working and learning tasks develops the capacity to construct work process knowledge, the central objective of the new approach. This approach might possibly enhance vocational education and training in other European countries, although the feasibility of implementing it outside Germany would depend crucially on how control of the curriculum process is shared between employers and educators. In a national system of vocational qualifications such as the UK's, where employers control the entire curriculum and tend to focus learning on narrow and immediate objectives, it might be difficult to achieve the necessary curricular breadth (Boreham, 2002a).

The crisis in the graduate labour market

To bring this section to a conclusion, a last example of how work process knowledge helps learners cope with the challenges of the contemporary employment situation in Europe can be found in the field of university education. Many European countries have seen an expansion of this sector. However, this has usually been accompanied by a fall in graduate employment, and characteristically this has not been matched by changes in higher education provision. One exception is Portugal, where to improve the preparation of university students for the labour market, the current trend in the higher education system is to empower them with a wider range of competencies provided by broadly-based courses. These courses emphasise the development of a general disposition for self-directed learning and a new set of non-technical competencies designed to help graduates navigate their way through the labour market. The acquisition of work process knowledge is an essential part of the new provision, as it provides the broad understanding which graduates need for deploying their specific competencies in contexts of flexibility and adaptability. The concept of work process knowledge presents a challenge to higher education, which has always concentrated on providing specialised academic knowledge and narrow skills. However, Oliveira *et al.* (2002) argue that it is possible to create favourable learning contexts for the development of work process knowledge within formal systems of higher education. Specifically, this means developing the capacity for the self-directed acquisition of work process knowledge during work experience, and necessitates rethinking the traditional learning models and strategies which reign in higher education.

Knowing the work process—a constructivist approach to human competence

Underpinning many, if not all of these issues, is the central question of the nature of competence at work. It is a central claim of work process knowledge theorists that the demands of flexible, customer-oriented kinds of work mean that employees must *construct their own understanding* of the complex and uncertain challenges that face them. This is particularly the case in those ICT-based organizations which use the new technology to meet the challenges of global competition by adapting rapidly to changing market conditions.

Many of the studies carried out for the WHOLE project illustrate the tructed nature of work process knowledge. For example, a study of electrical maintenance work on the Paris Metro by Samurçay and Vidal-Gomel (2002) shows how work process knowledge is constructed in the context of work by synthesising experiential know-how with theoretical understanding. Although safety rules for carrying out electrical installations and repairs are specified in maintenance manuals, Samurçay and Vidal-Gomel found that skilled operatives use their discretion with regard to the extent to which they observe them in any given situation. This is because they frequently encounter non-standard installations which the maintenance manuals do not cover. In-depth studies of the cognitive processes of electricians in these situations showed that they rely on their ability to construct mental models of the unexpected situations that confront them. These mental models include standard electrical theory as well as phenomena that could only have been known by direct personal experience. In fact, the electricians studied by Samurçay and Vidal-Gomel were *constructing* the work process knowledge which guided their actions by resolving contradictions between lived experience and the theoretical principles and procedures of electrical maintenance.

Another example is a study of a computer-based debt collection agency by Lammont and Boreham (2002), in which new technology (an automatic direct dialler and an electronic database containing records of the agency's dealings with debtors) functioned as a collective memory for the entire workforce, and provided the linguistic resources with which they solved problems. The telephone debt collectors interacted with the database by recording narratives of their conversations with debtors, and these became a shared resource out of which they could construct new conversations with new debtors. The technology made the work process transparent and accessible to all, and the work process itself was co-configured and known collectively by the employees who participated in it.

A last example of the constructivist principle can be found in Fischer and Röben's (2002) study of laboratory assistants. A significant finding of this study was that, despite the practical nature of their work, laboratory assistants in chemical laboratories need theoretical knowledge relating to the various analytical tests that are available. They combine this with personal experience of how the individual test instruments in the laboratory function, in order to devise the procedure which is most appropriate for each new situation. It is not accurate to say that they are *applying* theoretical principles, for detailed observations carried out by Fischer and Röben showed that the knowledge which guided action in these contexts was constructed dialectically out of theoretical understanding *and* experiential know-how during the process of problem solving.

Thus work process knowledge is located within a constructivist epistemology, in opposition to a representationalist one. Representationalism depicts knowledge as a state inside people's heads which mirrors, by means of internal images, what is occurring in the world outside. An example of a representational view of work-related knowledge is Ochanine's (1978) theory of operative images, which he defines as mental models of complex industrial plants formed inside the heads of the process controllers who operate them. The latter allegedly control the plants by consulting their mental models, a type of introspection which tells them what actions to take. However, constructivist epistemologies reject this dualism of inner and outer worlds, arguing that knowledge is fashioned publicly through social interaction, and that it is embedded in social structure (Boreham, 1988). The knowledge which employees use in the workplace can be found in the social artifacts which exist there, such as the language in use, the work routines and the organization's symbols. On a constructivist view, human beings develop concepts collectively by using artifacts to make sense of their experiences of work, and they decide how to act in these situations by following social norms which embody these concepts.

The learning citizen in the knowledge economy—central, but vulnerable

A central theme of the present book is the position of the 'learning citizen' in contemporary European work and society, and the way this is treated in EU funded research. This chapter has outlined some of the findings of the Framework IV project WHOLE, which demonstrate the importance of work process knowledge for employment in the emerging European knowledge economy. The link between this research and the theme of the learning citizen is the constructivist nature of work process knowledge which was discussed in the previous section. If flexible, adaptive and innovative economic activity demands workers who can construct work process knowledge in the course of their work, then they assume a place at the centre of the knowledge economy. The citizen should not be conceived as a cog in an industrial machine, nor as a receptacle for procedural training, nor as a slave to a programme of industrial development designed by others, but as someone centrally involved in creating the knowledge that drives industry and commerce (and public services, too). This is a clear implication of the research on work process knowledge cited in this chapter, especially Mariani's (2002) study of a knowledge-creating chemical company, Fischer's (1995) study of production islands, Lammont and Boreham's (2002) study of informated debt-collecting and Boreham's (1995) study of the supervision of complex, dynamic systems. An economy built out of flexible, informated, knowledge creating organizations cannot rely on workers who are denied opportunities for taking control of their own work, nor denied opportunities to engage in sense-making at work. Nor can it depend on workers who have received only a minimal level of theoretical instruction in their field of work, for as the WHOLE studies show, theoretical understanding is one of the intellectual resources out of which work process knowledge is constructed. It is time, therefore, to recognize the agency of the learning citizen.

Lundvall (2001) has advanced cogent arguments for replacing discrete industrial and educational policies by an integrated policy field focused on the creation of 'national systems of innovation'. Originally developed by a group of economists including Lundvall (1992) and Edquist (1997), the concept of a national system of innovation is defined as a range of institutions—companies, patent offices, universities, banks, schools and so on—which collaborate as a unitary system in the accumulation and diffusion of knowledge. It can be argued that work process knowledge is crucial for building the complex interrelationships between the organizations which constitute such a system. By recognising this, we create space for the citizen to exercise his or her agency. Arguably, creating work process knowledge is one of the core tasks of participants in national systems of innovation.

The finding which emerged from the WHOLE studies that the creation of work process knowledge is typically embedded in collective activity does not undermine the agency of the individual employee. To appreciate this, we need to take account of the theoretical recentring that has occurred in recent years in relation to the concept of the self. Gergen (1999a) challenges the longstanding tradition of conceptualising the self as individually-contained, tracing its origins to the time of the Enlightenment and arguing that it is now disintegrating in the face of social change, especially the decline of the old industrial culture. In the contemporary world, the need Gergen perceives is 'to generate an alternative mode of constructing self and other, with the ultimate aim of wedding such discursive moves to ongoing social practice... to position ourselves in a way that we can ask providential questions about our collective lives' (Gergen, 1999b, p. 114). His alternative to the concept of the individually-contained self is the relational self (1999a, p. 115). This incorporates aspects of Bakhtin's (1981) theory of dialogue, according to which individuals exist primarily in their relationships with others (cf Mariani's 2002 study of the knowledge-creating chemical company). Whilst the individually-contained self is an independent entity with fixed qualities, the relational self is a process of dialogic self-construction. Such a self develops as individuals make sense of lived experience by engaging in dialogue, identifying with categories and discourses and using these to position and construct themselves in successive situations.

The concept of the relational self demands a revision of long-established assumptions about personal autonomy. Sherwin (1998), for example, has argued that the concept of autonomous agents as people cut loose from all ties is unconvincing, and that it would be preferable to represent the autonomous person as one who is embedded in complex networks of personal and organizational relationships. Autonomy in learning and knowledge-creation depends on relationships because it is primarily through relationships that we can engage in the process of learning in the workplace. Ultimately, whether one theorises the self as individually-contained or relational is a matter of choice. But the employees interviewed in the course of a recent study of a knowledge-creating company (Boreham & Morgan, 2004) expressed the view that the collaborative construction of work process knowledge enhanced their autonomy by expanding their relationships in the workplace. They did not perceive knowledge-sharing in negative terms, but as something that freed them by spreading the burden of their hazardous and often frustrating work among a network of colleagues.

From the perspective of the WHOLE project, then, the learning citizen emerges as a person with a relational rather than an individually-contained self. Vocational education and training, and human resource development, need to fully acknowledge this. But he or she, as the creator of the work process knowledge that underpins flexible and innovative economic activity, is also a *vulnerable* citizen. In much of the literature on learning organizations and knowledge-creating companies, an image is presented of an enjoyable and liberating process of creating knowledge and sharing it with collaborators. Against this, the WHOLE project reported numerous cases which suggested that creating and sharing work process knowledge is a potentially conflictual activity. One example of this is the role professional knowledge plays in creating occupational identities. In order to protect its legitimate employment interests, a profession typically resists sharing this knowledge with others (Boreham, 2002c), and this sets the stage for conflict between occupational interest groups. Another example is the way sharing knowledge in the workplace can undermine traditional patterns of working relationships and destroy trust, especially in industries with paternalistic cultures—the norm in many parts of Europe (Krüger *et al.*, 2002).

To make sense of these findings, reference can be made to Larson (1990), who argues that control of knowledge creation is central to the process of professionalization because it enables occupational interest groups to create monopolies of practice. Other sociologists of the professions, such as Abbott (1988) and Collins (1990) even go so far as to argue that the bodies of professional knowledge developed in this way may not be relevant to practice because they serve principally to construct status and create barriers to prevent others practising in the same field. A similar point has been made by Armstrong (1993), who suggests that to achieve competitive advantage, a profession must develop a knowledge base that makes it distinct from that of its competitors. These forms of knowledge-creation are driven by occupational status-group conflict, and can undermine work process knowledge. As Krüger *et al.* (2002) point out, the form of work organization currently accepted by both employers and employees in a particular industry or company is a compromise which maintains a mutually-acceptable allocation of work tasks, power sharing and distribution of wealth between different actors. Krüger *et al.* argue that every proposed change to the current arrangement will signify threats and opportunities for all concerned. The learning citizen thus stands in the middle of contested terrain. As the creator of work process knowledge, his or her customary work activity lies at the heart of the innovation process, but it will alter the way knowledge is distributed in the workplace and provoke clashes of occupational interests. Addressing this problem ought to be a priority for future research within the European Union Framework programmes.

References

Abbott, A. (1988) *The System of Professions: An Essay in the Expert Division of Labour.* Chicago: Chicago University Press.

Armstrong, P. (1993) 'Professional knowledge and social mobility'. *Work, Employment and Society*, Vol. 7, pp. 1-21.

Bakhtin, M. (1981) *The Dialogic Imagination.* Austin: University of Austin Press.

Bernard, F. (2000) 'Forschungsmetodische Lösungsansatze zur Differenzierung und Integration von Technischem Wissen'. In J-P. Pahl, F. Rauner & G. Spöttl (eds) *Berufliches Arbeitsprozesswissen.* Baden-Baden: Nomos Verlagsgesellschaft.

Boreham, N. (1988) 'Models of diagnosis and their implications for adult professional education'. *Studies in the Education of Adults*, Vol. 20, pp. 96-108.

Boreham, N. (1992) 'Harnessing implicit knowing to improve medical practice'. In H. K. Morris Baskett & Victoria J. Marsick (eds) *Professionals' Ways of Knowing: New Findings on How to Improve Professional Education.* San Francisco: Jossey-Bass, pp. 71-8.

Boreham, N. (1994) 'The dangerous practice of thinking'. *Medical Education*, Vol. 28, pp. 172-179.

Boreham, N. (1995) 'Error analysis and expert-novice differences in medical diagnosis'. In J.-M. Hoc, E. Hollnagel and C. Cacciabue (eds) *Expertise and Technology.* Hove: Lawrence Erlbaum Associates, pp. 91-103.

Boreham, N. (2002a) 'Work process knowledge, curriculum control and the work-based route to vocational qualifications'. *British Journal of Educational Studies,* Vol. 50, pp. 225-237.

Boreham, N. (2002b) 'Work process knowledge in technological and organizational development'. In N. Boreham, R. Samurçay & M. Fischer (eds) *Work Process Knowledge.* London: Routledge, pp. 1-14.

Boreham, N. (2002c) 'Professionalization and work process knowledge in the UK's National Health Service'. In N. Boreham, R. Samurçay and M. Fischer (eds) *Work Process Knowledge.* London: Routledge, pp. 171-82.

Boreham, N. (2004a) 'Orienting the work-based curriculum towards work process knowledge: a rationale and a German case study'. *Studies in Continuing Education,* in press, 2004.

Boreham, N. & Lammont, N. (2001) *Work Process Knowledge in Technological and Organizational Development. Final Report of Project SOE1-CT97-1074 of the EU Targeted Socio-Economic Research Programme.* Brussels: European Commission, Directorate General for Research. http://www.cordis.lu/improving/socio-economic/publications.htm

Boreham, N. & Morgan, C. (2004) 'A sociocultural analysis of organizational learning'. *Oxford Review of Education,* in press, 2004.

Boreham, N., Samurçay, R. & Fischer, M. (1995, March 10-11) Presentation at the conference to inaugurate the education and training strand of Targeted Socio-Economic Research in the European Commission's IV Framework Program, Bordeaux, France.

Boreham, N., Samurçay, R. and Fischer, M. (eds) (2002) *Work Process Knowledge.* London: Routledge.

Boreham, N.C., Shea, C.E. & Mackway-Jones, K. (2000) 'Clinical risk and collective competence in the hospital emergency department in the UK'. *Social Science & Medicine,* Vol. 51, pp. 83-91.

Collins, R. (1990) 'Changing conceptions in the sociology of the professions'. In R. Torstandahl and M. Burrage (eds) *The Formation of Professions: Knowledge, State and Strategy,* London: Sage.

Dehnbostel, P. & Molzberger, G. (in press 2004) 'Decentralised learning – integration of learning and working at the workplace. In M. Fischer, N. Boreham & B. Brink (eds) *Work Process Knowledge and Work-related Learning in Europe.* Thessaloniki: CEDEFOP.

Edquist, C. (1997) *Systems of Innovation: Technologies, Institutions and Organizations.* London: Pinter Publishers.

European Communities (1997) *Green Paper: Partnership for a New Organization of Work.* Luxembourg: Office for Official Publications of the European Communities.

European Foundation for the Improvement of Living and Working Conditions (2002) *Report on New Forms of Work Organization.* Dublin: European Foundation for the Improvement of Living and Working Conditions.

Fischer, M. (1995) *Technikverständnis von Facharbeitern im Spannungsfeld von Beruflicher Bildung und Arbeitserfahrung.* Bremen: Donat Verlag.

Fischer, M. (2002) 'Work experience as an element of work process knowledge'. In N. Boreham, R. Samurçay & M. Fischer (eds) *Work Process Knowledge.* London: Routledge, pp. 119-33.

Fischer, M. & Rauner, F. (2002) 'The implications of work process knowledge for vocational education and training'. In N. Boreham, R. Samurçay & M. Fischer (eds) *Work Process Knowledge.* London: Routledge, pp. 160-70.

Fischer, M. & Röben, P. (2002) 'The work process knowledge of chemical laboratory assistants'. In N. Boreham, R. Samurçay & M. Fischer (eds) *Work Process Knowledge.* London: Routledge, pp. 40-54.

Gergen, K.J. (1999a) *An Invitation to Social Construction.* London: Sage Publications.

Gergen, K.J. (1999b) 'Agency: Social construction and relational action'. *Theory & Psychology,* Vol. 9, pp. 113-115.

Hoc, J.-M., Cacciabue, C. & Hollnagel, E. (eds) (1995) *Expertise and Technology*. Hove: Lawrence Erlbaum Associates.

Jessup, G. (1991) *Outcomes: NVQs and the Emerging Model of Education and Training*. London: The Falmer Press.

Knorr Cetina, K. & Preda, A. (2001) 'The epistemization of economic transactions'. *Current Sociology*, Vol. 49, pp. 27-44.

Krüger, K., Kruse, W. & Caprile, M. (2002) 'Work process knowledge and industrial and labour relations'. In N. Boreham, R. Samurçay & M. Fischer (eds) *Work Process Knowledge*. London: Routledge, pp. 201-214.

Kruse, W. (1986) 'Bemerkungen zur Rolle von Forschung bei der Entwicklung und Technikgestaltung in Sachverständigenkommission Arbeit und Technik'. In Universität Bremen (eds): *Perspektiven technischer Bildung*. Bremen: Universität Bremen.

Lammont, N. & Boreham, N. (2002). 'Creating work process knowledge with new technology in a financial services workplace'. In N. Boreham, R. Samurçay & M. Fischer (eds) *Work Process Knowledge*. London: Routledge, pp. 94-105.

Larson, M.S. (1990) 'In the matter of experts and professionals, or how impossible it is to leave nothing unsaid'. In R. Torstandahl & M. Burrage (eds) *The Formation of Professions: Knowledge, State and Strategy*. London: Sage.

Leach, D.J., Wall, T.D. & Jackson, P.R. (2003) 'The effect of empowerment on job knowledge: an empirical test involving operators of complex technology'. *Journal of Occupational and Organizational Psychology*, Vol. 76, pp. 27-52.

Lundvall, B-A. (1992) *National Systems of Innovation: Towards a Theory of Innovation and Interactive Learning*. London: Pinter Publishers.

Lundvall, B-A. (2001) 'Innovation policy in the globalising learning economy'. In Archibugi, D. & Lundvall, B-A (eds) *The Globalising Learning Economy*. Oxford: Oxford University Press, pp. 273-91.

Mariani, M. (2002) 'Work process knowledge in a chemical company'. In N. Boreham, R. Samurçay & M. Fischer (eds) *Work Process Knowledge*. London: Routledge, pp. 40-54.

Millot, P. & Mandiau, R. (1995) 'Man-machine co-operative organizations: Formal and pragmatic implementation methods'. In J.-M. Hoc, E. Hollnagel & C. Cacciabue (eds) *Expertise and Technology*. Hove: Lawrence Erlbaum Associates, pp. 213-28.

Nonaka, I. & Takeuchi, H. (1995) *The Knowledge Creating Company*. Oxford: Oxford University Press.

Norros, L. & Nuutinen, M. (2002) 'The concept of the core task and the analysis of working practices'. In Boreham, N., Samurçay, R. & Fischer, M. (eds) *Work Process Knowledge*. London: Routledge, pp. 25-39.

OECD (Organization for Economic Cooperation and Development) (1996) *The Knowledge-Based Economy*. Paris: Organization for Economic Cooperation and Development.

Oliveira, M.T., Pires, A.L.O. & Alves, M.G. (2002) 'Dimensions of work process knowledge'. In N. Boreham, R. Samurçay & M. Fischer (eds) *Work Process Knowledge*. London: Routledge, pp. 106-18.

Ochanine, D.A. (1978) 'Le rôle des images opératives dans la régulation des activités de travail'. *Psychologie et Education,* Vol. 3, pp. 63-79.

Rogalski, J., Plat, M. & Antolin-Glenn, P. (2002) 'Training for collective competence in rare and unpredictable situations'. In N. Boreham, R. Samurçay & M. Fischer (eds) *Work Process Knowledge*. London: Routledge, pp. 134-147.

Samurçay, R. & Vidal-Gomel, C. (2002) 'The contribution of work process knowledge to competence in electrical maintenance'. In N. Boreham, R. Samurçay & M. Fischer (eds) *Work Process Knowledge*. London: Routledge, pp. 148-59.

Senge, P. (1990) *The Fifth Discipline*. New York: Doubleday.

Sherwin, S. (1998) 'A relational approach to autonomy in health care'. In S. Sherwin (ed) *The Politics of Women's Health: Exploring Agency and Autonomy*. Philadelphia: Temple University Press, pp. 19-47.

CHAPTER SEVEN

Work and Workers in the Learning Economy: Conceptions, Critique, Implications

CATHERINE CASEY

Introduction

Recent years have seen an intensification of post-industrial trends toward a privileging of knowledge work, of information science and technology, and the production, trade and consumption of information-rich commodities and diverse knowledge products. The shift to globalising, deregulated economies of information and knowledge and to computer-controlled production are much debated (Beck 1992, Castells 1996, Drucker 1993, Harvey 1989, Lash and Urry 1994, Reich 1991, Rifkin 1996). The implications of these globalising economic developments for work, national economies, civic communities and persons are immense. Increased complexity in economic production in increasingly global markets generates a climate of heightened risk, uncertainty and contingency. In accordance with post-Keynesian neo-liberal economic models, which favour deregulated markets and a more laissez-faire role of the state, elite economic and business leaders encourage organizations to restructure toward flexibility, contingency, and rapid response to market environments. Within this climate of risk and uncertainty, and as part of the current economic initiatives for efficiency, flexibility, innovation, and production growth, there is a growing interest in the notion of the 'learning organization' and in employee learning at work. The privileged emphasis on knowledge-based production and exchange stimulates increased awareness that the processes and content of learning—more precisely, specific learnings—among employees affects organizational success in achieving continuous innovation and strategic advantage. The concept of the learning organization is premised on an idea that human knowledge as human capital is now the principal productive force in contemporary capitalism (e.g. Porter

1990, Senge 1990, 1999, Stewart 1997, Boisot 1998). The European Union has accordingly declared that efforts to develop Europe as a learning economy/ learning society are central to its strategic response to knowledge-based economic trajectories in globally competitive environments.

At the everyday level of organizational workplaces managers and their academic advisors now avidly advocate the development of particular organizational and employee learning strategies in pursuit of product and process innovation and adaptation. These worker learning imperatives present a different character to those advocated a generation ago in movements for worker education and life-long learning, which included emphasis on education for workers to advance their knowledge and skills in order to participate in the political and management activities of their workplaces (e.g. Blumberg 1973, Crouch and Heller 1983, Freire 1973). These movements for adult and worker education favoured a holistic model of the ideal worker learner for whom education and skills acquisition were directed toward goals of self and community development for living and working in participatory democratic society (Dewey [1916] 1966). Although these models of worker education have by no means receded (see Director-General of the ILO Juan Somavia's recent reiterations on 'decent work' 1999), their demands have been somewhat quietened by the currently louder chorus of advocacy for the organizational learning/worker learning conceived according to the singular imperatives of economic rationality, production innovation and efficiency.

Considerable socio-economic research is now directed toward the new agenda of worker education and training objectives. An influential iteration of this endeavour is the report prepared by Bengt-Ake Lundvall and Susana Borras for the European Union Commission (1997). The report, entitled 'The Globalising Learning Economy: Implications for Innovation Policy', has attracted much interest and application. It reflects and asserts a primary assumption that a 'new society' is on its way - a 'society based increasingly on knowledge and learning capacity of its citizens' (Lundvall and Borras 1997:3). The concerns and arguments of the Lundvall and Borras Report, which articulate at an intermediary level neo-liberal economic theoretical formulation, are now familiar, and its orientations and assumptions widely expressed in practitioner circles in Europe and other Western countries. They are also reflected in numerous subsequent research projects directed toward application and achievement of the knowledge-based economy. Some of these research projects, in particular those in the FP 4 & 5 Education and Training cluster, are discussed below.

As a preface to that discussion, I wish first to critically examine the economistic and managerial discourse on learning economy/learning society and learning workers. My starting point is a rejection of the often taken for granted concession that the currently dominant discourse must be accepted because 'there is no alternative' (Touraine 2001) and that socio-economic research must necessarily favour applied and practical foci. The questions posed of the paradigmatic assumptions and purposes of the learning economy agenda apply in particular to its implications for work and workers. The questions at the heart of this critical discussion are substantive ones. Their legitimacy, I contend, is sourced in a grand European cultural heritage that demands that questions of ultimate value, or socio-cultural ends, provide a definitive measure of economic and technological activities. Therefore, in the spirit of Aristotles' phronesis, one may ask: What are the substantive socio-cultural ends of the knowledge-based learning economy? Are the currently stated imperatives driving worker learning and production innovation policies serving such cultural ends? How do the conceptions of work and workers, and of their education and training, measure up?

For Lundvall and Borras (1997) and numerous other European Commission statements (e.g. European Commission 1999, 2000), the substantive socio-cultural ends of knowledge-based economies of learning and production are left unarticulated or elided in an explicitly stated economic orientation that conceives organizational and worker learning as instruments for innovation and productivity. This economistic orientation exerts an agenda setting influence over subsequent research activities which are apparently funded on their basis to further develop worker learning and innovation thus framed.

In this framework, education, learning and innovation are defined as economic activities and commodities which in themselves are presumed to be self-explanatory instrumental ends. Lundvall and Borras knowledge conceived 'as an economic resource' (1977: 32) 'determines the context in which the dramatic changes in knowledge generation and use' occurs. The ultimate end of innovation, which is both imperative and outcome of worker and organizational learning and knowledge, is for 'the shaping of institutions and structures of production so that the innovation system becomes better suited to future market developments' (pg. 164).

This clear statement of the current intense emphasis on innovation—in which it must be noted, innovation is a careful and strategic degree of product and process change—underscores the singular trajectory of economistic and business driven demands and strategies for organizational and worker learning in advanced capitalist society. There are three principal aspects of the economistic framework, which have direct bearing on conceptions of work and workers. The first is the assumption of the actor as hominus economicus, of rational economic man for which instrumental utility is privileged and for which operational environments are fundamentally competitive. Although classical liberalism acknowledged other moral constraints on acquisitive individualism, the neo-liberal models favour unfettered economic agents (Bourdieu 1998, Touraine 2001) and a-social individualism. Under this lens, work is conceived as solely or principally economic utility, and workers as actors or objects of such utility.

The second aspect is that of organizational and system rationality. Systems rationality is assumed as the abstraction of collective individual action and the means to accomplish rational goals. Notwithstanding unintended contradictions in terms of the systemic constraints on individuals and paradoxical outcomes of rational action, the elevation of abstract economic and technological system imperatives requires and achieves subordination of individual needs and interests. Even though organizations are replete with power struggles, counter-rationalities, paradoxes and inequalities, the organizational system is rhetorically privileged as being in need of resources and processes to which employees must defer. In particular, its demands that learning processes and knowledge acquisition be governed by system adaptation and innovation requirements and managerially directed, are presented to employees as rationally necessary and inevitable.

The learning organization is thus conceived in an over-arching economistic systems framework strategically coupled with managerial control. Further assumptions about the bearer of knowledge—both the organization system and individual workers—follow. Much of the contemporary literature addressing questions of learning and knowledge work for a neo-liberal and globalising economy, contains uniform assertions about the new 'knowledge worker' (see, for instance, Senge 1990, Stewart 1997, Boud and Garrick 1999). These assumptions are those of the familiar hominus economicus institutionalised as 'industrial man'—the rational, sober, instrumental individual conforming to the disciplines and rationality of economic organization systems. But they include in addition, assertions of knowledgeable workers accepting the logic of constant and unpredictable change, of flux and flexibility, and of the neo-liberal economic organization requirements for heightened managerial roles in determining strategic production innovations and employee utilisation.

Therefore, in accordance with the elevated role of strategic managerial action, the worker-learner is now constructed as a 'human resource'. The notion of the worker as 'human resource', a discursive reconstruction of the working person, has become remarkably widely accepted in little more than a decade. It reflects the instrumental economism of neo-liberal economics and organizational management. That a person may be treated solely as the object of another's utility, or of system ends, manifests the everyday elision of substantive human and cultural values and ends in preference for the needs of economic production systems. This similarly manifests in the abstraction of knowledge from the person as learner, and in the demand for worker learning to be directed by, and result in, economic imperatives. The construction of worker-learners solely as resources for innovation ensures that their diverse learning motivations and pursuits—which have long been recognised and accommodated in adult education principles—are inadmissible and disregarded.

A third critical aspect of the economistic discourse and accompanying the notion of human resource as instrumental object, is the avoidance of substantive assessment and treatment of various risks consequent of such models. The problem of risk generated by socio-technical systems of rationalising modernity is prominently elaborated work of Ulrich Beck (1992, 2000), Anthony Giddens (1990), and Scott Lash, among others (Beck, Giddens and Lash (1994). But notwithstanding these currents of thought in European and other Western scientific arena, the rhetorical models of the knowledge-based economy premised on innovation and productivity growth, are coyly silent about significant constitutive risks.

Aside from ecological risks, which cannot be addressed in this paper, an expansion of competitive knowledge-based economic activities that require rapidly learning, adapting and flexible workers produces social and personal risks. The risk of polarization and of 'winners and losers' in 'a game of change' (Lundvall and Borras 1997) is met in response with a reiteration of state institutions managing social policies of compensation and welfare redistribution. Yet the social bonds necessary to support redistributive institutions are weakened and eroded under neo-liberalised arrangements encouraging heightened individualism in acquisition and accumulation of wealth in the 'game of change'.

An unreflexive economistic logic displayed in many European Commission reports, notably the Lundvall and Borras Report (1997) belies a persistent, unarticulated, belief in the capacity of science and technology to control and manage the risks of its own activity, including those risks concomitant of technologised, competitive, growth-driven economic practices. This belief reveals a pre-analytic vision of an isolated economic system and an inexhaustible planet. It also reveals a persistent unwillingness on the part of policy-makers to reflect on the contradictions and crises of modern socio-economic discourses and institutions. Importantly, neither the Lundvall and Borras Report nor the research frameworks of E&T research reports explicitly recognize a consequence of the complicity of knowledge-based innovation-driven production organizations with the generation of contingent organizations and work practices, flexible and deregulated labour markets, and their social and personal consequences. The known risks of social exclusion and personal precariousness resulting from insecure or non- participation in employment consequent of capital mobility and labour market flux, along with unknown and unpredictable consequences of dislocation and polarisation, are glossed over in the assertion that extant social and state institutional responses will compensate for such risks.

From this general discussion of economistic approaches to the learning economy/learning society, I turn now to focus on a selection of research reports conducted under FRP 4 and 5 and co-ordinated for valorisation by the E&T cluster[1]. In making the following evaluative criticisms, I wish first to acknowledge that the organization of social science institutions, the competitive basis of grant funding, and the politics of the setting and legitimation of research agendas all play immensely influential roles in determining and circumscribing funded research activity and the reception of its outcomes. These contextual matters, which I have in part sketched out above, have necessarily affected the researchers' agendas and conceptual models in the projects this paper critiques. Even though I am proposing a broader critique of that very framework, I wish nonetheless to give fair recognition of the considerable accomplishments of the many and comprehensive projects conducted under FRP 4 and 5 across Europe, and to acknowledge the constraints and real politik of the work of research and a certain division of labour to which we are ineluctably subject.

While cognisant of the risk of under-appreciating strengths of particular projects, my primary task here is to offer a general critique of their collective endeavour. My discussion addresses in particular conceptions of work and workers, and it raises discussion of a number of implications.

The projects' conceptions of work and workers

Not unexpectedly in a large number of projects there are important differences in levels of focus and analysis. However, few of the projects paid explicit or detailed attention to current trajectories in the practices of economy and production or offered analysis of these meta-level changes, although they all in various ways fully recognise that significant developments are taking place. A good number of projects describe and reflect many of these changes as they affect certain industry sectors or occupational groups e.g. Wickham & Webster et.al; Smyth et.al. Others pointed out the ironies of increased attention to individual education and training for learning workers as a post-Keynesian state disengages from economic intervention and employment stimulation e.g. Cullen et.al. They all recognise that the drive toward the learning economy is a significant feature of contemporary capitalism.

The projects were, perhaps ineluctably, conducted within a framework circumscribed by the contemporary restructuring of the institutions of work and production. Although there were differences in degree of acceptance or of proffered criticism of some of these conditions, the projects appear to implicitly accept the current intensified rationalisation of work and production toward a globalising knowledge-based economy as already given. Interrogation of the particular sectoral interests, asserted rationales and agendas of these current policy drives, and their origins, were apparently considered beyond the legitimate foci of the projects.

The projects share a conception of work as synonymous with labour market employment. (This in itself reflects an economic rationalisation of human labour and creative endeavour). Work, as labour market employment, is a social practice in which the structures and trajectories are determined by and for economic and technical rationalities enacted through organizational structures and relations. Most of the projects appear to accept, apparently unreflectively, the managerial term 'human resource' in reference to workers (with the notable exception of Cullen et.al.). The general acceptance of the economistic construction of contemporary work, although with compelling reasons, reveals the normalisation of a powerful, but particular, point of view (as promulgated in various EC policy documents and in wider economic discourses).

An apparently wide public acceptance of employers' and shareholders' priorities and discursive referents—which are obscured in the reification of abstract systems imperatives—enables these current conceptions of work to achieve a virtually universal and solely legitimate dominance. Although other conceptions of work—which include its non-marketised motivations and relations—and workers' and trade union movements' demands for qualities of working life beyond the economistic model persist, few of the E&T project reports seriously acknowledged these plural and contestational models of work.

The E&T projects have been conducted in the context of, and in response to, the current prevailing climate of economistically determined and managerially governed work. My criticism, which is oriented in opposition to economic reductionism, and to obscured particular sectoral interests and power relations, focuses on three particular ways in which of economistically determined and managerially governed work is accepted or contested in the E&T cluster projects.

1. The first is the conception of work governed by economic rationality. In this approach work is conceived as singularly a rational economic activity. Its performance, although of benefit to individuals, is organized toward the productivity and innovation needs for the organization. These needs and their means of accomplishment are themselves determined by management and markets. The conceptions of education and training of workers

engaged in economically and managerially defined work is to further advance productivity and innovation for the organization. The concept of the worker-learner is that of resource for organizational advantage.

2. For Sauquet et.al. this conception of work is, necessarily, explicitly stated in order to pursue their investigation of the ways in which 'learning processes lead to increased competitiveness of the small to medium sized companies'. They reported: 'In first place, there is a strong link between innovation and competitiveness' and innovation requires 'strong learning skills' pg. 11. 'In second place, there is a link between competitiveness and organizational change; learning has been linked to the ability of organizations to change their structure, systems, and culture. Lastly, learning has been related to superior skills in the interpretation of a fast growing environment.' Pg. 11.

3. It is perhaps churlish to criticise Sauquet et.al. for replicating so explicitly the economistic rationale of their research into learning processes and competitiveness of SMEs. That is precisely what they were funded to do, and their results may well find sound practical application. But the risk in an apparently unreflective application of the circumscribing economistic model lies in promulgating worker learning as only, or as necessarily, legitimated according to its usefulness for innovation and competitiveness.

4. Similarly, Tjepkema et.al. declared their project's task according to the instrumentalist agenda of economic learning: 'How do HRD departments in learning oriented organizations throughout Europe envision their own role in stimulating and supporting employees to learn continuously, as a part of their everyday work (with the intent to contribute to organizational learning, and thus enhance organizational competitiveness)?' Their findings lead to the recommendation that 'HRD functions should increase their strategic orientation in order to be involved in strategic processes', and to develop 'collective intelligence within organizations... and overcoming the remains of fordism at different levels'.

5. Steedman et.al and Brandsma et.al. emphasise the application of skills training programmes to enhance employability among the low-skilled or long-term unemployed. Yet, as Brandsma reports, it is not so much the provision and quality of training and education courses for these people and the delivery of higher skills learning that results in their increased utility in the workplace. Rather, 'it is quite clear that it is the labour market as such, which is particularly relevant for the effectiveness of the training in terms of its outcomes.' (pg. 8). The researchers express disappointment that the expected stronger relations between training programmes for unemployed workers and their success in gaining employment were not realised: 'For

example with regard to the outcome, a stronger and more clear relation had been expected between the provision of practical training in an enterprise, and the extent to which former trainees managed to get a job' (pg. 22). This is an important recognition of the role of labour markets and organizational contingencies in utilising re-trained workers. Skills redevelopment through professionally provided education and training programmes, and workplace placement schemes, had little effect on these workers' labour market participation.

a) A modification of the employer-privileged instrumentality of work appears in some projects that endeavour to utilise the conception of work as economically and technologically determined in ways that may advance individuals and groups. In particular Wickham & Webster et.al.'s project (Serviemploi), accepted the context of 'considerable technological and organisational innovations and upheavals'. They launched their project to investigate the situation of women working in two sectors of the accepted information economy of retail and financial services with the explicit aim to examine the prospects for women working in the low-grade jobs in these sectors to 'develop skills and knowledges which would allow them to move into better work or 'good work'.

b) Importantly, this project (one of the few) reported the disparities between training and learning opportunities actually provided for employees and the discourses on the learning organization that advocates such opportunities. The project reports: 'with the exception of companies which operated retail apprenticeships, the majority of retail companies in the study provided only very basic and very brief training for their junior (female) staff'. (pg.xv).

c) In the financial services sector there was slightly better but decidedly limited opportunity for women to advance into more senior positions. To redress this situation the researchers recommend, in keeping with their project objective, that: 'Regular training and lifelong learning opportunities should be routinely made available to junior employees. Training for skills and knowledge enhancement should be systematically available to all' (pg. v). These opportunities, they hope, will enable women's advancement into 'better work' in these sectors. Notwithstanding the practical attractiveness of these aims for the advancement of women, the retention of assumptions of upward mobility for individuals or groups subsequent to education and training is currently problematic. Moreover, these aspirations beg the question as to who will do the poor jobs from which these individuals have escaped. Current directions in the structures of organizations, work arrangements, and employment relations pose a disjuncture of the correlation between education and employment opportunity, as labour economists point out (e.g. Borghans and de Grip 2000). Poor work and low-grade jobs (which do not have to equate) are not eradicated even as some individuals or groups gain improvements.

d) A third approach in the conception of work and workers recognises that economically rationalised work may not necessarily be the sole model of human work, but it is the model that prevails over other, conflicting, human and cultural imperatives. Education and training in this view could potentially serve plural ends, from individual or group advancement to public service. But the immensity of the rationalisation trajectory of modern economy and organization appears to defeat oppositional aspirations through a totalising process of subjectification. Cullen et.al.'s Delilah project offers exemplary illustration of these concerns. In identifying what they term a 'learning patrimony'—a modus operandi and a set of values and dispositions (pg. 4) the authors report: 'The learning patrimony follows a dynamic which is partly internal to education and learning themselves and partly shaped by socio-economic and political factors and processes—which means that the learning patrimony cannot be modified at will; nor can it be conceived of and understood as completely determined by economic circumstances, much as the economic sphere be currently 'ruling' over other social spheres' (pg. 4).

In addition, the project explicitly addressed 'social disadvantage and exclusion as both a research/theoretical issue and as a more practical concern' (pg. 5). This concern with social disadvantage and exclusion led to their development of policy for the provision of education and training for disadvantaged and excluded groups. Recalling and reiterating a 'long tradition of liberal-humanist education in Europe' the authors criticise the inadequacies in the current 'neo-liberal and vocational views of education and learning' (pg. 6).

They report that 'a critical conflict between the view of education as an end in itself for living a human life and the view of education as a mere instrument of the economy and man/woman as workers" (pg. 6 original emphasis) poses serious implications for education and society.

Their discussion of research evidence of 20 cases proposes that: 'there seems to be a considerable scope for change in relation to the use of ICT, neither is the scope for change unlimited nor does the rhythm and pace of such change appear constant across sectors and countries; rather the rhythm and pace of change varies according to sector-dependent features and also according to the cycle of innovation and change in which the different countries may be located' (pg. 8 original emphasis).

Here the researchers importantly recognize the socio-economic context of education practices, specifically ICT education and training. They point out that opportunities for 'innovation attached to ICT only become 'reality' (in educational and learning terms as opposed to purely economic terms) when ICT is embedded in a well organised pedagogic practice and institutional arrangements' (pg. 8).

The authors concede that the economistic re-alignment of the education and training spheres in relation to the economic sphere has weakened the autonomy of the educational sphere, but they point out that wider socio-cultural currents, and not just the economy, demand 'a truly educated work force which is able to think imaginatively and creatively in relation to the new challenges' (pg. 8). In addition, they point to the pressures of 'citizenship movements, multiculturalism and internationalisation' (pg. 8).

Of course, for most of the projects the theoretical and practical constraints under which they were conducted precluded substantive analyses of the broader contexts of contemporary work and organizations in which the learning economy is practically enacted. A closer examination of contemporary work may be helpful in further assessing the contributions and further implications of the projects. As well, considering some of the important trends currently occurring in the world of work which are generating the drive toward to the learning economy and constructing the imagined 'learning human resource', or learning worker, may assist the interrogation of dominant ideological models and assist the reassertion of alternative educational imperatives.

Trends in contemporary work

In a deregulated, neo-liberalising economy, a heightened emphasis on strategic managerial action arises as the pragmatic response to uncertainty. Strategic managerial demand for flexible organizational forms capable of rapid response, lean production, and maximising innovation in product and process, requires correspondent flexible and contingent employment relations. Heightened organizational uncertainty concomitant of contingent dynamism, is thereby displaced onto a deregulated and increasingly individualised workforce.

At the same time, the drive toward hyper-efficiency and innovation requires organizational and worker learning to accomplish innovation in production and worker conformity to organizational contingency and aggressive shareholder demand. Consequently, simultaneous demands for innovation and heightened employee discipline are regularised as essential components of workers' jobs and performance measurement. These demands, of both learning and compliance, are immense. Therefore, these manifestations of hyper-rationalisation require the normalization of the employers', and managerial, viewpoint and the delegitimation of alternatives.

Among the inefficiencies—and resistances—which strategic neo-rational management (in contrast to organic structural functional theories of organization) seeks to eliminate are counter-managerial worker perspectives, These include demands for humanistic, participatory reforms of older models of 'scientific management', which industrial and organizational democracy movements achieved until their strategic undermining and effective decline in the 1980s. Humanistic demands not only for worker participation but for the satisfaction of plural human needs and interests in the workplace, such as self-development through occupational expertise, pride in mastery and skill, esteem in creative and good work, sociality and solidarity in shared labours and so forth are, in a hyper-rationalized trajectory, cast as inefficient and extraneous to organizational 'core business' of profit making and shareholder satisfaction. The thwarting of these interests currently contributes to the generation of demands, for instance, for reduced working hours, and family-friendly workplaces.

In a trajectory of hyper-rationalisation strategic learning in the workplace is regarded as an essential requirement of most, if not all, jobs. Innovation, which is regarded as the crucial factor in strategic advantage, is a continuous demand and deliverable from all industry sectors in a knowledge economy. The managerial, and therefore worker trainer's, task is the continuous elicitation and utilisation of specific worker learning toward instrumental ends. However, notwithstanding the organizational benefits of learning and the possibilities for workers to appropriate their organizational learning for self-development, many of the realities of contemporary work consequent of a hyper-rational organizational model and strategic organizational management present a different picture to the favourable images of managerially designed learning workers in a learning economy. In contrast to assertions of a neat correspondence of the economic model of the learning economy and learning-for-innovation workers with a learning society—as is typically promoted in the learning economy discourses—divergent, uneven and polarising tendencies affect many industries and sectors, and effect social and personal precariousness.

Intensification and dispensability

In Europe, and in other OECD countries, we can observe an expansion of two major and divergent trends in contemporary hyper-rationalised economy and production (Beck 2000, Block 1990, Heery and Salmon 2000, Castells 1996, Harvey 1989). These trends are that of intensification and of dispensability. Intensification of production demanded by neo-rational management strategies in highly competitive, flexible organizations has been observed significantly since the 1990s. In contrast to the progressive participatory management efforts of the 1960s through 1980s, such as the exemplary Uddevalla Volvo factory in Sweden, in which workers managed production intensity and work design, and employment relations were conducted under external legislative regulation, a rise of GM-style 'lean production' is evident (Durand 1994, Gorz 1999, Szell 2001). Lean production promotes the displacement of overhead and labour costs through various out-sourcing and contracting arrangements and intensification of work. Intensification, which includes higher rates of productivity, increased work tasks or work elements, faster output rates, eradication of inefficiencies, and predetermined work design, is evident in various forms in traditional blue-collar work, and in white-collar and new forms of service work.

The intensification of lean production coupled with organizational outsourcing and the displacement of variable costs onto labour leads to the second and concomitant trend: The expansion of contingent and deregulated employment practices. The strategic requirement for contingent labour encourages a flexibilisation of the employment contract in order for labour to be retained and discarded, as organizational contingency requires. As a consequence, across Europe and other OECD countries the rise of intermittent workers and those holding portfolios of part-time and discontinuous jobs with different employers is widely evident (Casey 2002, Felstead and Jewson 1999, Heery and Salmon 2000, Lind and Moller 1999, Williams and Windebank 1998). Both of these two major and divergent trends, one toward the intensification of production and managerial rationality, the other toward employment flexibility and worker dispensability, undermine the reliable conditions in which not only more participatory workplace structures may be practised but in which worker learning serves personal and social ends in addition to those of organizational economy.

A post-Keynesian neo-liberalism in economic regulation exacerbates the technologically enabled trends toward contingent, flexible work forces and strategic managerial demands for readily adaptable 'human resources'. There is much evidence that post-industrial production practices and strategic organizational practices effect conditions of sustained high unemployment—

along with increased productivity—and underemployment and precipitate greater levels of social fragmentation and exclusion (Beck 2000, Castells 1998, Heery and Simon 2000, Lind and Moller 1999, Rifkin 2000, Strath 2000). Furthermore, a range of new service industries take advantage of a deregulated labour market and, in many instances, workers' diminished expectations of 'standard' work in a continuous, full-time employment relation.

The trends toward intensification and dispensability generate many realities of contemporary work that in turn negatively affect workers and social institutions reliant on work-based social cohesion. Irrespective of the upward mobility enabled by education and training for some, and manifest productivity and market gains, numerous industry sectors—including the knowledge-intensive—not only retain but generate low-knowledge, low-skill, neo-Taylorised jobs simultaneously with knowledge-rich jobs. Importantly, the persistence, and even growth, of drudgery jobs—jobs that are dull, repetitive, intensely managerially controlled—and the wide expansion of deregulated, contingent employment practices, including zero hours contracts is widely evident (Gallie 1991, Felstead and Jewson 1999, Lind and Moller 1999, Ritzer 1996). A growth of low-paid and casual employment in service industries from food and entertainment services to globally marketed call centres represents a competing trajectory to that of a highly paid and over-employed technological and knowledge-rich service sector.

Liberalised workers

Another emergent trend to that of a dominant rationalisation and managerialism outlined above is that of a heightened individualism animated in part by a broader cultural climate of neo-liberalism in the West. The strategic management of the flexible organization entails a displacement of organizational uncertainty and contingency, which erratically require intensification, and discarding, of labour, onto an increasingly de-collectivised workforce. The expansion of contingent, discontinuous and intermittent work facilitates the decollectivisation and individualisation of workers as union organization is weakened and membership declines. The worker, as simply a human resource for organizational utility, is managerially encouraged to be an entrepreneur in competition with other entrepreneurial workers in selling her resourcefulness—and in gaining education and training for prospective employability. Entrepreneurial individualism obscures a desocialisation of the social costs of corporate organizational power in shaping production relations—which were once more vigorously contested by collective workers' movements—and social fragmentation and exclusion are exacerbated.

Alongside the desocialisation and decollectivisation of economic work participation, a heightening cultural turn of interests mobilises different currents of action. This cultural turn (theorised in the work of Beck 1992, Castells 1998, Taylor 1989, Touraine 1995, 1997 among others), manifests in both a new individualism and in identity movements, and in diverse self-expressivist interests, in which many people, especially the young, raise new socio-cultural demands and agendas. Contemporary people are demanding rights to pursue diverse interests in all domains of life. In particular, the turn of self-expressivist individualism fuels demands for new forms of citizen rights and expectations. The emergence of expressive individualism, which is now readily visible in contemporary western cultures, and in workplaces (Casey 2002, Lewin and Regine 2000), poses an emergent second substantive trend in the world of work to that of strategic managerialism that I have elaborated above.

All of these trends, although to a lesser extent the latter, are fully recognised by trade union and worker movements. But the rationalisation imperative, which sociologists regard as a defining characteristic of modernity, affects trade union movements and organizations as much as it does it production enterprises. The rationalisation of trade union demands, which manifest a diminishment of a more complex array of plural rationalities and socio-cultural aspirations (see Casey 2002 for elaboration on this point), has shaped articulated response to economistic imperatives in only limited ways. Yet demands for delimitation of economic and technological rationalities, as in the French success in the reduction of the working week (35 heures) are by no means insignificant. They represent in part a set of implications consequent of production intensification. These particular implications include heightened demand for freedom from intensified work, even as demands for inclusion in economic work remain predominant.

Implications

In considering the orientations and outcomes of the research projects under scrutiny here in relation to current trends in work—conceived as labour market employment—a number of political and social implications may be discerned. I sketch out three main implications that may stimulate further discussions on the learning economy and its relation to notions of learning society and of citizenship.

A non-learning economy

As controversial as this claim may appear in a learning emphasised knowledge-based economy, there persists a sector of work, production, and employment that must be termed a Non-Learning Economy. The non-learning economy—which is amply demonstrated if not articulated or analysed in many of the projects (especially Wickham and Webster et.al.) - is an accompaniment to the rationalisations driving the learning economy. Notwithstanding extant critical evidence (e.g. Borghans & de Grip 2000, Gallie 1991, Lind and Moller 1999, Ritzer 1998) the non-learning sector is widely refused recognition in contemporary economic-modelled discussions of the learning economy and learning society. Contemporary organizational management of knowledge-based organizations favours a strategic management of knowledge and learning. It strategically requires selected knowledge-rich sectors and knowledge-poor sectors; e.g. liberally managed technologists and 'creatives', and hyper-managed call centre workers and process workers. As a consequence, numerous industry sectors not only do not require learning and innovation among workers, but require intensified subjugation to predetermined rigid structures and systems of work activity and predetermined rates of pay and employment conditions. These heteronomous controls also delimit other opportunities for learning and development at work which participatory workplaces, and organizational democracy initiatives formerly stimulated. Jobs of this sort are readily found, as the projects illustrate, in retail, low-end service work, in call centre work and diverse data entry and processing work. As the Wickham and Webster project demonstrates, retail workers are required to know less than former sales workers in some sectors—that is, to know little about the product, the pricing system, or their own employing organization. Learning is restricted instead, to company-preferred styles of self-presentation and customer appeasement.

Moreover, managerially determined strategic learning and knowledge legitimation selects and represses specific knowledges. For instance, the repression of democratic and participatory structures and the knowledge sources for their engagement restricts learning and development avenues for workers. Engagement in participatory and democratic workplaces can enable workers, even in low-end jobs that are ineluctably dull or dirty, sources of social and personal development and of dignity and esteem. In a climate of managerially determined strategic learning these opportunities or learning and knowledge are disfavoured. Their absence is most obvious in, but not restricted to, hyper-rationalised and controlled industry sectors including custodial and cleaning services, manufacturing, retail, and call-centre activities.

The implications of large numbers of learning deprived workers in a non-learning economy sector, and of hyper-managed workplaces pose considerable challenges to ideological assertions of an economist correspondence of the learning economy and the learning society. They pose direct implications and challenges to education and training in industries and organizations.

Hyper-rationalisation and socio-cultural rift

A second implication arises in the rift exposed between the imperatives of the learning economy and strategically learning workers, and the learning society of learning citizens. The developments outlined above of an intensification of rationalization and efficiencies requiring strategic management and ceaseless innovation occur increasingly in conflict with other social and cultural imperatives. The heightened privileging of imperatives of technological and economic rationalities opposes notions of society valuing a high correspondence between economy and socio-political life. That is, these imperatives weaken or rupture modern industrial correspondences between economy and culture. This rupturing of correspondence, or weakening of notions in which participatory democratic society exerts effective regulatory controls or at least manages capitalism, poses immense challenges. An erosion of the efficacy of democratic politics and civil society—as conceived in modern society—in which notions of citizenship and 'the good life' are highly valued portends. The singularly instrumental model of the learning economy— which expends all resources in its service - is at odds with socio-cultural models of democratic society long valued in European cultural heritage.

The learning economy conceived according to the imperatives of a hyper-rationalisation trajectory of contemporary economic and technological practices represents a strategically selective application to specific industry sectors, regions and workers. It ineluctably generates uneven and polarising effects. The economistic model, manifesting what sociologists term a hyper-modernity of intensified rationalisation (Beck 1992, Bourdieu 1998, Touraine 1995, 2001), proposes an unintended opposition to substantive socio-cultural ends.

III: Cultural Turns: Expressivism, Citizenship, Democracy.

A third set of implications may pose, I suggest, greater opportunities for social action toward the reconstitution and revitalisation of European and other western societies. Consequent and constitutive of the rift between economy and socio-cultural imperatives is the rise of a heightened individualism and self-expressivism (Beck 1992, Castells 1998, Taylor 1989, Touraine 1995), which reflects in part the rise of post modern and counter-modern currents of thought and action. They include demands for self-expressivist and identity movements—from gay life-styles to reinvigorated ethnic and tribal movements to 'New Age' seekers. Notwithstanding the regressive elements in some of these movements (which cannot be elaborated here, see Casey 2002) they share in common demands for quality of life choices and citizen rights in plural cultural and political arena in the pursuit of satisfying and dignified life. These aspirations and demands also, and even ironically, stimulate revitalisation of notions of citizenship and democracy.

Contemporary notions of citizenship, of civil society and of revitalised democracy, are gaining renewed attention among social and political theorists (Archibugi et.al. 1998, Held 1993, Touraine 1997). Yet, these revitalised humanist ideals of European culture are frustrated or refused in contemporary strategically managed workplaces—as most of the E&T projects attest. Hyper-rationalisation, strategic resource-oriented learning and non-learning economies refuse their recognition and aspirations. The ideal of the city of modernity encouraged a civil society and congruence between individual rights and responsibilities in participating in the general will of society—as a fundamental democratic principal. This idea of democracy enabled a somewhat greater correspondence between cultural values and economy (notwithstanding class fracture and struggle). Yet in contrast to the cultural ideal, the organizational workplace of the factory, shop or office—especially in the increasingly large and corporate organization—demands integration not through democratic citizenship, but through conformity and compliance to elite-established rules and systems. Even one's learning and passions in today's organizations are required as resources for instrumental utilisation toward organizational goals. In most contemporary workplaces—including those of learning organizations—workers means to advance citizenry rights of democratic participation and diverse learning interests are undermined and frustrated.

Yet the intensified rationalisation of work and workers generates counter-movements. Among the revitalisation of older European cultural resources are revitalised ideas of citizenship and civil society, and movements for the pursuit of life interests that include diverse self-directed learning for diverse activities. Although it is widely assumed that workers learn at work according to the curricula, and for the benefit, of the organization and its economic production imperatives, and serendipitously for the advancement of their skills for careers in such organizational activities, diverse other learnings actually occur or are informally pursued (Casey 2002, Hirschhorn 1988, Kondo 1990, Lafferty 1989). Diverse learning in adult life contributes significantly to the dynamic construction of self-identity and meaning making. Adult employees utilize their various formal and informal learning experiences in ways additional, or contrary to, those intended by their employing organizations. As emerging research attests, a raft of competing currents of interests and learning aspirations among contemporary workers in the West presents as contestation to the economistic norms of subjugation as human resources (Casey 2002, Lewin and Regine 2000, and Walther's draft report 2003) Significant among these alternative currents of interest are demands for self-expressivism and self-identity which are governed by non-economic imperatives, and which considerably influence the composition, value, and ultimate ends of diverse knowledges.

The implications of the diversely learning citizen, who refuses reduction to utility and commodity and with her or his always-plural interests and agenda, are considerable. The diversely learning citizen has the potential to disrupt economistic imperatives and to articulate an alternative vision of educative learning, and of a learning society.

Conclusion

The possibilities for a revitalisation of democratic ideas and values and their notions of rights and citizenships—even within the complexities of the self-expressivist and heightened individualist turn—offer rich sources for reformulating and re-visioning the economic model of the learning organization. In the case of production organizations and workplaces, which are currently officially thwarting the exercise of citizen participatory forms and demands for plural imperatives in the worker's conduct and experience of work, a revitalisation of ideas of organizational democracy and participatory management may assist the socially necessary limitation of hyper-rationalisation. Workers plural interests for satisfying work relations and non-economic pursuits of value and meaningfulness may have a greater chance of accommodation in a dynamic political context. The divergent agenda and competing demands of hyper-rationalised organizations and self-expressivist individuals in a contingent workforce pose further challenges to educators and possibilities for revitalised organizational democracy. Prospects for both workers' education, and for citizens' education beyond the knowledge requirements of economic production find new horizons.

Policies encouraging learning and innovation in organizations that do not recognize diverse sources of, and values in, adult worker learning unreflectively repeat the rational abstractions of a modernity conceived only as rationalisation. Alternatively, a reflexive awareness on the part of policy makers may encourage policy development able to stimulate social imagination beyond neo-liberal, marketised trends of the present time—as Cullen et.al.'s project on learning and education innovation exemplifies. In addition to critical awareness of ideological managerial agenda and models, renewed attention to forms and practices of education cognisant of the currents of socio-cultural and self-identity demands, must figure highly on a reconstructed agenda.

A reconstruction of models of learning for economic development and organizational reformulation in renewed and reasserted correspondence with socio-cultural aspirations for learning and development is the immense task at stake, and at hand. An emphasis on education for socio-cultural ends and political participation and for reinvented forms of citizenship may go some way in addressing the problems of social fragmentation consequent from a globalising economic liberalism.

Note

1. J. Wickham & J. Webster, et.al. 'Innovations in Information Society Sectors'; J. Cullen et.al. 'Looking at Innovations in Education and Training'; A. Sauquat et.al. 'Small Business Training and Competitiveness'; R. Sarcina et.al. 'Developing Organisational Learning in SMEs and SME clusters'; L. Svensson et.al. 'In-company Training and Learning in Organisations'; S. Tjepkema et.al. 'The Role of HRD within Organisations in creating opportunities for life-long learning'; E. Smyth et.al. 'A Comparative Analysis of Transitions from Education to Work in Europe'; Brandsma et.al. 'The effectiveness of labour market oriented training for the long-term unemployed'; H. Steedman et.al. 'Low Skills: A Problem for Europe'.

References

Archibugi, D., Held, D. & Kohler, M. (eds) (1998) *Re-imagining Political Community.* Stanford CA: Stanford University Press.

Block, F. (1990) *Postindustrial Possibilities.* Berkeley California: University of California Press.

Beck, U. (1992) *Risk Society: Toward a New Modernity.* London: Sage.

Beck, U., Giddens, A., & Lash, S. (1994) *Reflexive Modernization: Politics, Tradition and Aesthetics in the Modern Social Order.* Stanford: Stanford University Press.

Beck, U. (2000) *The Brave New World of Work* (trans. Patrick Camiller). Cambridge: Polity Press.

Blumberg, P. (1973) *Industrial Democracy.* New York: Schoken Books.

Boisot, M. (1998) *Knowledge Assets: Securing Competitive Advantage in the Information Economy.* Oxford UK: Oxford University Press.

Borghans, L. & de Grip, A. (eds) (2000) *The Overeducated Worker?: the Economics of Skill Utilization.* Cheltenham UK: Edward Elgar.

Boud, D. & Garrick, J. (eds) (1999) *Understanding Learning at Work.* London and New York: Routledge.

Bourdieu, P. (1998) *Contre-feux.* Paris: Raisons d'agir.

Bradley, H., Erickson, M., Stephenson, C. & Williams, S. (2000) *Myths at Work.* Cambridge UK: Polity Press.

Casey, C. (2002) *Critical Analysis of Organizations: Theory, Practice, Revitalization.* London: Sage.

Castells, I. (1996) *The Rise of the Network Society.* Oxford: Blackwell.

Castells, I. (1998) *End of Millennium.* Oxford: Blackwell.

Crouch, C. & Heller, F.A. (eds) (1983) *Organizational Democracy and Political Processes.* Chichester: John Wiley.

Dewey, J. [1916] (1966) *Education and Democracy.* New York: Free Press.

Durand, J.-P. (eds) (1994) *La Fin du Modele Suedois.* Paris: Syros.

European Commission (1999) *The European Employment Strategy.* Luxembourg: Office for Official Publications of the European Communities.

European Commission (2000) 'A Memorandum on Lifelong Learning', Working paper, SEC (2000)1832, Brussels: European Commission.

Felstead, A. & Jewson, N. (eds) (1999) *Global Trends in Flexible Labour.* Basingstoke UK:Macmillan.

Freire, P. (1973) *Education for Critical Consciousness.* New York: Continuum.

Gallie, D. (1991) 'Patterns of Skill Change: Upskilling, Deskilling or the Polarisation of Skills?' *Work, Employment and Society,* Vol. 5 (3), pp. 319-51.

Giddens, A. (1990) *Consequences of Modernity.* Cambridge: Polity Press.

Gorz, A. (1999) *Reclaiming Work: Beyond the Wage-Based Society.* Cambridge: Pluto.

Harvey, D. (1989) *The Condition of Postmodernity.* Oxford: Blackwell.

Heery, E. & Salmon, J. (eds) (2000) *The Insecure Workforce.* London: Routledge.

Held, D. (eds) (1993) *Prospects for Democracy.* Cambridge: Polity.

Hirschhorn, L. (1988) *The Workplace Within.* Cambridge Mass: MIT Press.

Kondo, D. (1990) *Crafting Selves: Power, Gender and Discourses of Identity in a Japanese Workplace.* Chicago: Chicago University Press.

Lafferty, W. (1989) 'Work as a Source of Political Learning among Wage-Laborers and Lower-level Employees'. In R. Sigel (eds) *Political Learning in Adulthood.* Chicago: University of Chicago Press.

Lewin, R. & Regine, B. (2000) *The Soul at Work.* New York: Simon and Schuster.

Lind, J. & Moller, I.H. (eds) (1999) *Inclusion and Exclusion: Unemployment and Non-standard Employment in Europe.* Aldershot: Ashgate.

Lundvall, B.-A. & Borras, S. (1997) The Globalising Learning Economy: Implications for Innovation Policy, Report DGXII, European Union Commission, Brussels.

Reich, R. (1991) *The Work of Nations: Preparing Ourselves for 21st Century Capitalism.* New York: Alfred Knopf.

Rifkin, J. (2000). *The Age of Access.* New York: Putman.

Ritzer, G. (1996) *The McDonaldization of Society.* Thousand Oaks, CA: Pine Forge Press.

Senge, P. (1990) *The Fifth Discipline: The Art and Practice of the Learning Organization.* New York: Random House.

Senge, P. (1999) *Challenges of Sustaining Momentum in Learning Organizations.* New York, NY: Doubleday.

Somavia, J. (1999) Report of Director-General of the International Labour Organization 87th Session of the ILO Conference.

Stewart, T. (1997) *Intellectual Capital: The New Wealth of Organizations.* New York: Doubleday.

Strath, B. (eds) (2000) *After Full Employment: European Discourses on Work and Flexibility.* Brussels: Peter Lang.

Szell, G. (eds) (2001) *European Labour Relations.* Aldershot: Gower/ Ashgate.

Taylor, C. (1989) *Sources of the Self: the Making of Modern Identity.* Cambridge MA: Harvard University Press.

Touraine, A. (1995) *Critique of Modernity* (translated by David Macey). Oxford UK: Blackwell.

Touraine, A. (1997) *What is Democracy?* (trans. David Macey). Boulder CO: Westview Press.

Touraine, A. (2001) *Beyond Neoliberalism.* Cambridge UK: Polity Press.

Walther, A. (2003) Preliminary Report on Youth Policy and Participation: the Role of Participation and Informal Learning in the Transition of Young People to the Labour Market. Paper presented at Living, Working and Learning in the Learning Society Workshop, University of Bremen, Germany 27-28 February 2003.

Williams, C & Windebank, J. (1998) *Informal Employment in the Advanced Economies: Implications for Work and Welfare.* London: Routledge.

CHAPTER EIGHT

The Subject and Work Related Identity

GABRIELE LASKE

About the FAME Project

The FRP 5-Project 'Vocational Identity, Flexibility and Mobility in the European Labour Market (FAME)' was a three year project that started in March 2000 with the aim to investigate how increasing flexibility and mobility in European labour markets effect the development of vocational identities. The project consortium consists of partners from seven European countries: the Czech Republic, England, Estonia, France, Germany, Greece, and Spain.

The project's aim was initially to investigate and analyse the phenomenon of vocational identity in seven European countries, the need or neglegtability of vocational identity regarding the individual and about critical aspects or shortcomings of work and occupational identity to meet current and future labour market developments. The project intended to show if labour markets and sectors of the selected countries showed an increasing requirement for workforce flexibility and mobility and if so, how employees respond, adjust or refuse to meet these demands.

The individual receives his social identity through the attribution of certain specified characteristics that have the nature of normative expectations. The individual is expected to subordinate himself to these expectations or to act according to them and behave as others do in the same social context. This can be also designated as acting in conformity with a role within a given social context, such as an occupational group. By contrast, in the case of personal identity, there is a demand to distinguish oneself from all others, i.e. to be like no other. These conflicting expectations require a balance, otherwise there is a risk of non-identity in two ways. In one case the completely objectified blending into different depersonalized role contexts, in the other case stigmatization on the basis of behaviour deviating from norms. 'Knowing who one is creates meaning and gives a person's own endeavours a direction for the future. Identity helps us to fit in the community and to mark our special features and distinctions from others. In the classical approaches towards describing the formation of an identity during youth and early adult age the profession was always the focus as the anchor of one's view of oneself. Failing here was considered to be the key risk factor for what could be a lifelong mis-adjustments' (Silbereisen1997, p. 184). Today the role identity breaks down during the adolescence phase, and the ego identity has to be developed as the ability characteristic of the adult to build up new identities and integrate them with those overcome. 'This advanced stage of identity (...) is a high cultural achievement of people and cannot be understood without a retrospective historical look at the creation of human culture' (Habermas, 1976). This stage of identity holds particular importance for the work in the Fame Project. The question of the increased demand for flexibility and mobility is directly related to the process and ability to build up new identities and integrate them with those overcome.

The process of creation and formation of identities is determined both by societal conditions affecting the individual and by individual talents, inclinations and activities. Developing an identity is an achievement of the individual (a learning process). It is an internal process whereby societal influences and individual capacities and dispositions meet and generate an internal process that can lead to the formation of identities. An individual's work or occupational identity is determined by external, societal influences that are adjusted, responded to or rejected based on the individual's personal talents and inclinations. A process of 'negotiation' or a search for some balance of individuals' internal and external activity and selective process takes place that adjusts, responds or rejects elements on either side of the internal or external disposition and circumstances. Contradictions that arise during a more or less successful processing of interaction between societal and individual demands have to be endured and digested by the individual.

The project used the tool of investigating different perspectives, the perspective of employers and employees, regarding work related or occupational identity. The research on employers' perspectives aimed to investigate the societal, organisational conditions and changes of workplaces regarding the occupations/professions the project focused on. The project tried to extract what employers currently expect from their employees and what features they anticipate for the future. When looking at the findings of the different national employer perspectives, it is striking how much the recognised problems or new demands differ. One also has to take into consideration that problems or tensions reported are subject to national political discussions and, due to this, offer a specific awareness of necessities for change or resistance towards change. However, the results of the employers' perspectives are valuable precisely because of their subjective bias.

They derive from different national discussions and perceptions of change and structural problems concerning the sector of which employees are aware and exposed to. Predominant economic and entrepreneurial concepts are openly discussed in the media. They also are conveyed to employees within the company through human resource management strategies. Inevitably employees are confronted with and have to respond to these demands, also in terms of reaction and reflection. A process of response and negotiation between employer and employee occurs while new demands or new work paradigms are introduced. Employees are forced to develop strategies to cope, adjust, negotiate or refuse employers' expectations that arise from newly defined concepts about work performance and employment. They have to integrate new tasks, working behaviour and attitudes into their work.

It is clear that the development of work related and vocational identity is strongly determined by structural, educational and organisational conditions. Under favourable conditions sound vocational identities can form, given that an interest and attachment of employees concerning their work exists. On this basis employees are able and willing to adjust to higher demands on flexibility, learning and even spatial mobility. Unfavourable conditions (which are partly subject to individuals' expectations and perceptions) lead to low identification, low commitment and indifference towards the job. However, between these polarities a wide range of different work related and vocational identity patterns can be found which differ from sector to sector, partly from country to country and are more or less modified by structural conditions.

In order to look for typical occupational or work related identity formations in each country, the project partners proved which sectors and occupations or professions could suit the project's objectives best. The sectors, metal industry, health care, and telecommunications were chosen in the first place on the assumption that they represent three different types of changes or challenges at nowadays workplaces:

– Production in metal industry has historically developed strong traditional patterns of occupational identities, which now are challenged by implementations and use of computer aided technologies and new organisational concepts.
– Health care also has strong historical roots. The sector amongst others faces changes from distinct hierarchies and regulated occupations due to partly outsourcing of services. Private organisations sell services which substitute health care or in some countries are mainly provided at home by female family members until now. Therefore the existence of strong traditions and in addition a newly developing labour market due to new service providers made this sector an interesting subject of the project.

Finally 'telecommunications' as a sector under major structural changes including the revolutionary introduction of IT and other latest technologies was supposed to show ways how occupational or job identities are generated in a fast changing structural and technological environment. These changes strongly effect tasks and job descriptions and ask for permanent learning of employees.

It was decided to broaden the scope of the sectors and also to investigate the areas of IT and tourism. Telecommunications and IT are closely linked. However, it also became obvious, that telecommunications, with a history of having been publicly owned at least in the UK, France and Germany, the Czech-Republic, and was only recently privatised, shows different sectoral features in comparison to the small and larger IT businesses that have evolved during the last 10 to 15 years. In addition, the Spanish partner suggested looking into the field of tourism as a traditional sector of their country, as a larger Spanish telecommunications sector does not exist.

As the project findings show, one can distinguish four major elements or dimensions that influence and partake in the development of work related and occupational identities:

- The individual,
- socialisation,
- organisational embeddedness and
- social recognition.

All four can either, depending on their mutual influence, dominate, weaken or balance work identities or vocational identities.

The 'individual' dimension encompasses personal inclinations, for example, what a person is identified with at the job. This can be a personal interest in providing a service, the product the company is famous for, the institution where one works, or the pleasure in working with customers, people, etc. The" individual" dimension also includes specific talents in response to the work to be done and towards the ability to meet demands at the workplace. Therefore the focus is on an individual's personal and psychological features, through which he or she reacts towards environmental and structural conditions.

Regarding 'socialisation' the area of particular interst, which influences the way that the individual relates to the work and the workplace includes initial, continuous and further education and training. Also socialisation through the membership of a community of practice is taken into account, as is the corporate culture of the institution and company to which a person belongs. In the first place socialisation is something that the individual experiences through education he or she receives, the system of values and norms regarding work and professions she is confronted with while learning to work and through communication and co-operation with colleagues. With time, these socialising factors become internalised and an integral part of the individual's personality, so to speak, a work related personality. It is clear that there is a strong interaction and interlocking between both dimensions, the individual and socialisation (Leithaeuser, Volmerg).

As a third dimension the project findings showed the importance of the 'organisational embeddedness' in terms of the development of work related and occupational identities. This dimension not only implies the organisational structure and situation of a specific workplace and company, but reaches out to the conditions of sectoral and governmental structures, that effect the way work is organised in a given sector and organisation. The individual with his/her work personality will respond towards for example higher demands on flexibility, time pressure, the use and implementation of technology, poor or rich learning opportunities etc. the organisation and sector offers.

Finally the way a specific vocation is viewed in society has an essential effect on the development of vocational identities. The dimension 'recognition from society' comprises elements like wages, societal status given to an occupation or job, policy concerning the different segments of the labour market, reorganisation and privatisation of economic sectors as well as the legal frame of a occupation or job (full or part time, social security, education and certifications, legally or illegally employed ...) determine to a large extent how the individual's work related identity grows or deteriorates.

Individual	**Socialisation**
– Personal inclinations,	– initial and further education
– talents	– continuous education
– subject of identification	– membership of community of
– individual response towards change	practice
at the workplace and work profile	– corporate culture of a company
Vocational Identity	
– wages	– policy of personnel development
– status	– organisational structure
– legal frame of work	– organisation of work
– policy	– rich/poor learning environment
	– use of technology

As the above described dimensions indicate, societal and organisational structures might foster or restrict learning as well as the formation of work related identity. Existing social and economic structures mainly determine the nature of work and lead to different modifications regarding the need for change. Thus far, one cannot speak about a common European pattern with respect to how demands for flexibility and mobility affect the European workforce and what this means for the development of occupational identities. A striking feature when one looks at the project is, how much the recognised problems, solutions or new demands on employees differ, for each national, sectoral, and organisational set of problems or demands is of a different nature (due to the national economic-ideological bias, nationally or regionally perceived problems...). In this context the full range of the project's findings cannot be addressed.

However, a few examples will illustrate the great variety of circumstances that lead to different forms of vocational and work related identities. The tourism sectors in Spain and the Czech Republic will serve as an example of a sector that is affected by the global trend of tourism that to a large extent creates unfavourable working conditions and lacks career opportunities and personal development. The example taken from the healthcare sector, specifically from radiographers in Spain and England will serve as an example to illustrate how, despite global technological development and the use of medical technology, the national and sectoral policies regarding education and professional status strongly effect the development of occupational identities. Finally, examples of the IT sector in Germany, Estonia, Czech Republic and England will be viewed in the light of new job profiles and demands in the New Economy.

Global trend and deregulation: Tourism in Spain and the Czech Republic

Tourism is one of the most vital industries of today's economy. In international tourism Europe holds a prominent and dominant post. Worldwide business in tourism has become very competitive and Europe has to react on the changes and demands of the sector. During the last years, Spain has been successful in gaining the second place among tourist destinations, following France that ranks first. After a process of democratisation, abolishment of visa requirements and the opening of boarders, also Central and Eastern European countries first experienced booming tourism that by now has slowed down but still provides good prospects.

The range of job opportunities in tourism is wide and offers employment to unskilled workers, workers who are educated in traditional occupations, and to highly qualified workers. Due to the sector's specific capacity to provide many jobs, which do not require high qualifications, jobs can be generated in areas that are less economically developed or suffer from structural unemployment. Another prevailing feature is the high percentage of small companies. The average number of employees per company in the Czech Republic in 2000 was 4,1 compared to 4,6 employees in the EU. However, a tendency can be observed that the sectors undergo reorganisation and (especially in Spain) centralisation occurs in terms of penetration and expansion of national and multinational hotel chains. In the Czech Republic tourism is still undergoing a phase whereby many companies are starting up, a phase that the rest of the EU experienced during the 1990s (Martinez; Strietska-Illina).

Another essential feature of tourism is that the sector is subject to seasonality. This means that companies which work in areas where tourism is limited to one or two seasons a year as for example summer or winter, must acquire the necessary income during this short period of time to cover their fixed costs for the rest of the year. However, it is not only the factor of seasonality which creates a substantial instability. Tourism as an industry in general is highly vulnerable in terms of natural catastrophes, political events etc. as recently September 11th 2001 and the SARS disease in 2002/3 have shown. These features imply a lack of long-term perspectives for employees. Workers hardly know how long they are going to work and cannot plan for a long term professional career. Their unemployment during low season makes them seek other job opportunities or involvement in activities mostly outside of tourism. They often stay on unemployment benefit whilst awaiting job opportunities in the high season. These facts detract the prospect of having a career in tourism which results in employees' low interest regarding professional development and training. As a consequence, service in tourism often is of low quality.

As a result of the structural features described, to a large extent employers do not seek for a qualified workforce that is educated in vocational programs that tourism can offer. They rather look for cheap, unqualified, and occasional workers such as students and young people, who are looking for a temporary job. Due to these personnel policies and attitudes, the reputation of vocational education and training in tourism is undermined.

For tourism in the Czech Republic, another unfavourable element was pointed out. The sector is characterised by the high degree of job insecurity and involvement of a 'grey' labour force (i.e. hired without contractual obligations) and the low commitment of employers to develop the human potential of their company. Therefore staff in hotels and the catering trade often display low commitment to their job, company and the sector in general and demonstrate low interest in work performance. In summary, employers use their workers flexible and in accordance to seasonal demands, but without providing social guarantees and occupational promotion, while the workforce suffers from irregular working hours, working overtimes and the psychological pressure that comes with the constant human communication most workers are exposed to in tourism. 'The unfavourable working conditions and lack of career and personal development prospects badly damage the generally attractive sectoral image and prestige, cause high staff turnover and outflow of skilled personnel from the sector' (Martinez; Strietska-Illina).

National structures can make a difference: The example of radiographers in Spain and England

The profession of radiography is currently meeting with major changes in respect to new technological and medical developments. These do not only require technicians that operate x-ray images and get x-ray images, but technology which has broadened towards digital screening, for example. In addition, new demands have been added regarding radiotherapy, in the treatment of cancer, for exmaple. With the increase of instruments and methods some diagnoses may even be left to the medical technicians. In summary, in health care there is an increasing demand in the medical-technical field. In general, one can expect that these facts will push forward the occupational demand for learning and the medical importance of professions like radiography. Facing this change through new technologies and treatment, traditional radiography becomes obsolete. However, the way that the profession of radiography is currently developing varies significantly from country to country. Spain and England provide good examples how different approaches of the national healthcare sector create very different profiles of the same profession. As a consequence they offer the individuals in these jobs quite different conditions to develop their professional identity.

The Spanish example rests on research and findings in the region of Valencia. The employees of the Spanish health care system are to to a large extent, civic servants. Employment and the workforce distribution are regulated by governmental institutions. Staff selection functions in respect to the medical-technical staff through a public register of available workers. Hospitals as employers cannot request any employee with specialist knowledge, for the principle of list-seniority has priority in the register. Also compensatory staff are provided by this mechanism. The work period of the compensatory staff tends to last between three and six months and because unemployed technicians of the public register they also get the advantages of being employed. Experience and CVs are not taken into account. A person's merit has no influence on employment.

The organisation of the Spanish health care sector has very strict hierarchies. Doctors as the top of the hierarchy are highly qualified and provide a high level of competence and qualification. The hierarchy on the level below are nurses, usually with the status of civil servants but without specialisation. To become a nurse, one has to get a University Diploma. Medical technicians belong to the lowest hierarchy level with the lowest status. Their possibility of autonomy in the field in which they work is very limited. Also doctors can take on the task of technician or medical auxiliary, if necessary. As mentioned above, radiology as a field has grown tremendously, but this is not reflected in the curriculum. This means that a lot of work associated with this new technology has to be carried out by the medical staff. One reason why this frequently occurs is due to the fact that doctors have the advantage of being trained by the suppliers of the latest medical equipment. Compared with the doctors' training situation, technology in vocational centres, where radiographers are trained, is partly outdated.

Initial education and training is generally well adapted by trainees for radiodiagnostic technicians, although it occurs at hospitals under quite some pressure from the other hospital departments, which require their service. High workload and tight schedules are common. However, the basic vocational training does not really supply sufficient qualifications for certain posts, where work with new technological equipment is required. Then the highest level in the hierarchy, the doctors, have to take on the responsibility to do the job of the workers on the lower level, either to cover momentary staff shortages or to train the new worker, selected from the public register.

It is very noticeable that low level health care such as the technicians have less interest in continuous training courses. There is almost no attendance due to the lack of motivation. The reasons may be for those who see being a radiographer as a job for life due to the lack of autonomy and responsibility given to them at work. Also it is not yet considered as a solid occupational status. Those radiographers who are not permanently employed and on the public register of available health workers may lack interest due to the instability of their work.

Contrary to their Spanish colleagues, radiographers in the UK have strong occupational identities. It has recently become a graduate entry profession. Their workplace is principally restricted to hospitals, but few also work for equipment suppliers. Their professional responsibility is of a much wider scope than that of their colleagues in Spain. Recruitment and retention of this occupational group is of major concern to the English healthcare sector. Professional radiographers can and do move to other hospitals, either to complete their initial and further training or for promotion. However, the initial skills formation in a practical sense is not always as strong as hospitals would like or need. Therefore learning and training support is seen as an important factor and so is learning while working, although this cannot always be fully supported in practice because of the additional demands it puts on the already stretched senior staff.

Continuing professional development is statutory and the staff have to maintain record of it. This does not necessarily mean attendance of formal training events. Time spent on learning in more informal ways also counts. The broad scope of variations in work generally makes a rich learning environment. However, the pressure of work sometimes constrains the possibility of further learning.

Tensions between staff can be observed when boundaries and responsibilities overlap between occupations, between radiographers and doctors, for example. It can be difficult for doctors to accept that a radiographer may be more competent to give diagnoses about x-ray images. However, hospitals have expanded roles and responsibilities and are experimenting with different patterns of work organisation which requires varying skill mixes. Also career opportunities have been opened up for practitioners with special responsibilities.

In addition, changes to professional training and development about the ideas regarding the nature of practice and philosophy of care are changing the patterns of work and service in healthcare service and the adoption of new technologies create a turbulent environment for practice and work in hospitals. However, there is not a single model of best practice. Hospitals and their departments have to find their own way to best optimise the service delivery and skill development.

As this short draft shows, an individual radiographer in England is given more autonomy and responsibility, but in a context of increasing demand for services.

The development of work related identity in a sector of the New Economy

Information technology as part of the new economy is a relatively young and dynamic sector. Driven by the fast technological developments and their applications, up to now the sector is continuously facing rapid changes. Information, as the core subject around which this technology revolves, has taken on the form of an industrial property and commodity. As a result, working in the IT sector means acquiring and working with a new set of skills that the labour market of the old economy hardly had required. Consequently, new occupational profiles have developed. One profile for example is that of a multi-skilled specialist with technical skills, good communication skills, and team working abilities.

Most countries face a shortage of qualified workers in the IT sector. This significantly affects their capacity to use new technologies. Although the IT sector uses traditional ways to train and educate in order to generate their workforce to some extent, new and informal ways for learning and skill upgrading have also been developed. Given the fairly new emergence of this sector, driven by a global diffusion of information in combination with a global access to the latest technologies of this field, the IT sector in different countries is nevertheless embedded in country-specific contexts and traditions. For this reason solutions regarding the development and recruitment of the workforce are different in Germany, England, Estonia and the Czech Republic.

Indeed, the German vocational education tradition of the dual system has also entered the IT sector in Germany. Occupational profiles have been defined and corresponding training paths developed to meet the needs of this new labour market segment. One must remember, however, that the number of trainees per year does not meet the need of the IT labour market. Due to the fact that the IT sector in Germany is one that consists principally of small companies and a few large departments or daughter companies of corporations from other sectors that want to make use of IT for their products, there are not many companies with the capacity to incorporate trainees for two to three years. Instead, many companies employ graduates from universities or colleges. Information science graduates are most welcome, but students with maths or engineering backgrounds who have developed some skills in information technology are also desirable.

Training and education traditions in the UK are more of a trade oriented education system and school-based training. Universities and colleges offer degrees on undergraduate and graduate levels. These graduates receive a profound foundation in computer science and engineering. They are envisioned as a future workforce for research and development, either in the public or private sector or at universities. Companies prefer to hire young people with a background of practical-oriented courses in information technology than to prepare students for work in an industrial environment, or people who have acquired IT experiences outside the formal education structure.

In Estonia vocational education programs do not provide the qualifications that the IT industry needs. This is partly due to the very rapid development of the sector that outdates curricula during the two to three years training period. At the same time as the sector is very young, its institutional structures of education and training are not fully developed. Higher education of universities and technical schools in information science is regarded as being too theoretical for practical use in industry. One recruitment strategy which companies currently favour is to employ school-leavers and to expose them to work experience. This results in unfinished educational paths of most of the technicians. Due to intense workloads, a continuation of their studies becomes very difficult.

The major training sources of IT specialists in the Czech Republic are special programs at secondary schools, higher professional schools, and in higher education. IT specialists are also recruited from other study programs that provide some courses in computing and programming, as do electrical or mechanical engineering courses. Some secondary schools also arrange for their students to do practical education in computing in workshops or firms. It is however, apparent that organisation or students' obligations for such practices are not clearly defined.

As illustrated, strategies to educate and recruit the workforce in IT differ in the described countries. Generally, employers' requirements in this sector are very similar in all countries. 'The multi-skilled IT technician constructed by employers contains a variety of aspects: Confidentiality and loyalty, language skills, hybrid technical skills, communication skills, readiness for change and continuous self-development, stress handling ability, team work skills, and general knowledge about administration and economy' (Loogma, Ümarik, Vilu). Thus people working in IT are facing high expectations and stressful working conditions. IT-specialists therefore emphasise the importance of a good climate at the company and positive relations between colleagues. Autonomy and responsibility held by IT specialists in their job seem to strengthen their identification with the position. Although the sector is fairly new and not yet fully developed organisational-wise, to work in IT activates strong feelings of professional identity. They are not so much related to specific occupational profiles, rather to a feeling of belonging to a new and aspirant industry and professional field that ranges among the 'knowledge' professions. In connection to this, the development of informal communication networks (club-type communities, web-based communities) is very important. They not only play a significant role in employee's professional self-development process. These informal communities also give a feeling of togetherness and often serve as a field for the solution of work problems and learning. This rather informal development of communities of practice in IT seems to be a characteristic feature of the new industry.

Conclusions

As the three examples show, structural and social conditions have a major impact on the development of work-related and vocational identities. The examples chosen demonstrate that in the case of radiographers, national educational and human resource strategies of the health care sector can offer either a high status and challenging profession which employees like to identify with, or on the contrary as the Spanish example of radiographers shows, provide a structural setting that neither encourages learning nor the commitment for a low status job that neither offers career opportunities nor the possibility to work with a sufficient degree of autonomy and responsibility. Tourism serves as an example of an industry under the structural influence of globalisation. National peculiarities do not seem strong enough to meet the overall trends in employment policy that are unfavourable in terms of the development of work related identities. The irregular and insecure working conditions in tourism lead to little interest in qualifications and to low service qualities. Many jobs are just seen as an opportunity to earn money. Work related identities therefore on average are fairly undeveloped. IT again shows a different picture. Although still a new industry and confronted with many shortcomings and structural difficulties, it nevertheless provides employees a dynamic milieu with challenges and excitement. Possibly also because of a certain climate of getting ready to go and being on top to face new technological challenges for the future, including high wages, the industry (despite the high demand on flexibility, mobility and stressful working conditions), is seen as a very attractive workplace with high social status. Regarding the development of vocational identities, the sector provides sufficient features that foster the identification to work in this industry.

References

Alan, Brown (2002) Initial findings from the UK employee interviews. For Athens FAME meeting. Internal paper.

Habermas, J. (1976) 'Können komplexe Gesellschaften eine vernünftige Identität ausbilden?' In J. Habermas *Zur Rekonstruktion des Historischen Materialismus*. Frankfurt am Main: Suhrkamp.

Laske, G. (2001) 'Profession and occupation as medium of socialization and identity formation'. In G. Laske (eds) *Project Papers: Vocational Identity, Flexibility and Ability in the European Labour Market (Fame)*. ITB-Arbeitspapiere 27, Bremen: Unpublished report.

Leithaueser, T. & Volmerg, B. (1988) *Psychoanalyse in der Sozialforschung: eine Einführung am Beispiel einer Sozialpsychologie der Arbeit*. Opladen: Westdt. Verlag.

Loogma, K., Ümarik, M. & Vilu, R. with contributions from Czeck Republic, Germany, UK (2003) Work identities and readiness for flexibility and mobility in the IT sector (Czech Republic, Estonia, Germany, United Kingdom).

Marinez, I. & Strietska-Illina, O. (2003) 'The Context of the Tourism Sector: the Cases of Spain, Czech Republic and Greece'. In I. Marinez & F. Marhuenda *Annex for the tourism sector*. FAME Final Report. February 16th 2003.

Silbereisen, R. K. (1997) 'Das Veränderungsoffene und Grenzenbewußte Ich—Seine Entwicklung über die Lebensspanne. In E.U. Weizsäcker (eds) *Grenzen-los?: Jedes System braucht Grenzen—aber wie durchlässig müssen sie sein?* Berlin: Birkhäuser.

3

ICT and Learning

CHAPTER NINE

Learning and ICT in the Learning Economy / Learning Society

P. Robert-Jan Simons

When the learning economy/learning society theory becomes the leading idea for the European economy/society, and learning will become one of the leading process of organisations and societies, new ideas about learning and knowledge will be needed. This chapter sketches two of these: Acquisition versus participation learning and explicit versus implicit knowledge and skills. The changes in the direction of the participation metaphor and implicit knowledge and skills will mean new roles for ICT within education, in work contexts and outside of those two. A new digital pedagogy is needed. Furthermore, we expect a further emphasis on collective learning. Several kinds of collective learning are discussed as well as the role of ICT in facilitating collective learning.

Consequences for learning when Europe becomes a learning economy/learning society

The learning economy/learning society is an economy/society that is good in innovation. It is a prescriptive/normative idea focusing on the ability of an economy to renew itself constantly. Clearly, since this an economical theory, the impetus comes from economical ideas and plans. There are several critics on this idea, mainly focusing on the fact that economical thinking is too much central. In the idea of a learning society, also a prescriptive/normative idea about ideal societies, a much broader perspective is taken. Learning is not only needed for economy, but also for its own sake, because it is a most human process that gives people future perspective and ideals. The learning society puts learning central because this is an ideal in its own and not just because of the economical advantages of learning people. Moreover, the learning of all people is emphasized and not only that other people who contribute to the economical growth.

Although the opinions differ about the exact image of a learning economy/ learning society and there might be differences between the two concepts, there are some general consequences for learning that are compatible with both concepts. These can be summarised as follows:

1. Learning is no longer owned by educational institutions alone.
2. Educational institutions should prepare their students for the other kinds of learning.
3. New competences and new kinds of and perspectives on knowledge are needed.
4. New conceptions of knowledge and competences are needed.
5. There is a growing need for collective forms of learning.
6. All organisations in societies should become learning organisations.
7. Societies at large should become good in learning themselves.
8. New roles for ICT in facilitating learning.
9. Alignment of the different ways of learning.
10. European learning.
11. New roles for research.

Table 1 gives a more detailed overview of point of attention.

New ideas about learning and knowledge

The possible consequences of the learning economy and learning society thinking, as described in the previous section, imply new conceptions of learning and knowledge. This difference can be described in terms of two metaphors: The transmission (also called the acquisition) metaphor and the participation metaphor.

Implicitly or explicitly, most of us tend to use the transmission metaphor of learning and knowledge distribution. According to Bruner (1996) the basic assumptions of this metaphor are that

a) knowledge of the world is treated as the objective truth that can be transmitted from one person to another;
b) a medium, such as a teacher or a book is needed to transport the knowledge of the one person who 'knows' to an other person who does not;
c) learning has to be institutionalised in a building (school).

TABLE 1: Overview of points of attention for the learning economy/learning society

1	Learning is no longer owned by educational institutions alone	
	Learning at the workplace Innovative learning Life long learning Learning though ICT	Self-directed learning Implicit learning. experiential learning Coaching
2	Educational institutions should prepare their students for the other kinds of learning	
	Learning to learn New ways and new outcomes of learning Use of ICT in educational institutions	Multiprofessional, multiperspective learning New contacts between educational institutions and other actors in society
3	New competences and new kinds of and perspectives on knowledge are needed	
	Learning competences Tacit knowledge and skills Other competences such as collaboration, networking, self-regulation, creativity, autonomy and innovation competences	New ways to assess competences outside of educational institutions New ways to relate assessments to ways of learning
4	New conceptions of knowledge and competences are needed	
	Social-cultural knowledge conceptions Holistic competences Deeper understanding	The social life of information New conceptions of professionalisation Trainable and less trainable competences
5	There is a growing need for collective forms of learning	
	Communities of practice, communities of learners Team learning	Organisational learning New forms of knowledge management
6	All organisations in societies should become learning organisations	
	The learning school, the learning university Learning companies Sme's as learning organisations	Learning cities, learning regions, learning governments New networks of companies and other organisations
7	Societies at large should become good in learning themselves	
	Innovation in society Innovation in companies	Innovation in governmental organisations The learning citizen / citizenship
8	New roles for ICT in facilitating learning	
	Individual learning Collective learning	Related to knowledge management
9	Alignment of the different ways of learning	
	Roles of different organisations Facilitating actors	New kinds of networks Coaching and mentoring
10	European learning	
	The European learning economy / learning society Multinational thinking and learning	Multicultural thinking and learning
11	New roles for research	
	Research in relation to innovation Research into learning	Action research and action learning

The alternative assumptions of social-constructivism and social learning theory (Wenger, 1998), called the participation model (Sfard, 1998) state that

a) there is no objective truth and knowledge is constructed in social-interactions between people;
b) learning should be done by people themselves; at most they can be helped with this; we cannot do it for them;
c) learning is gradually becoming a member of a community of practice (or a culture, or a profession, or a field of science); this happens for an important part outside of institutions and tacit knowledge and skills play important roles in it.

Although many of us believe in these constructivist assumptions nowadays, few are able to fully implement them in their actions (see Brown & Duguid, 2000). This is, on the one hand, because this is not an easy job to perform. Time and time again one has to realise that knowledge cannot be transmitted, that different perspectives exist on even very 'logical' kinds of knowledge, that knowledge develops in cultural interactions between people, and that much of our most important knowledge is tacit, thus difficult to discuss. On the other hand, it is also the case because the basic assumptions of the transmission model are so dominant in our culture that it is difficult to escape from them. Even in the debates about the learning economy/learning society, learning is often confined to formal education and training and processes of informal and social learning are undervalued or underestimated. The beliefs in the possibilities of transmitting information through formal schooling, written texts and websites are still very dominant in the learning economy/learning society thinking too. We should not, however, remove the transmission model from our thinking totally. As Sfard stated the transmission and the participation metaphors are not completely contradictory. Combinations and integrations are needed.

The consequences of the participation metaphor are

a) that knowledge cannot always be distributed;
b) that knowledge distribution is knowledge (re) creation;
c) that knowledge distribution cannot take place outside of real interactions between people. This means that organising knowledge distribution is organising interactions between perspectives of (groups) of people.
d) That exploration and communication become more important processes than information transmission. Besides an information tool, ICT is more and more also a communication and an exploration tool.

The social learning theory thus requires new ways of dealing with knowledge distribution and creation, much more embedded in social interactions where the clashes between different cultural perspectives are used to create ideas. This has important consequences for (vocational) education and training as well as for learning outside of education and training, related to all three of Bruners' assumptions, to name a few:

a)   Focus on other contents (not the known facts but the development of new ideas in a domain; where the uncertainties and the developments are);
b)   focus on exchanges of perspectives and social interactions; revaluation of implicit knowledge and skills;

d)   more self-directed learning;
e)   preparing people for life long learning;
f)   learning in communities of practice;
g)   learning communities;
h)   learning outside institutions and buildings;
i)   learning in relation to real authentic problems.

Above two metaphors of learning were distinguished, the acquisition and the participation metaphor. Bereiter (2002) makes a further distinction in two kinds of social learning/participation focusing on the one hand on the individual meaning construction, where people develop opinions and explore their views of reality and on the other hand on the implicit cultural knowledge that is shared between members of a community or culture. According to Bereiter meaning construction in the second sense differs from the individual meaning construction and different kinds of learning are required for these two. He uses the word 'knowledge building' for the last category and defines this as creating, articulating, and building different kinds of conceptual artefacts. Knowledge building is a practice of working for producing cultural knowledge typical of scientific research groups or other expert communities.

The changes in conceptions about learning metaphors co-occur with a change in the value of certain kinds of knowledge: From explicit knowledge and skills towards implicit knowledge and skills. Whereas in earlier days the focus especially in educational contexts was on explicit knowledge and skills, nowadays-implicit knowledge and skills came back to the front of the stage. More and more theorists plead for a revaluation of knowledge and skills of which people are relatively unaware. These kinds of implicit knowledge and skills are probably learned in social practice and thus related to the participation metaphor.

The changes in conceptions about knowledge and learning form a part of broader changes in thinking in relation to the way organisations and societies are supposed to function (Tomassini, 2002). These can be summarised as in Table 2.

TABLE 2: Changes in ways of thinking

From	To
Engineering model: Creation of one best product	Dialogue model: Creation of platforms for joint co design of plural – multiple purpose product and for sharing of information and experience
Focus on outcomes: A specific technology	Focus on process: an ecology of solutions
Success or failure logic	Serendipity logic: Introducing softly procedures in order for users to find uses
Search for direct applications	Also valorisation of indirect impacts
Clear-cut problems and solutions	Wide range of problems and solutions: Understanding needs Fostering multi-level collaboration Suggesting different solutions Finding shared ways for use Cultivating stable communities of practice who are aware of their role.
Research Researchers vs. implementers: Problem–research–solution	Action–research Researchers as active co-designers (local actors): Extending tacit knowledge Socialising solutions Combining information Internalising new competences

The shift in emphasis from the acquisition/transmission metaphor towards the participation metaphor brings new roles for ICT, both in schools, in work organisations and learning outside of education and work. These three will be discussed in the next sections. Information and communication technology (ICT) is defined as all kinds of technology that can facilitate the storage, transfer and distribution of information as well as the communication between (groups of) people.

ICT and education

What should the role of ICT within education be in the learning economy/ learning society? Should it change? There are four answers to these questions:

a) ICT within education should prepare students for the kinds of learning that are needed in organisations, life long learning and society (see above). The ways of learning that are important there, should also be the focus of ICT within education. This means a high emphasis on learning to learn: Preparing students for their future ways of learning.

b) On the other hand ICT should also focus on competencies needed in the learning economy/learning society: How can competencies such as collaboration, regulation and problem solving competences be developed?

c) ICT within education could help to facilitate and promote social learning according to the participation metaphor (see above). What kinds of learning environments are needed for social learning? Powerful learning environments are described in the literature as learning environments that
   • increase the students activities and constructions,
   • stimulate self-regulation,
   • create opportunities for authentic learning, networks and collabora-tion, relating to communities of learning and of practice,
   • help to develop thinking and learning competencies, both general and domain specific ones, creating classroom cultures with emphasis on reflection on and articulation of learning and thinking processes (process oriented instruction).

d) The further implementation of ICT in education should focus on digital pedagogy: How to use ICT in education. Digital pedagogy refers to the use of ICT within education. Simons (2003) proposed 7 basic principles on which digital pedagogy can be built. These are:

Relating

ICT can open the doors of schools. Trough ICT students can be in contact with all kinds of outsiders in companies, museums, other schools, other countries, etc. Moreover ICT can have important roles in the organisation of collaborative learning, both inside classrooms (less noise; better structure) and outside of classrooms (with students in other classrooms, international collaboration, learning communities). Electronic discussion forums offer new possibilities for exchange of ideas. Although it is by no means easy to interact virtually because one misses important non-verbal and personal information, it can become an important new way of interacting that supplements instead of replaces other forms. New forms of peer-assessment and peer-feedback become possible through ICT.

Creating

Five ways to create knowledge can be organised with the help of ICT: Learning through problem solving, learning through decision making, learning through inquiry and research, learning through design activities and learning as meaning construction. All five ways gives the student a more active role.

In solving problems students search for the best (or the only) solution for a problem. In decision-making there is no best answer. It is more a matter of opinion. Advises should be formulated and legitimised. In inquiry or research activities, students try to answer questions and to test hypotheses. In design activities the task is to make a (new) product that fulfils certain criteria, for instance a website, a poster or a manual. Meaning construction pertains to critical reflection about central concepts and principles. Through discussion students construct new (collective) meaning.

Extending the audience

The third important function ICT can have is to extend the audience of the outcomes of learning. Students do not only learn for themselves and their teachers but also for an other audience. These can be other students, parents, employers, or even a general audience. One important application is the use of competition. Prices are given for the best design, the best inquiry or the best advice. Another application is the use of real clients. Student's activities have a role for real clients: They solve real problems, give real advises, make real products, do real research of construct new meaning for clients.

Transparency of thinking and learning

ICT can make thinking, learning and collaboration processes more visible. The transparency of learning processes becomes better through the on-line analysis of activities and patterns of interaction. Which students are active and which one passive? Who collaborates with whom? Who brings new ideas and who only responds? What are processes behind learning outcomes?

Learning to learn and metacognitive development

ICT makes it also possible to teach and learn how to learn. Learning problems and collaboration problems become more visible (see 4). Students see how they are learning and how their approach differs from that of other students. Through feedback and reflection on learning processes metacognitive awareness can be increased and learning competences can be monitored and developed. Teacher feedback as well as peer-feedback on learning is the motors for these kinds of higher order learning.

Focus on competences

Competence based education needs ICT as a base where all information about the progress in competence development is collected. There can be a competence matrix with an overview of all competences as described in vocational or professional job profiles with explanation of the reasons why these are important, the behavioural criteria that show that one acquired the competences and with ways to learn. In electronic portfolios students bring their progress reports, their evidence and their results and products together. They can make a show dossier for specific purposes (job-application, CV, entrance in new education). Electronic assessment, peer-assessment and self-assessment.

Increasing flexibility

Through ICT it becomes possible to increase the flexibility of learning.

- Independent of time and place.
- Differences in prior knowledge.
- Variation in regulation: teacher regulation, student regulation and shared regulation.
- Variation according to learning.

One particularly important development is computer (CSCL) supported collaborative learning. CSCL is important for the learning economy because students learn to construct new products, to build knowledge together. In this way they learn to be part of innovation and research. The introduction of CSCL in classrooms, however, asks for a fundamental change in the curriculum and is in no way an easy process. See for further information about CSCL Ligorio's chapter in this book.

A main conclusion from several projects is that the way research projects are designed are not favourable for innovation and commitment of teachers and schools. Kollias and Kikis treat this topic in their chapter in this book in detail.

ICT and complex learning environments in and between organisations

Research on the position of training and development departments in companies and the relations between schools and companies (Sloane, 2002) concluded that it is important to run projects that combine input from organisations and from the educational context. Training and development departments have a marginal role in many companies. They find it hard to integrate their activities in the company. Researchers and the Knowledge Fora they take with them are used to strengthen this position. As long as the researchers are present this works, but when they leave the process stops. Schools and enterprises tend to ignore each other while they are responsible for education and training collaboratively in the dual system. In one project the researchers organised focus groups to discuss the collaboration between schools and enterprises. Here people acquainted themselves with each other and with the software. In learning to use the Knowledge Forum together, they also learned to cooperate. It is important not to focus on the ICT alone. People will not start to cooperate through technology alone. When they did not cooperate before, they will not do it through ICT. Thus, it is important to start cooperating first and then start to use ICT. An important conclusion of the research was that it is important to run projects together: A project-based organisation seems the best way to collaborate. Another conclusion is that student/workers are much better in working with the Fora then the trainers and educators. The benefits of the collaboration are especially in the knowledge development, not in other kinds of rewards like money. Therefore the time and costs play inhibiting roles.

What are characteristics of ICT related powerful complex learning environments? Sloane (2002) stressed the possibility an environment offers to act in a surrounding. Learning is happening everywhere, but people are not always learning and changing in desired directions. Change and learning are not always positive. Important is that the learning environment becomes a teaching environment, where change and learning are facilitated into positive directions. Further characteristics of powerful learning environments refer to a) a good fit between what is offered and the needs of the learner and b) focus on (meta-)cognitive strategies. A major problem of some complex ICT based learning environments is that it remains unclear what the aims of learning and teaching are or could be. Main aim should be the contribution to learning to learn.

ICT can tear down barriers between the levels of organisation (the shop floor site, the board room, the shell) and that ICT based knowledge management is an important way to reach that. Moreover ICT can open up the world outside the organisations for the insiders. The German learning areas approach seems to be a promising way of schooling for learning societies. It brings cross-curricular topics within reach. It helps schools to get away from bookkeeping approaches. Moreover, problem based and interdisciplinary approaches seem more suitable for the learning society. New very open curricula help teachers to organise their lessons in new ways.

ICT and the information society

Schienstock (2002) discussed the information society in relation to exclusion risks. Four themes were in focus:

a) Is there a new production model described as the ICT based network organisation? The main conclusion was that there is such a new kind of organisation. It is described in terms of five dimensions that are highly interrelated in a process of co-evolution:

- Technology platform ICT as organisation and communication technology;
- innovation and learning as strategic goals;
- multiskilling, digital and social skills;
- hierarchical de-integration, functional integration and
- trust-based business culture, reciprocal exchange.

The driving forces behind this network organisation are factors like globalisation, deregulation, new opportunities related to complex of knowledge production and innovation as a competitive factor. In the competition game, innovation and learning are related. This asks more reflexive learning. The basic assumption is that people who are able to innovate should be able to reflect on the environment and different ways to act. The network organisation is a structural reflexivity needed for individual reflexive learning.

b) How is the transition from Fordist to network organisations? The assumption is that there is a direct way from Fordist organisations to network organisations. This assumption, however, cannot be upheld. There is no direct way, there are still many not-network organisations and there are different pathways. Moreover, there are many mixed forms in between the two extremes. Partly this occurs because there is no global orientation in more than 50 % of the organisations. Partly, this is because standardisation is not diminishing as might have been expected. Four kinds of organisations are to be discerned: low-tech Fordist, high tech Fordist, low tech network and high tech network.

c) What are the new skill demands?

The new skill demands are not so much ICT skills but more soft skills like social skills, management skills, work orientation skills and virtues like entrepreneurship and reliability. The ICT skills involved are rather simple skills.

d) What are the exclusion risks?

There are especially the 'reflexive losers'. Not ICT is the problem but lack of reflexivity. Slow learners are at risk. They will be transferred to the less demanding jobs without connection to ICT not using the flows of information. A second risk is the individualisation of work. The risks are not with the elderly people or the part-timers as often thought but with the temporary work contracts. The work by outsiders who are not strong networkers becomes vulnerable. Outsourcing, high mobility, downsizing and mergers create the greatest risk and not automatisation per sé.

The main conclusions from the research on the information society are that in the competition game, innovation and learning are related. This asks more reflexive learning. There is no direct way from old organisations to the network organisation. The new skill demands are not so much ICT skills but more soft skills like social skills, management skills, work orientation skills and virtues like entrepreneurship and reliability.

ICT outside of education and work

One idea in the new ways of thinking about learning is that there is a shift from education to learning outside of institutions. More and more people are learning all of their lives (life long learning). Which roles can ICT play in facilitating and sustaining life long learning? More learning takes place in organisations, both profit and non-profit. Workers are learning on the job, mostly rather implicitly. Apart from individual learning, there is also a lot of collective learning (team learning, communities of practice, organisational learning). How is ICT used in these contexts and how are the relations between knowledge management and learning? More and more learning outside of VET can take place through ICT. Distance learning can probably take over some of the new needs for learning. How important can this distance learning be? What kinds of pedagogies should be developed for this?

Especially, a focus on the learning citizen is needed. The concept of citizenship is both a descriptive and a normative concept. It is embedded in membership of a community. It is fragmentary and it shifts over life. It used to relate to sets of duties and rights. It is, however, best seen as a set of cultural and economic practices.

New modes of governance especially from national states ask for new ways of interacting with and consulting of citizens. Prodi sketched a new civil society at both the European, national and regional level, where citizens have more influence than they used to have. The more it is pushed down to lower levels the tighter the time schedules become. We do not know much about the learning of citizenship. The only knowledge is about attempts to teach citizenship in schools. One thing we know is that citizenship learning is located in social practices and takes place over long periods of time. It is not a one-time event, which can be completed. Citizens develop and grow on their own. It is continuing throughout life.

The concept of active citizenship combines the active citizenship with active learning. In a focus group study 69 life interviews were carried out with educational interventors, teachers, community workers, trade union people, etc. The results made clear that active citizenship is not universal and that informal learning is the dominant way to learn it. It is learnt in specific contexts, using biographies and networks. The changing forms of governance create new contexts for learning active citizenship, but governments do not think about the creation of learning opportunities. The contexts have their own internal diversity, meaning that culture is shaping the learning of active citizenship. Very important is the result that unequal access to contexts shapes active citizenship differently for subgroups of citizens. Key issues refer to the way to the methodology to study informal learning (through life interviews) and interventions for informal learning.

ICT can have a role in the learning of active citizenship, but we do not know much about it. Virtual communities exist and can perhaps become more important now it is easier technically. Furthermore, we need to develop ICT learning materials and games as well as exercises. The relation to new forms of governance is important. Especially, the internet (websites) brings new ways to intervene. Multifunctional ICT tools can be used for learning active citizenship (like in Finland). Access to information is an important aspect. Access to information seems to be gender and power related. Therefore technology should be given to the people.

ICT and collective learning

In all three contexts discussed so far (education, work and life) there is a growing interest in collective learning. There are different variants of collective learning. These should be discerned conceptually from each other and from individual kinds of learning, because especially the collective ones are difficult for people to conceptualise. Some people think, for instance, that they are learning collectively when they are just involved in teamwork or a network. Learning as a team or network is, however, not the same as learning in a team or network. Some people believe that organisations and teams cannot learn because only individuals can learn. When these kinds of confusion occur, people fail to organise the possible, more explicit collective outcomes. Sometimes, people undergo or undertake learning together, but without any actual or intended collective outcomes. Then the learning processes are collective, but the learning outcomes may be only individual ones. In other cases, however, actual or intended outcomes of learning (in terms of learning and/or in terms of changes in work processes or outcomes) are collective. Thus there is a distinction between learning in social interactions (with and from others) and collective learning (where the members consciously strive for common (learning and/or working) outcomes). These forms of collective learning are also called 'group learning' and 'organisational learning' We prefer to use the term 'collective learning' for ways of learning where the intended outcomes (and maybe, but not necessarily, the processes of learning) are collective. How can one make the step from individual outcomes to collective outcomes? We think that there are three answers to this question: (a) When groups or organisations reflect upon the common implicit outcomes of learning, (b) when they reflect on or plan common explicit learning outcomes and (c) when they define common plans for externalisation in the group or the organisation.

Next we will discuss three types of collective learning in more detail: Learning in networks, learning in teams, and learning in communities. After that we focus on the possible roles of ICT in facilitating collective learning.

Learning in networks

Learning in (social) networks is the most loosely form of collective learning. People in a network share a common interest, exchange ideas, and help each other. People call on each other when they have a problem to solve or something to offer (Dekker & Kingma, 1999). The people in a network participate voluntarily and have a great deal of personal freedom. Although individuals within the network frequently meet person-to-person, the whole network rarely meets (McDermott, 1999). Networks facilitate individual collaboration and leave it to the individuals to determine the content and form of knowledge sharing (Walton, 1999).

Learning in teams

Where networks are loosely coupled, teams have a more structured pattern. Collective learning in teams is task oriented. Where people in a network contact each other to solve a work related problem, teams are initiated or created around a certain task or problem that has to be solved. Characteristic of learning in teams is the temporary nature of teams. They are established for a certain task, when this is completed the team breaks up. When thinking of learning in teams a distinction must be made between working teams (organisation related collective learning) and learning teams (professional related collective learning). The learning that goes on in working teams is implicit but more and more recognized as an important asset for the organization (Nonaka & Takeuchi, 1997; Engeström, 1999a; 1999b; Eraut, 2000).

The learning in working teams remains not only implicit; a working team itself can also be temporary. Instead of being part of a stable working team, the combinations of people collaborating to perform a task may change constantly. Yet in their basic pattern, they are continuously repeated (Engeström, 1999b). Engeström recognizes the temporary notion of working teams and suggest the concept of knotworking to capture the innovative and creative nature of team learning. Knotworking suggests a longitudinal process in which knots are formed, dissolved, and reformed. The notion of a knot refers to rapidly pulsating, distributed and partially improvised orchestration of collaborative performance. Engeström therefore suggests that the knot itself should be the focus of attention.

The intention to learn within a learning team is different from a working team. A learning team is formed to explicitly study a certain task or problem. The members of a learning team organise meetings and make agreements on how to complete the task. Huczynski & Buchanan (2001) speak in this context about project teams. According to them a project team consists of individuals who have been brought together for a limited period of time (from different parts of the organization) to contribute towards a specified task. Once this has been completed, the team is either disbanded or else its members are given new assignments.

Project teams are created when:

- Creative problem solving is required involving the application of different types of specialized knowledge;
- there is a need to closely co-ordinate the work on a specific project.

The project teams are overlaid upon the existing functional structure of the organisation, and hence are an addition to it.

Learning teams in sum have the following characteristics:

- Representative: They are representative in that their individual members usually retain their position back in their 'home' functional department.
- Temporary: They have a finite life, even if their end is years in the future.
- Innovation: They are established to solve non-conventional problems and meet challenging performance standards.

Learning in communities

Teams are, as we just mentioned, created to solve a predefined problem. Communities are emergent (Brown & Duguid, 1991). Their shape and membership emerges in the process of activity, as opposed to being created to carry out a task. Communities emerge around a topic of interest shared by voluntary members. According to Ackroyd and Thompson (1999) groups organize themselves around shared interests, through establishing autonomy by defining what their community is about and creating boundaries, and by establishing identities (individual identities through group membership and group identity by which groups can be distinct from each other). Barth (1981) argues that a group can be described in terms of how members imagine the community's boundaries. Some are core members; others participate more peripherally (Wenger, 1999).

In communities the intention to learn is based upon individuals who have a certain learning goal for themselves but come together to learn as a group to help out each other. They share insights and negotiate and create knowledge together. Over time a sense of belonging to arises between the participants. Membership to a community is voluntary and people stay a member as long as they are interested in the theme that is discussed within the community. In this article we focus on the emergence of communities in two fore mentioned different contexts. One is situated in a professional context; the other draws its attention on an organisational setting. When we speak of the professional context we refer to communities of learners. In work settings we refer to communities of practice.

First we will discuss communities of learners. According to Brown and Campione (1994) a learning community is a pedagogical model that is designed to take advantage of the distributed expertise and cognitive diversity. The approach is focused on adopting the goals, values, beliefs, and forms of discourse characteristic to scientific practice. Conceptual advancement is made by cultivating each member's own expertise. The participants engage in a self-regulated and collaboratively inquiry being responsible for the task as a group. The participants are apprentice learners, learning how to think and reason in a variety of domains. In a community of learners they try to foster supporting overlapping zones of proximal development that stimulates growth through mutual appropriation and negotiated meaning.

In the context of learning in work practice the term communities of practice is used (Brown & Duguid, 1991; Wenger, 1998; 1999). In a community of practice, participants, who share a common interest for the field they work in, come together to help out each other, solve problems, and share and create knowledge collaboratively.

A community of practice therefore is a group of people informally bound by a shared practice related to a set of problems [...] they typically solve problems, discuss insights, share information, talk about their lives, and ambitions, mentor and coach on each other, make plans for community activities, and develop tools and frameworks that become part of the common knowledge of the community. Over time these mutual interactions and relationships build up a shared body of knowledge and a sense of identity. They constitute an informal, social structure initiated by members and reflecting on their collective learning (Wenger, 1999, p. 4).

A community of practice defines itself along three dimensions (Wenger, 1998; 1999):

- *What it is about* – A joint enterprise as understood and continually renegotiated by its members.
- *How it functions* – Mutual engagement that bind members together into a social entity.
- *What capability it has produced* – The shared repertoire of communal recourses (routines, sensibilities, artefacts, vocabulary, styles, etc) that members have developed over time.

The role of ICT in collective learning

How can this collective learning be stimulated and supported within organizations through ICT?

a) ICT has an advantage in bringing people together without time and place constraints. Organisations nowadays make use of knowledge management systems, stimulating its workers to share and create knowledge. Brown & Duguid (2000) argue in their book 'The social life of information' for more attention for the contextual and social processes that are present while using certain ICT-tools, focussing on the group dynamics that are needed to organise and coordinate learning and to support the clarification and the aim of the discourse by providing insight in how knowledge is created.

b) Tools like groupware applications play an important role in bringing people together and offer a platform through which collectives communicate, share information and learn. More and more organizations make use of knowledge management systems, which are not only designed to retrieve knowledge from databases, also possibilities are offered to discuss and update this knowledge-based upon new experiences by their employers. In modern organizations, workers are stimulated to share and develop knowledge together.

c) Are many different ICT-tools available for this purpose, we argue however that for learning it is important is to focus the attention on how to organize and support learning independent from which tool is being used. Groupware applications offer the possibility for a shared workspace, but do not seem to provide enough support for the group to regulate their own learning activities, argue that members in a networked environment are not able to work productively with knowledge alone, but need a lot of pedagogical guidance and expert modelling. For online communities of practice to become used to share knowledge, deepening their own and common understanding and creating further insights, it seems to be crucial for them to be able to coordinate, clarify and regulate the discourse themselves.

d) De Laat and Simons (2002) propose two kinds of support. The first type of support derives from a content driven perspective by introducing a discourse model, the latter from a group dynamics perspective by assigning roles to the members of the community. These two kinds of support can be used separately but also in combination as they can strengthen each other.

e) They introduce the model of progressive inquiry in order to clarify the content and the aim of the discourse. This model developed by Hakkarainen (1998) addresses the way knowledge is created in scientific communities. Progressive inquiry engages members of the community in a step-by-step process of question- and explanation driven inquiry. An important distinction (or addition) with other problem solving cycles is the emphasis on the development of shared expertise. Making use of the distributed expertise of the community members, the aim of this model is to support the collaboratively problem solving process resulting in a shared understanding.

The successive elements of progressive inquiry are:

Creating the context. To be able to explore the problem more deeply, members have to get familiar with it. A context needs to be created to clarify why the issues in question are relevant and worthwhile to investigate (Hakkarainen, 1998). This way the community develops a body of understanding that serves as an anchor for the formulation of the problem statement or research question.

Setting up research questions. The next step is to set up questions that guide the process of inquiry. Scientific inquiry can be seen as a problem solving process. Initial questions guide and direct the search for information.

Constructing working theories. Once the community has agreed on an initial research question, the members are invited to construct their own interpretation. Construction of personal working theories guides the participants to use their background knowledge to offer an explanation for the problem. A first knowledge base of the communities understanding of the problem is being created.

Critical evaluation. This knowledge base or inventory of distributed expertise needs to be evaluated. Critical evaluation is important to assess advancement in the theories or explanations being offered. Through evaluating whether and how well the working theories explain the chosen problems, the community seeks to assess strengths and weaknesses of different explanations and identify contradictory explanations, gaps of knowledge.

Searching deepening knowledge. Considerable advancement of inquiry cannot be made without obtaining new information. By examining prior problem statements or working theories with the help of new information, the community may become aware of their inadequate presuppositions. New information may help them to reconstruct their conceptual understanding of the problem.

Engagement in deepening inquiry. Progressive inquiry is a process of further refinement; at first the community has a broad conception of the problem that leads to general questions. After inventory of prior knowledge and searching for new information more specific questions emerge. Advancement in inquiry is captured by examining a chain of (deepening) questions.

Constructing new working theories. By finding answers to subordinate questions, the community approaches step-by-step toward answering the initial question or problem statement.

Shared expertise. All the above-mentioned elements of this model will be performed and shared by all the community members. Cognitive research indicates that advancement of inquiry can be substantially elicited by relying on socially distributed cognitive resources, and collaborative efforts to advance shared understanding and expertise (Hakkarainen, 1998)

Introducing this model of progressive inquiry offers support to structure and regulate the learning activities of the participants.

f) In the second type of support, several roles are introduced to stimulate interdependence and collaboration (Johnson & Johnson, 1999; Forsyth, 1999). The roles are: Chairman, process evaluator, content evaluator, log keeper, and technical support. These roles offer the community some support in how to organize collaborative learning and to reflect on their problem solving, collaboration and shared expertise. The person who is assigned to a certain role does not necessarily have to carry out all the tasks by him or her self. Tasks can be delegated to other members in the community; most important is that people feel (or can be addressed to) the responsibility to keep the discussion alive and towards the desirable direction.

Recommendations

1) ICT within education should prepare students for the kinds of learning that are needed in organisations, life long learning and society.
2) ICT within education should also focus on competencies needed in the learning economy/learning society.
3) ICT within education could help to facilitate and promote social learning according to the participation metaphor.
4) Priorities for ICT in education should focus on digital pedagogy, focussing on 7 principles: Relating, creating, extending the audience, increasing the transparency of learning, thinning and collaboration, learning to learn, focus on competences and increasing flexibility.
5) ICT for work organisations should focus on project based collaboration between education and work as well as on complex learning environments connected to learning by doing in the workplace.
6) For the further development of network organisations learning and knowledge management and innovation should become connected.
7) ICT learning programs for network organisations should focus on soft skills and not on ICT skills.

8) ICT programmes and tools should become available to help the learning citizen develop and to prevent exclusion.
9) Pedagogical support models that can help communities to develop and continue to exist need to be developed and studied.

References

Ackroyd, S. & Thompson, P. (1999) *Organizational Misbehaviour*. London: Sage.

Barth, F. (1981) *Process and Form in Social Life*. London: Routhledge & Kegan Paul.

Bereiter, C. (2002) *Education and Mind in the Knowledge Age*. Hillsdale: Erlbaum. http:// csile.oise.utoronto.ca/edmind/edmind.html

Brown, A. & Campione, J. (1994) 'Guided Discovery in a community of learners'. In K. Mc Gilly (eds) *Classroom Lessons: Integrating Cognitive Theory and Classroom Practice*. Cambridge: Bradford books.

Brown, J.S. & Duguid, P. (1991) 'Organizational learning and communities of practice: Toward a unified view of working, learning, and innovation'. *Organizational Science*, Vol. 2(1), pp. 40-57.

Brown, J. S. & Duguid, P. (2000) *The Social Life of Information*. Boston: Harvard business school press.

Dekker, J. M. & Kingma, J. (1999) 'Managen van leernetwerken'. In J. M. Dekker (eds) *Netwerkend Leren; Opleiders in Organisaties: Capita Selecta Vol. 38*. Decentre: Kluwer.

De Laat, M. F. & Simons, P. R. J. (2002) 'Collective learning: Theoretical perspectives and ways to support networked learning'. *European Journal for Vocational Training*, Vol. 27(3), pp. 13-24.

Engeström, Y. (1999a) 'Innovative learning in work teams: Analyzing cycles of knowledge creation in practice'. In Y. Engeström, R. Miettinen & R. Punamaki (eds) *Perspectives on Activity Theory*. Cambridge: University press.

Engeström, Y. (1999b) *Expansive Learning in Interorganizational Contact Zones*. Helsinki: Centre for activity theory and developmental work research.

Eraut, M. (2000) 'Non-formal learning, implicit learning and tacit knowledge in professional work'. *British Journal of Educational Psychology,* Vol. 70 (1), pp. 113-136.

Forsyth, D. R. (1999) *Group Dynamics*. Belmont: Brooks/Cole-Wadsworth.

Hakkarainen, K. (1998) *Epistemology of Inquiry and Computer-supported Collaborative Learning*. Ph.D. thesis. University of Toronto.

Huczynski, A. & Buchanan, D. (2001) *Organizational Behaviour: An Introductory Text*. London: Pearson education.

Johnson, D.W. & Johnson, R.T. (1999) *Learning Together and Alone: Cooperative, Competitive and Individualistic Learning*. Boston: Allyon and Bacon.

McDermott, R. (1999) *Building Communities of Practice*. Cambridge: Social Capital Group.

Nonaka, I. & Takeuchi, H. (1997) *De Kenniscreerende Onderneming: Hoe Japanse Bedrijven Innovatieprocessen in Gang Zetten*. Schiedam: Scriptum.

Schienstock, G. (2002) Contribution to the domain 2 workshop of the Learning Economy project. Crete, May 24-26.

Sfard, A. (1998) 'On two metaphors for learning and the dangers of choosing just one'. *Educational researcher*, Vol. 27(2), 4-13.

Simons, P.R.J. (2003) 'Eindelijk aandacht voor de didactiek van e-learning!' *HRD Thema,* Vol. 4, No. 3. Deventer: Kluwer. 18-26.

Sloane, P. (2002) Contribution to the domain 2 workshop of the Learning Economy project. Crete, May 24-26.

Tommassini, M. (2002) Contribution to the domain 2 workshop of the Learning Economy project. Crete, May 24-26.

Walton, J. (1999). *Strategic Human Resource Development*. London: Prentice Hall.

Wenger, E. (1998) *Communities of Practice: Learning, Meaning and Identity*. Cambridge, (Mass.): Cambridge University Press.

Wenger, E. (1998) 'Communities of practice: learning as a social system'. *The Systems Thinker*, Vol. 9, No. 5.

CHAPTER TEN

CSCL Contributions to the
E-Learning Economy

M. BEATRICE LIGORIO

Computer Supported Collaborative Learning (CSCL) has gathered a broad range of experiences that made it possible to give guide-lines for the implementation of E-learning economy in educational contexts. CSCL has been strongly encouraged also by the European Commission that funded several projects. Some of them had a fairly large size: Many countries involved with large number of students, teachers and researchers, applications to different school domains and topics, use of different types of software. This chapter will review three of those European projects considered as best practices: CL_Net, Euroland, and Itcole.

Some relevant aspects are highlighted: The specific effects on students' thinking and learning strategies, teachers' needs, the relevance of the local contexts, the effects on the identity, the new skills required not only to students and teachers but also to researchers and academics.

Finally, the CSCL contribution to E-learning economy is summarized into the following guidelines: a) Using single site's diversity as a resource; b) classrooms forming new blended learning contexts; c) CSCL should help E-learning to move from a 'knowledge building' to a 'knowledge creation' society.

Introduction

CSCL is the innovative branch of the more traditional ICT stream of research. This new branch originated from the need to use computers as tools and artifacts to sustain particular forms of learning, such as collaborative learning and metacognitive development within a community of learners. The advantages of collaborative learning over individual learning are broadly acknowledged. The term 'collaborative learning' refers to a general method of working, where learners at various performance levels, work together in groups of different size toward a common goal. Every individual is responsible for one another's learning as well as their own. Thus, the success of one student helps other students to be successful.

Supporters of collaborative learning claim that the active exchange of ideas within groups not only increases interest among the participants but also promotes critical thinking. According to Johnson and Johnson (1986), there is persuasive evidence that cooperative teams achieve at higher levels of thought and retain information longer than students who work quietly as individuals. The shared learning gives students an opportunity to engage in discussions, take responsibility for their own learning, and thus become critical thinkers (Totten, Sills, Digby, Russ, 1991).

Slavin (1990) points out that collaborative learning enhances learners' motivation because:

- It leads to success which in turn increases student views of their own self-efficacy;
- students enjoy being in cooperative classes;
- students in cooperative learning situations like their classmates and are liked by them;
- students working cooperatively become more cooperative and strengthen their own interpersonal skills.

In general, we can say that collaborative learning (or cooperative learning, as Slavin preferred to say) intertwines the cognitive and social aspects of learning. In this way learning is no longer an individual fact but highly involves the group and the context where the learning occurs. The main and more convincing reason for not considering learning as an individual event is a change in views: Learning is no longer seen as reproduction of knowledge only. Instead, new views of learning emphasize deeper processing of knowledge. The typical occasion for reproducing knowledge is when novices are exposed to experts who transmit knowledge or when learning is based on individual work (reading text-books or performing some tasks). But there are many more occasions where learning occurs, and in particular when people interact to exchange information, solve problems, gather new ideas. In this sense learning exceeds the reproduction of knowledge and reaches an active and collaborative knowledge building.

By moving the focus to the social context, also the artifacts used to promote collaborative learning became important. In particular, tools that enhance communication and interaction, the two factors underling the social dimension of learning, can promote collaborative learning. CSCL has as main object the study of all kinds of situations where technology covers the role of an artifact promoting collaborative learning. As Lipponen (2002) has clearly noted, within the CSCL framework there are many different controversial aspects and different interpretations of the empirical evidence available. For example, studies differ in terms of the size of the sample, the duration of the research, the topic and task students work on, the unit of the analysis (ranging from students dyads to the entire classroom or even larger community). Even with those unsolved diversities, or maybe thanks to them, CSCL contributes to the enhancement of the understanding of collaborative learning at least in two ways:

• By providing new occasions for more sophisticated learning: new and higher processes of thinking, reasoning, and interaction can be activated when technology is an active part of the learning scenario;
• by fostering the design of technology deliberately aiming to support collaborative learning. As consequence better interfaces and better functionalities are designed.

Using these particular perspectives, CSCL has today gathered enough experiences, data, and reflections that it can give valuable contributions to better understand and implement the E-Learning economy.

Review of some CSCL best practice

In order to add evidence to the statement that CSCL research results can improve E-learning, three European projects will be briefly reported. The three projects are selected on the basis of different criteria:

– Each of these projects has a fairly large size in terms of students, teachers, researchers, and schools sites involved,
– all of them have a cross-national nature, which is considered as one of the strongest added value of using E-learning,
– all the activities undertaken during these projects are different regarding the educational nature of the tasks as well as the work methodologies used in the classrooms and on-line,
– even if each project aims at impacting the cognitive, meta-cognitive, social, and cultural nature of the results gathered, the contribution of the platforms is always analyzed in terms of dynamic processes.

The three projects described in the following are already finished and the many analyses performed allow us to consider them as best practices in the field of CSCL. Furthermore, the lesson learnt from these research offers some suggestions about how E-Learning can profit from the CSCL experience.

Cl_Net

Cl_Net (Computer Supported Collaborative Learning Networks) is a two-year project funded in 1998 by the European Commission under the TSER fourth framework program. The main objective of this project was to compare different computer-supported collaborative learning networks (CLNs) looking for advantages and obstacles when implemented in real education contexts. The central question of the project was: How can effective knowledge building in CLN's be supported in European primary and secondary education? Five European countries were involved (Belgium, Finland, Greece, Italy, The Netherlands) with almost 600 students from primary school (age 10-12), secondary (age 13-16) and vocational education (age 18-24), together with 25 teachers from 20 schools. Different types of technological settings were used and compared (Van der Meijden, Simons, De Jong, 2000).

The technological platform used by the participating sites differed as to (a) content, (b) curriculum, and (c) target group characteristics. For example, WorkMates is a common tool for information delivery and communication, used by the research group for the exchange of documents and project-bound information. Our World—a data base for classifying environmental data—, Discovery Your Town—a multimedia game to learn about the Middle Age—, and Our Castle—a web-site to build an hypertext—(all used by the Italian sites) are instances of highly content oriented and multimedia software, referring to both different groups of children and specific curriculum content. Computer Supported Intentional Environment (CSILE) and Knowledge Forum (KF) (Scardamalia and Bereiter, 1994) are discussion forums consistent with the notion of 'co-construction' of knowledge, using very open software to support cooperation and collaboration in many subject-matter domains, like arithmetic and literacy. The quality of the software highly depends upon the quality of both the information put into the database and the concomitant support offered by teachers and peers.

This project produced two types of results:

- Cases studies. Eight different case studies where carried out within the Cl_Net project.

From this type of data it is visible how different each local setting could be in terms of school structure and culture, teachers' attitude and training, general impact of the school on the society, etc. All these diversities allow reflecting upon the not homogeneous state of the European education under the institutional point view. In fact, if the theoretical background of the project (primacy of collaborative learning over individual learning, socio-constructivism approach, CSCL framework) could be shared (with different degrees of difficulty) by all the countries involved, the implementation was very sensitive to local factors such as curriculum structure, timetable, general organization of the school, and teachers' attitude toward technology. All these factors strongly impact reasons for successes or failure of the CSCL implementation in the classroom. For example, better results were often gathered when teachers were more willing to introduce innovation into their classroom and when the whole school (the principal and the colleagues) was willing to contribute to the project.

- Comparative results. Three kinds of common measurement instruments were used by all the sites:

1) Protocols of communications among students and between students and teachers were saved and analyzed;
2) small questionnaires and interviews to teachers and students were used to find out what tools, support structures, and manuals functioned the best;
3) tests that measure the cognitive, metacognitive, and motivational effects of CLN's were designed and administrated.

Especially the third type of instruments allows to generalize some of the results obtained, since they were administrated in all the sites as pre and post test. In particular, consistent evidence was found suggesting that during the course of the project many students showed less emphasis in superficial engagement and more interest in real collaboration. Motivation increased in almost all test sites. The findings gained from the different test-sites where cognitive effects were measured and reported, show significant advantages of introducing CSCL in classrooms. An improvement of the score was obtained by the students participating and answering to standardized test scores for curricular domains, such as language and mathematics as well as process-oriented measures, like quality of question-raising, and depth of explanation.

Interesting findings come out from the analysis of the metacognitive questionnaire, especially in those sites where the project lasted the whole academic year. The questionnaire was composed by open-ended questions inquiring three types of metacognitive aspects:

a) Knowledge source perception: the knowledge sources quoted in the answers could be totally external (books, teachers, media), internal (my own thoughts and reflection), or mixed (both internal and external);
b) monitoring of the comprehension and achievement of the learning process. Again, the monitoring could be external, internal, or mixed;
c) communication perception that could vary from not relevant at all to an essential part of the learning process.

In particular, the second question ('How do you know you really understand something?'), inquiring the monitoring strategy, and the third question ('Do you think it is useful to communicate with the others? Why?'), about the communication process, show interesting results. Students initially delegated others the monitoring of their own learning process and the exposition to CSCL activities fosters a development of self-regulated learning, which is considered one of the fundamental skills to acquire in order to achieve higher types of learning (Kulh & Kraska, 1989; Van Hout-Wolters, Simons, Volet, 2000).

Typical answers collected at the out-set of the project were:

'I know I really understood something when the teacher gives me a good score';
'I know I understood when the teacher tells me so'.
At the end of the project there is a significant increase, recorded in many sites, of answers of the second and third type (internal and mixed monitoring):
'I really understand something when I can figure it out and I can summarize it in my mind';
'I can understand whether I really understood it, then I compare my considerations with that of other friends'.

Students develop also a more sophisticated sense of what communication is. At the pre-test many students do not recognize the value of communicating with others and when they think it is useful, the advantage of communication is restricted to information accumulation or to generic social reasons. In this sense the most representative answers are the following:

'Because it may be that the others know more stuff that I know, and talking to them I can exchange information. In this way we can accumulate a lot of information';
'Because it is nice, funny, and you may find new friends'.
At the post-test we found the following types of answers:
'It is only by communicating with others that one knows to know something';
'Because by explaining to the other what I know I can learn more';
'You can get into the discourse more in depth and you can better understand when information is not necessary and when it is needed; what you must say and what can be omitted'.

Communication is definitively an occasion to learn and to better organize what has already been learnt, in other words communication is fully entitled to be considered as part of the metacognitive process.

In synthesis, we can say that by introducing the Cl_Net project into schools it became clear that we introduced three types of innovations at the same time:

a)   The didactic of collaborative and cooperative learning: collaboration was not always easy to implement (regardless the use of the computer) and it depended on many factors;
b)   learning with computers: computers could provoke a specific type of learning, especially involving metacognitive skills;
c)   knowledge building: to implement this educational radical changes are required in the organization of the classroom as well as in the teachers' role.

Euroland

Euroland is one-year project funded in the 1999 by 'Training and Mobility of Researchers' (TMR) Marie Curie Research Training Grants. The project sought a strong collaboration between Italy and The Netherlands. Seven schools were involved, ranging from primary to high school. A total of 268 students, 13 teachers and a cross-national research group composed of 8 researchers participated very actively. Two of these researchers acted as tutors on-line always connected during the weekly synchronous meeting scheduled. The aim of this project was to sustain and develop a virtual community that would be able to integrate activities on-line (both synchronous and asynchronous) with activities in the classrooms.

The virtual community populated a learning environment composed of a three-dimensional virtual world, created with Active Worlds (AW) (www.activeworlds.com) combined with Web Knowledge Forum, designed by Scardamalia and Beretier (1994).

AW is desktop, internet-based, user-oriented software and it belongs to the non-immersive type of virtual reality. Within the virtual worlds built with AW, users can walk through, navigate, and fly over three-dimensional (3D) objects. The presence of a user is made visible thanks to 'Avatars' which are animated 3D objects that may range from a puppet to a penguin or some other animal. AW supports mainly synchronous communication via text-based chat, visual Avatars, and 3D objects interactions and manipulation. The integration of AW with KF is easy under the technical point of view: it is enough to build a 3D object with an active link to KF. The figure here below shows how AW and KF look like when running together.

FIGURE 1: The computer screen as it appears when AW and KF are running at the same time

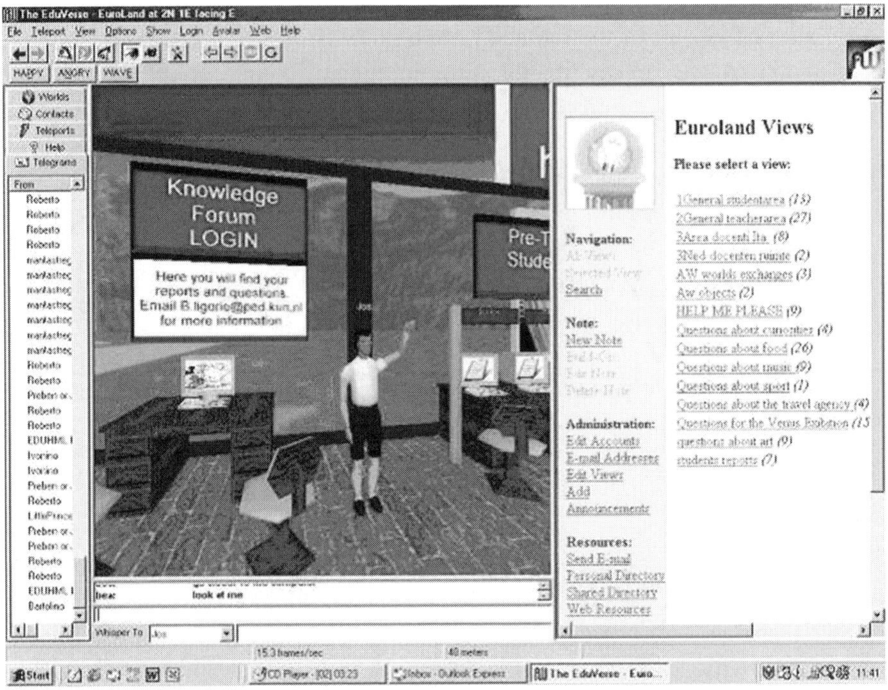

With this type of integration a complex and rich environment was obtained where different types of communication were possible: text-based (chat and forum) versus visual (the 3D objects of AW); and synchronous (the AW chat) versus asynchronous (the forum). This mix allowed fulfilling different types of needs and fostering the participation of people with different capabilities and competencies.

The final result of this project was a virtual world full of houses with educational content, developed by the students themselves. In particular it was possible to distinguish:

• Cultural houses: A house of music, art, food, sport, and a travel agency. The construction of these houses was based on subject-matter issues. Since these houses were considered as the most relevant under the curricula point of view, the researchers forced students to use collaborative learning strategies, not only while working into the classroom but also when working at a distance. The group in charge of a specific cultural house had to build the house of the partner country. Therefore, Italians had to build the house of Dutch music, art, food, and sport, while Dutch students were taking charge of the Italians houses. In this way each group was positively and genuinely interdependent (Salomon, 1998) to the partner at a distance, since they were not simply those to show the final products but competence and expert sources of information, which could be involved in all the phases of the project, from the planning to the decoration of the houses.

- Individual houses: Houses where each group could represent its own identity. For this type of houses, groups worked mainly by collaborating on the site. The need to show who 'I am' and to familiarize with the other partners by visiting their houses seemed to be a fundamental pre-requisite for triggering a productive collaboration at a distance.
- Social spaces: These are spaces where the community could meet to talk and discuss (for example, the Conference room) or to share relevant information about the project (the Welcome area built by the researchers).

These organization of the space allows to reflect on how a virtual environment should be structured in order to sustain collaboration both in the classrooms and on-line, and how to foster the collective and social dimension and, at the same time, the individual dimension, both necessary to develop efficient collaboration strategies (Slavin, 1990). In this respect, the roles of nicknames and avatars were crucial. Even though each participant makes his/ her own choice, help of other connected users is request during the process of choosing the Avatar to wear.

Of course identities are not confined exclusively to nicknames or avatars. Emotions were very often a central topic of the interaction, both through special symbols called *emoticons*—such as J to smile and L to express sadness – and through the use of just-in-purpose coined words.

Results from the Euroland data analysis proved that

self presentation is context-shaped—the particular social environment allows certain ways to express emotions—, and at the same time context-renewing because new elements introduced by the participants are used afterwards by the experts to label others' identity (Atkinson & Heritage, 1984).

Virtual environments allow playing most of the interactions around unreal identities, based on the type of avatar chosen and on the type of discourse established.

The specific nature of the identities played into the virtual environment needs to get more attention. In fact, all the games around the identities can be great 'control levers' of the learning occurring. The educational nature of this virtual world implies that all the identities, or better the positioning (Harrè & Van Langenhove, 1991), shown and 'built' contribute to the construction of the participants' image of themselves as learners. Telling who we are and who we are able to be as consequence of what we learn is a 'dialogical' game (Hermans, 2001) that makes learning experience strongly connected to the emotional dimension.

The analysis of this project leads also to some points of discussion:

a) Time. The virtual environment was easy to be used under the technical point of view; nevertheless a lot of the time was allocated to train teachers about the educational way of using the virtual environment. The playful dimension given by the availability the chat and 3D objects made the environment looking like an entertainment place and not so much as an educational one. Teachers, but also others, tend, however, to believe that an electronic space for learning and training has to be a serious one and this leads to resist to game like environments such as the ones used in this project. Extra-was needed to prove the educational value of game-like virtual environments.

b) Cross-national value. Although cross-national communication seems to be an exclusive value given by electronic environments, it is not easy to take place in an efficient way. A lot of support was needed from experts and tutors on-line. Students and teachers were often frustrated by the initial not spontaneous interaction, despite the motivation and the excitement of meeting people from another country. The initial inhibition of expressing themselves in other language needed to be overcome.

c) Didactical material. Specific didactical material needed to be developed. Multi-disciplinary and innovative content seemed to be more suitable to electronic environments, but how to develop and integrate this material in the existing curricula?

Itcole

ITCOLE (www.euro-cscl.org/site/itcole) is a two-year project funded by the European Commission within the 5th framework. Four European countries participated by providing many experimental sites, 84 teachers (experienced and novice) and 1.413 students were involved from primary, secondary and university level. Sixty-six local projects were carried out within the main program, some of them were designed as cross-classroom collaboration and others required cross-national collaboration. The main objective of ITCOLE was to design a pedagogically meaningful modular knowledge-building environment, called Synergeia, which supports students' joint efforts, tailored on different European school cultures (Ligorio, Rahikainen, 2003).

Synergeia (http://bscl.gmd.de/bscl2) was developed through two testing phases: Phase 1 was aimed at sharing participating teachers' first impressions on Synergeia and their conceptions of pedagogical principles. Phase 2 provided information about the activities carried out into the classrooms, as well as teachers' and students' during first phase of the project.

Besides quantitative data concerning the number of notes and materials posted on Synergeia, this project used many types of teachers' and students' questionnaires, interviews, and user stories in order to have a clear picture of what students and teachers were experiencing.

The teachers in all four countries expressed the opinion that the use of the electronic learning environment supports collaboration among their students. However, they remarked that students' new knowledge building is a complex process, especially when not explicitly guided by teachers. Furthermore, they concluded that in addition to virtual meetings, face-to-face meetings are necessary for the learning process.

Students report that they collaborated successfully within the project, despite the fact that, according with their teachers, collaboration was not 'natural' for students. This discrepancy was stronger for secondary education than for primary education. Nevertheless, teachers always acknowledged that Synergeia supported collaborative learning in an effective way, because it made the process of collaboration visible to everyone. Their own and others' products and ideas could easily be seen and accessed because posted on the common web platform. However, many teachers claimed that deeper levels of collaboration and shared development of products needed extra teachers' support and guidance. Both students and teachers claimed that they would like to practice collaborative activities more often.

Students reported that they enjoyed collaborating. Many of them improved their feeling of self-respect, due to their contribution to the shared discussions. Working in electronic learning environments stimulated the sense of belonging to a large community, although this was not an automatic process. In order to fully participate to the process of building community, teachers and probably students needed to put in practice novel and original skills.

Two dimensions seemed to influence the teachers' stance relative to this project: a) Teachers' previous experience with CSCL, and b) differences between primary and secondary school teachers (for primary teachers the project was in general more successful).

Successful computer supported collaborative learning projects depend on time and training for teachers: Enough training on both pedagogical and technical aspects, and enough time to 'translate' the project into the classroom. Teachers already experienced with CSCL can dedicate more time and efforts to more complex aspects of the projects, whereas novice teachers need time to get acquainted with new technological skills, pedagogical models, and new processes taking place into their classrooms. Generally, primary school teachers have more time to implement projects, which may explain why they are relatively more successful. Another important factor deals with the novelty, for secondary students, of the collaborative learning paradigm. Pupils in high schools are usually more reluctant when embracing new learning approaches, whereas primary students fell less the 'weight' of traditional education and they may be more open to new learning strategies. The introduction of Computer Supported Collaborative Learning in secondary education could be improved only by reshaping the official curriculum around it and by adopting project-based approaches that reinforces links between different subject-matters and with the extra-school.

Another relevant results coming from the ITCOLE project concerned teachers training. A European-wide discussion forum on computer supported collaborative learning (www.euro-cscl.org) was started within the project with the intention of helping teachers to learn from each other and to form a community of practitioners. Teachers participating to the ITCOLE project play a major role on animating this forum. One of the outcomes of the forum is a set of guidelines for setting up courses for teachers' professional development, concerning CSCL topics.

In conclusion, ITCOLE produced free and open source software, a group of trained teachers, a forum on CSCL, and guidelines for professional development. These are good ingredients for fostering a CSCL movement around Europe. However, this is not enough. What has become clear is that teachers (and students) need time and training to really master CSCL and, furthermore, they are not yet independent (they need researchers and experts support) on planning and accomplishing high quality CSCL projects. The further step expected, based on this experience, is that national educational boards and educational institutions will allocate adequate time and recourses to teachers' CSCL training.

Contributions to the E-learning economy

Learning economy seems to assume that education can be submitted to the same economical laws that apply to any other commercial product. It is also expected that the introduction of internet and intranet technologies into educational contexts will offer tremendous opportunities to bring learning into the mainstream of business.

Based on the results discussed above and gathered by three European best practices of CSCL we can outline the conditions under which this may happen:

• Platforms should be able to support pedagogical theories, in particular collaboration at a distance, knowledge building, reflective thinking, and virtual community building. Electronic platforms will be really used as tool for learning only if, before building technical tools, there is a clear idea of what type of learning should be promoted. This may mean a different location of the economical investment. When e-learning platforms are designed on users' needs, more time and energy is needed at the very initial stage of the planning (usually the biggest investment is at the stage of dissemination and distribution of the platform). Already before starting to design the platform, time and money are needed to build a few bridges: between final users and educational researchers; and between these latter and computer scientists. Mixed competencies may also be needed, such as educators with technical skills, computer scientists specialized in educational software, and users trained in knowing what can be expected from an e-Learning platform.

- Platforms have to be rich and flexible. Although the presence of several tools can cause an initial confusion, we experienced that users enjoy activities where they can use different tools and where the environment can be tailored on individual or group needs. Initially users may not have a clear idea of how to use a new tool, but it is the tool itself, when well designed, that suggests new activities that could not be done without it. Of course, E-Learning platforms should focus mainly on educational activities, although a playful dimension can often foster not intentional learning. In suggesting original and educational activities a fundamental role is also played by the on-line tutoring offered by experts having technical, pedagogical, and communication skills. The final aim of on-line tutoring is to distribute competences among the participants in a way that the tutors will no longer be needed and that the community will be able to tutor itself.

- Pedagogical models should be innovated along with technology. The growing and successful use of e-learning is necessarily going to modify the pedagogical models that initially inspired it. If collaboration at a distance, knowledge building, reflective thinking, and virtual community building proved to be the most valuable educational frameworks within which design and implement e-learning, these models show their limits and weak sides when looking deeper into the results gathered by the best practices. Collaboration is not easy to be achieved, especially when partners with different competencies, languages, cultural backgrounds are involved. Knowledge building appears to be possible only when technical problems are solved and when teachers are enough experienced. Reflective thinking and metacognitive skills are impacted only when projects have a fairly long duration (at least one academic year). Community building should better take in account all the processes through which virtual identities and positioning are formed. Therefore, new pedagogical models are needed, or at least these models should be improved.

Recommendations

Finally an attempt follows here to present some guidelines to improve e-Learning based on CSCL lessons:

- A better understanding of the relationships between local settings and the implicit expectations that participants of e-learning projects have, will converge toward a common model of learning and teaching. An E-learning implementation can be difficult due to the diversity of participants that are often in remote sites. The effort on planning and implementing E-learning does not have to be focused on the reduction of diversity but on using diversity as a resource. Each organisation/site that wants to implement E-learning has to analyse very carefully and in a specific way its own context and find ways to make visible and valuable the specificity of the local site.
- Blended learning. E-learning is not just about using the latest technology in order to replace the classroom. Nor is it about posting content on the Web to be downloaded or read. E-learning provides a new set of tools that can add value to all of the traditional learning modes, from classroom experiences to learning from books. As learning becomes more a 'commercial' product, we have to address the need for more just-in-time and project-based learning, performance support, open and distance learning, expert assistance and a generally greater variety of educational events and experiences.
- Through e-learning experiences, learners can create new knowledge and cultural 'manufactured' objects. This may require a theoretical revision of the idea of a 'knowledge building' society. An e-learning economy needs a culture of knowledge creation based on dialogue and on balance between being part of a community and developing personal and small group identities. Replacing 'building' with 'creation' is not a mere play of words. It is a serious attempt to replace rational/scientific thinking with a way of thinking and being with a central space for intuition, creativity, and ability to think ahead (Runco, Albert, 1990). These skills are soon going to have a commercial and economical value also for training and work places. Standard psychological theories view creativity as arising largely from the unique or extraordinary characteristics of individuals (e.g., mental processes, background knowledge, intellectual style, personality, and motivation), reinforcing social attitudes and beliefs about the folklore of such terms as the lonely genius, brilliant inventor, estranged artist, or ruthless entrepreneur. In fact, however, any creative product emerges from a unique coincidence of individual intellective abilities; the nature and relative sophistication of a scientific, artistic or entrepreneurial domain; the

complexity and structure of the field; and the distribution of power and resources within a group, community or society. E-Learning should provide this type of opportunity by forming new and complex groups and bringing diverse cultures and attitudes into contact with each other. The accent on creativity is a natural consequence of the de-materialization of the modern economy, of the transaction from the industrial to the post-industrial society, where the first is based on information and the latter on the ability to create. This implies that human resources are the more important economical resources.

References

Atkinson, J.M. & Heritage, J. (eds) (1984) *The Structures of Social Action.* Cambridge: Cambridge University Press.

Harrè, R. & Van Langenhove, L. (1991) 'Varieties of positioning'. *Journal for the Theory of Social Behaviour*, Vol. 21, pp. 393-407.

Hermans, H.J.M. (2001) 'The dialogical self: Toward a theory of personal and cultural positioning'. *Culture & Psychology*, Vol. 7 (3), pp. 243-281.

Johnson, R. T. & Johnson, D. W. (1986) 'Action research: Cooperative learning in the science classroom'. *Science and Children*, Vol. 24, pp. 31-32.

Kuhl, J. & Kraska, K. (1989) 'Self-regulation and metamotivation: Conceptual mechanisms, development, and assessment'. In R. Kanjer, P.L. Ackerman & R. Cudeck (eds) *Abilities, Motivation, and Methodology*. Hilssdale, NJ: Erlbaum.

Ligorio, M.B. (2001) 'Integrating communication formats: Synchronous versus asynchronous and text-based versus visual'. *Computers & Education*. Vol. 37(2), pp. 103-125.

Ligorio, M.B. & Rahikainen, M. (2003) Implementing a pedagogically meaningful electronic learning environment in four different European school contexts. Symposium presented at the E.A.R.L.I. Conference, 26-30 August 2003, Padua.

Ligorio, M.B., Alamo, A. & Simons, R.J. (2002) 'Synchronic tutoring of a community on-line'. *Mentoring and Tutoring*, Vol. 10(2), pp. 137-152.

Lipponen, L. (2002) 'Exploring the foundations for computer-supported collaborative learning'. In G. Stahl (eds) Proceedings of CSCL 2002: The Fourth International Conference on Computer-Supported for Collaborative Learning, January 7-11, 2002, Boulder, Colorado (USA).

Runco, M. A. & Albert, R. S. (eds) (1990) *Theories of Creativity.* Newbury Park, CA: Sage

Salomon, G. (1998) 'Novel constructivist learning environments and novel technologies: Some issues to be concerned with'. *Research Dialogues in Learning and Instruction*, Vol.1 (1), pp. 3-12.

Scardamalia, M. & Bereiter, C. (1994) 'Computer support for knowledge-building communities'. *The Journal of the Learning Sciences*, Vol. 3, pp. 265-283.

Slavin, R. (1990) *Cooperative Learning: Theory, Research and Practice.* Englewood Cliffs, NJ: Prentice Hall.

Talamo, A. & Ligorio, M.B. (2001) 'Strategic identity in the cyberspace'. *Journal of CyberPsychology and Behavior*, Vol. 4(1), pp. 109-122.

Totten, S., Sills, T., Digby, A. & Russ, P. (1991). *Cooperative Learning: A Guide to Research.* New York: Garland.

Van der Meijden, H., Simons, R.J. & De Jong, F. (eds) (2000) Computer-supported collaborative learning networks in primary and secondary education. Final Report for the European project CL_Net no 2017 , University of Nijmegen (NL).

Van Hout-Wolters, B., Simons, R.J. & Volet, S. (2000) 'Active learning: self-direct Learning and independent work'. In R.J. Simons, Van Der Linden J. & Duffy T. (eds) *New Learning*. Dordrecht: Kluwer.

Von Krogh, G., Ichijo, K. & Nonaka, I. (2000). *Enabling Knowledge Creation*. Oxford: Oxford University press.

CHAPTER ELEVEN

Developing Synergies among Researchers and Teachers to Support ICT-related School Teaching and Learning Innovations

ANDREAS KOLLIAS AND KATHY KIKIS [1]

Introduction

The overall aim of this paper is to contribute to the strengthening of links, collaboration and the development of shared understanding and action among teachers and researchers in the design, implementation and further utilisation of pedagogic innovations with the use of information and communication technologies (ICTs). The ideas that are discussed here were crystallised in the frame of the Sypredem project [2] and emerged during our involvement in a number of research and development (R&D) projects on ICTs-related innovations in the field of education and training and our collaboration with research institutes, universities, schools, teachers and students from several EU countries. What motivated us most to elaborate on these ideas was our concern about what happens after an R&D project in schools has been formally completed. Will the involved schools, teachers and students continue and extend the ICTs-related innovative practices developed during the project? Will other schools, local and regional school administrators get to know them and, more importantly, will they integrate them in their own school development plans? How the outcomes of ICTs-related effective innovations can inform decision making regarding the integration of ICTs in schools? Such concerns, was not difficult to discover, were shared among researchers and long standing partners in European projects, as well as, teachers and local school administrators with whom we had the chance to collaborate with. What more, there was a shared feeling among researchers and teachers alike that no matter how promising the outcomes of a particular research might be and despite the hard work and dedication of the people involved, ICTs-related innovations implemented during R&D projects have little chances of being sustained let alone diffused at local, regional and, of course, national level.

Not few people would find it justified to respond to the above by blaming teachers for inertia and school education as a bureaucratic and aged institution which is slow to follow the advances in the fields of technology and social science or the breathtaking changes that take place in the wider society and especially in economy and work. It is, for example, quite widespread the belief that despite the theoretical and research efforts accumulated over the last two decades which strongly suggest that constructivistic, experiential and socio-cultural approaches to cognition are much more powerful than behaviouristic models in explaining how people learn, create meaning and understand, school education often appears to rely on frontal teaching and rote learning. Similarly, despite intensive policy making efforts and the implementation of huge funding schemes aimed to equip schools with ICTs and provide teacher training, regular use of ICTs for school teaching and learning is quite rare; it is often limited to a small sub-set of its educational potentials and, quite understandably, has not as yet provided us with clear evidence that all this have actually improved the quality of education. Being rather unconvinced that this is the whole picture we decided to take another, hopefully more constructive, route, trying to identify and investigate factors that play a potentially crucial role in the conductiveness (or, apparently, the lack of conductiveness) of schools to ICTs-related pedagogic innovation. This effort required from us, first of all, to critically reflect upon our own assumptions and practices as researchers and to challenge their relevance to the schools' community. To this end we performed a meta-analysis of the reported research processes and outcomes of recent projects the Education and Training Group at FORTH was involved in, as well as other selected Europe-wide research strongly related to innovative implementations of ICTs in schools. Valuable feedback to our reflective analysis was also provided by fellow researchers and teachers who participated in these projects through their contributions to the Sypredem workshop we organised a year ago. Critical issues identified in this paper are focused on the ways innovations in schools and, in particular, ICTs-related teaching/learning innovations can be conceptualised, implemented and utilised.

Understanding ICTs-related innovations in school teaching and learning

A few years ago, Frade (1998, p.47), reviewing several innovation case studies in education and training in many European Union countries arrived at the conclusion that 'the area that clearly appears as lagging behind is the very core of pedagogy, i.e. the teaching-learning process itself, as innovation efforts have not been very successful in bringing about new teaching-learning methods and functions matching the possibilities of ICT'. Similar concerns are persistently expressed in both sides of the Atlantic. In the USA for example, according to a recent report prepared by PITAC[3] , 'information technology accomplishments in education and training lag those in other areas, whether in research, commerce, or communications. It is hard to find another application area of information technology where the promise-to-performance gap is wider, and some assert the gap is widening' (PITAC, 2001, p.5). In yet another report prepared by The Web-Based Education Commission for the President and the Congress of the United States it is argued that 'schools often use technology to mimic this pattern of a top-down, lecture or text-driven model of instruction. Similarly, we have used the Internet in a narrow fashion, like vast textbooks or lectures online, instead of exploring its interactive potential.' (The Web-Based Education Commission, 2000, p. 59). Recent evaluation reports on the actual use of ICTs for teaching and learning in schools in United Kingdom and the Netherlands, two countries with a long tradition in the implementation of ICTs-related educational policies, express similar concerns. According to a preliminary evaluation report on the NGfL Programme,[4] the largest and most costly single initiative ever to be undertaken by local authorities in the UK, teachers often focus on basic rather than higher-order thinking and reasoning skills (ImpaCT2, 2001, p.14). Another recent preliminary report revealed that innovative ways of integrating ICTs are rare among teachers (NGfL Pathfinders, 2001, p.15). Similarly, a recent government report from the Netherlands admits that 'more didactically innovative use of ICT is still in its infancy' (OCenW, 2002, p.5).

The building of understanding on how innovations may be effectively applied in schools is something more than the compilation of a list of 'factors' that enable or hinder innovations in schools. The production of such a list implies a 'point of view' which often goes unnoticed although it may, as well, be part of the whole problem of how ICTs-related teaching/learning innovations are conceptualised, implemented and diffused in schools. A fist step in developing synergies among researchers and teachers to support ICT-related school teaching and learning innovations is the development of a common ground which both researchers and teachers may find as a relevant and useful starting point. The development of such a common ground is a task that is further necessitated by the great, often misleading, vagueness with which educationalists, practitioners, software designers, policy makers, administrators and researchers talk about such innovations in schools.

The most widely adopted definition of innovation appears to be that offered by Rogers (1995, p. 11) who, almost 40 years ago, suggested that an innovation is an 'idea, practice or object perceived as new by a unit of adoption'. According to Rogers, innovators are the 'early adopters' of the ideas, practices or objects which are perceived as 'new'. Understanding innovation, however, requires first to go beyond 'newness' and seek for the driving forces behind these ideas, practices or objects. Pedagogues and educationalists tend to believe that pedagogic theory formation, scientific inquiry and pedagogy-driven technologies are responsible for the new pedagogic visions, practices and objects that bring newness and innovation in education; however, what makes them relevant and feasible is often not the world of education but economy and technology. Changes in economy and society are, in many respects, an important driving force behind innovations, even school innovations. According to Frade et al (1996, p. 98), innovations seen from wider socio-economic perspective are processes which emerge out of a conflicting interplay between established school learning patrimonies (i.e. prevailing socio-institutional, educational and pedagogic practices, values, dispositions and expectations regarding schooling) and socio-economic trends and policy reforms mainly driven by such trends. At European Union level powerful socio-economic trends and reforms are hugely expressed in the strategic vision of the EU[5] to become most competitive and dynamic knowledge-based economy in the world. The role of innovation in achieving this strategic vision is of paramount importance as it is considered the single most important engine of long-term competitiveness, growth and employment (see EUR, 2001, p.11; COM, 2000, p. 4). This vision has implications for education as it is required to respond to the needs of a knowledge-based society and economy, offering learning and training opportunities tailored to target groups at different stages of their lives and especially young people, unemployed adults and those in employment who are at risk of seeing their skills overtaken by rapid change (Bulletin EU 3-2000). These requirements are of extreme importance as the rapid development of new technologies and the gradual de-regulation of European labour markets - which lead to the virtual disappearance of guaranteed lifetime employment with a single employer - create huge demands for life-long professional learning to increase the employability of individuals. Major European companies, on their turn, believe that the education systems of EU countries do not deliver the attitudes and skills Europe needs for the knowledge economy and push for the acceleration of changes in education and training that would make them more responsive to their own needs as power players in knowledge-based economies. As the ERT[6] Task Force recommended to the 2001 Stockholm European Council summit '…one of the keys to future competitiveness through the knowledge economy will be Europe's ability to equip all of its citizens with the appropriate attitudes, skills and competencies to enable them to be receptive to life long learning and mobile (willing and able to re-train and relocate to new roles in new and emerging enterprises)' (ERT, 2001, p. 4). In parallel, the ERT suggested that 'the current teaching curriculum is not always in line with the broader needs of business, which means that there is an immediate need for an interchange of ideas and collaboration between education providers and the business world.' (o.p.). European Union's strategic eLearning initiative, which aims to adapt European education and training systems to the needs of the knowledge-based society, identifies the development of collaboration between education and the business world as a key element to achieve the eLearning Action Plan. The European eLearning Summit on May 2001 brought together for the first time representatives from the private sector with education experts and public sector officials in a dialogue on developing education and training provision in Europe, emphasizing '… the potential for public-private partnerships (PPPs) to contribute to expansion and innovation in education and training delivery' (eLearning Summit Declaration, 2001, p. 2). These public private partnerships have strategic importance for the implementation of the eLearning Action Plan as '…active private sector participation in eLearning and ongoing dialogue with the public sector is no longer an option but an urgent necessity' (o.p., p. 3). In this context, businesses are invited to contribute not only to the development of reliable high performance computing infrastructures, broadband technologies and other technology equipment but also to be involved in key educational provision areas which in European learning patrimonies were primarily (and for most exclusively) a responsibility of public governments and educationalists. Key areas where businesses are invited to make contributions are the definition of the e-learning pedagogic paradigm (also in relation to classroom teaching), the redefinition of the role of teachers under the emerging e-learning paradigm, the development of content and flexible curricular and assessment frameworks (see o.p.). The eLearning Industry Group (eLIG), an autonomous working group, now consisted of around 40 companies and organizations, was formed as a response to the invitation made by EU aiming to work with the European Commission, national governments and academia to undertake innovative projects to promote e-learning deployment in Europe. In its recent set of recommendations, the eLIG argues that 'deploying the latest technology does not solve a learning need if there is not a sound pedagogical approach associated with it' (eLIG, 2003, p. 4). According to eLIG, this pedagogical approach is related to the new learning paradigm which is in the making and challenges education and educationalists in many respects: 'the transformation of our educational systems—and new opportunities and ways to learn outside of traditional classroom settings—is one of the largest challenges facing Europe today. Teachers, trainers, mentors and subject matter experts will have new roles to play, and they should participate actively in helping other stakeholders understand the implications of eLearning, particularly at primary and secondary school levels' (o.p., p. 5). As is evident for the above, the business world has a strong interest in pedagogic innovations in schools and is not just waiting in the corner for them to happen but actively seeks to raise and define the agenda. Schools and educationalists have already lost a battle as no-one from the world of economy would recognize schools as an example of 'knowledge-based' organizations, although their primary assets are not the school buildings, books or computers but the people (the teachers and the pupils) who work in them and their knowledge creation and learning activities. This is mostly because teachers have to re-invent pedagogic knowledge and solutions counting little on codified effective practices and scientific knowledge on teaching and learning, a problem that is not, as we shall discuss later, solely a problem of teachers' professional practices but also a problem of pedagogues and educational researchers as well. In brief, the dialogue about pedagogic innovation is not (any more) driven by enlightened educationalists, educational researchers and pedagogues who strive to bring their new ideas, practices and products into school life and wider culture. This is even more evident considering the impact of technological advances that took place during the last two decades of the previous century on educational theory and practice. Pedagogic theorists, researchers, practitioners and policy makers in the field of education often found and continue to find themselves in the position to struggle to cope with the pace with which information and communication technologies advance and it appears that it is not the emergence of new pedagogic theories and knowledge but the invention of new technologies that bring this aura of 'newness' to the field of education and training. A first important step for developing synergies among pedagogues, educational researchers and teachers to support ICTs-related school teaching/ learning innovations is then to build shared strategic visions on the role of schools in technology-rich knowledge-based societies and furthermore develop a shared understanding of their own (complementary) roles and responsibilities in shaping the current and future agenda regarding innovations in schools.

A second step would be that of establishing a shared understanding of the relation between theory and praxis, research-based and experience-based knowledge and their relevance to school innovation and change. Pedagogic theorists and researchers were always tempted by the idea that schools and teachers are the recipients of their findings and not partners in a common cause to improve the quality of education; pedagogues and researchers' 'new' ideas, practices or objects were 'always' there for schools and teachers to pick up and use. Discussing, however, the concept of ICTs-related teaching/learning innovations in schools it would be quite useful for both theorists/researchers and teachers to go further than the perceived or actual newness of an ICTs-related teaching/learning theory, knowledge or product (for example the perceived newness of a theory on how ICTs should be used in teaching/learning processes, or of a software product that is designed on the basis of such a theory), to focus on the process of integration of an ICTs-related pedagogic theory, scientific knowledge and/or an ICTs product in the actual school teaching/learning activities, and the outcomes of such an integration. This is because what distinguishes an ICTs invention, a new pedagogic model or new scientific knowledge from a school innovation is the actual integration of the former into a school-related teaching/learning activity. For example, a theory can be considered as innovative within the field of pedagogic theory and research if its application leads to important re-conceptualisations and opens up new research areas but it may not constitute a school innovation exactly because it has not yet been transformed, in one way or another, into school practice. As implied by the above, one can be innovative in school education without engaging in the process of inventing a new ICT tool, or of developing a theory and new scientific knowledge through formal research and development. Teachers can be highly innovative by implementing, for example, existing ICTs tools into their own practice thus transforming both the process and the outcome of teaching and learning. Integration into praxis is important in school innovations but they need something more than that to be considered as innovations per se. School innovation should not be equalled to experimentation that one can engage in to investigate, for example, how an ICT tool or a theory may be applied to school teaching and learning. Experimentation is an integral part of any innovation process but it is not innovation per se because innovation, unlike experimentation, needs to be proved that is effective, i.e. that it leads to the improvement of existing educational/pedagogic practices or that it results to new processes and outcomes of profound educational value.

Defining ICTs-related teaching/learning innovations

Providing a working definition of ICTs-related teaching/learning innovations in schools we suggest that ICTs-related teaching/learning innovations in schools are those activities where innovation agents integrate existing or new ICTs-related pedagogic theories, knowledge, processes and/or products in schools where these theories, knowledge, processes and/or products have never being applied before, leading to evidence-based improvements or desirable changes in the teaching/learning processes and their outcomes. This definition is 'pedagogy-independent', in other words, it is purposefully wide enough to include any potential improvement or desirable change in school teaching/

learning processes and their outcomes with the use of ICTs. However, there is a dominant trend to identify as 'innovations' only those improvements or desirable changes which depart from the traditional, and in many cases traditionally perceived, 'teacher-centred' school ethos. For example, the SITES[m2] project[7], which studied 174 cases of pedagogic innovation with the use of ICTs in 28 countries worldwide, suggested that ICTs-related pedagogic innovations are likely to involve significant changes in the 'traditional' roles of the teachers and students. A large majority of case study reports indicated that the teachers acted as organizers of students' learning activities, students' guides and advisors, and collaborators with other teachers as part of the innovation process, while only in a small minority of innovation case studies teachers also acted as lecturers. On the other hand, students tended to assume the roles of researchers (mainly in information seeking activities), designers or creators of products, publishers and presenters of their work, and collaborators with other students. Furthermore, changes in pedagogy were associated mostly on two patterns of practice, one focused on information management and another on collaborative research (see Kozma, 2003). In two other international projects, the Merlin[8] and Sypredem projects which were particularly focused on the identification of innovative practices with the use of ICTs on the basis of meta-analyses of EU funded R&D projects in education, similar changes in teacher-student roles and patterns of school practice were identified as indicators of pedagogic innovation. Characteristically, teachers in ICTs-related teaching/learning innovations tend to assume the roles of co-learner and collaborator with the students, facilitator, supporter, coordinator and/or guide of students' work, (co)developer of learning materials and software, researcher and life-long learner. On the other side, students' roles in pedagogic innovations tend to converge with these of the teacher. Significant changes on the roles of teacher and students as those described earlier are associated with changes in the patterns of teacher-students' interactions which shift from traditional logo-centric, teacher-oriented interactions towards informal, exploratory and meaning making negotiation discourse, and changes in the organisation of school life towards more flexible time-tables and learning spaces and expansion of school activities to include collaboration with other schools and local communities (Scheuermann et al., 2001, pp. 86-89). Underling these changes are shifts in school knowledge epistemologies which depart from knowledge and truth as possessions of the teacher or as contents of a textbook which have to be transmitted to students, to knowledge and truth as cognitive constructions and socio-cultural experiences which require active students' involvement.

Discussing ICTs-related teaching/learning innovations in schools a distinction needs to be made between the emergence and diffusion of such innovations in schools. Emergence of an innovation is an activity of early integration of ICTs-related pedagogic theories, knowledge, processes and/or products in schools, while diffusion is the gradual adoption of an innovation by more schools at local, regional, national or even international level. Activities where innovations emerge have their own internal logic and structure and their study is essential in order to develop strategies which would enhance ICTs-related teaching/learning innovativeness in schools. On the other hand, while the diffusion capacity of a particular innovation is definitely affected by the processes through which an innovation is implemented, the diffusion of an innovation also crucially depends upon the overall capacity of an educational system to adapt to and absorb ICTs-related teaching/learning innovations. In the following chapter we will narrow our focus on two generic types of innovation emergence activities and their diffusion capacity, also discussing some shared characteristics between the two.

The emergence of ICTs-related teaching/learning innovations in schools: two generic types of innovation activities

While any real-life innovation in quite unique in many respects, we have identified and further discuss two generic types of conducting ICTs-related teaching/learning innovations in schools, the 'Experiential' and the 'Research and Development' (R&D) type. These two types share a number of common characteristics and conditions which will be discussed in the following paragraphs.

Innovations as formal and informal learning activities

The creation of new knowledge, the recombination and transformation of existing knowledge and learning are processes inherent to the emergence of innovations. Knowledge and learning related to innovations can be created well beyond formal research, development and academic practices. Among others, important sources for innovation-related knowledge and learning can be: a) Everyday school teaching and learning with the use of ICTs, b) formal and informal interaction and collaboration with other schools, classrooms, individual teachers and pupils, with parents, local communities, teacher training or R&D institutes, communities of practitioners, etc., c) activities related to the implementation of ICTs into new curriculum areas and extracurricular fields, d) activities related to the implementation of new school or classroom organisational arrangements to support the integration of ICTs into school life, and e) formal and informal professional development activities.

Innovations as value-laden and risky activities

ICTs-related teaching/learning innovations in schools, as any innovation indeed, are inextricably linked with risk taking. This is not merely because it is risky to try out new things but, and perhaps more importantly, because ICTs-related teaching/learning innovations in schools are value laden activities which may challenge individuals, groups, existing organisational practices and institutional structures in many different ways and may create potentially enormous tensions among interested agents and institutions. Innovations may challenge teachers', students' and even parents' or local communities' roles and responsibilities; they may challenge formal or informal/implicit theories on teaching and learning, as well as established and 'routinised' ways of doing things (teaching/learning praxis and research).

At organisational and institutional levels, they may challenge classroom or school management and administration practices, curriculum philosophy, design and implementation, and, further, established teaching/learning traditions, as well as economic and other priorities in education. At societal and cross-cultural levels, they may challenge established dispositions on how young people should be educated and what for, or wider social and economic policies related to education.

Innovations almost never come along 'on their own'

Innovations on the ways teaching and learning are practiced in schools often cannot fully realise to their potential without implementing changes in other dimensions of the school practices and consequently culture. Changes (and even other innovations) well beyond the implementation of new ICTs-related teaching/learning processes may be required which may affect the school plans and priorities and the allocation of responsibilities among the staff, the ways regular classroom and school life is organised or the ways curriculum is delivered. Such changes can be within the powers and capacities of the researchers, teachers or the school board to manage, while others (for example, curriculum reforms which are necessary for some ICTs-related teaching/learning innovations to develop into their full potential), need the implementation of large scale policies. Related to the above is Bateson's (1979) distinction between 'first order' and 'second order' changes. While the former require from people involved to 'learn something new', the latter are about 'learning new ways to learn', which require changes that go deep into the structure of organizations and the very culture of schools.

Innovations often do not require but a few, relatively modest, initial conditions to trigger

Unlike innovations in the field of science and technology which rely upon highly complex and demanding structures (institutional, organisational, economic, technological etc) all dedicated to research and innovation, ICTs-related teaching/learning innovations can trigger not only in traditionally 'innovative', well equipped and highly performing schools but in a wide variety of school contexts. Ely's (1990, 1999) findings regarding 'micro' level conditions that facilitate the implementation of educational technology innovations and the meta-analysis of numerous case studies in the context of the Sypredem project (see Kollias and Kikis, 2002) both indicate that the emergence of ICTs-related teaching/learning innovations often do not require but a few, relatively modest, initial conditions to trigger. What is required is essentially a teacher or a group of teachers, sometimes also involving researchers, who are dissatisfied with current school practices or need to explore the potentials offered by ICTs, believe that something needs to change to improve a situation, are sufficiently motivated and committed to do what they plan to do, have (or are willing to acquire) some knowledge and skills in relation to the ICTs-related teaching/learning innovation to be implemented, have (or do whatever is required to have) access to ICTs and other resources to make the implementation of the innovation work, find extra time which is needed to acquire knowledge and skills, make their plans for use, adapt, integrate, and reflect upon what they are doing, and make sure that they develop a level of consensus on what they do among their colleagues, the school administration, the students and their parents. In view of the above it is not unjustified to argue that even a single teacher or a researcher and a classroom of students with a few pcs at hand can engage in ICTs-related teaching/learning innovation. At this nucleus level where innovation is exercised by a single or just a few innovation units (for example a classroom, a school or a few schools) sustainability of the innovation, i.e. its capacity to survive over time within its context of implementation, is largely depended on the commitment of the people involved. Going, however, beyond that level to achieve diffusion of successful innovations into more classrooms and schools at local, regional, national and even cross-national levels is a whole different story, which, as it was already pointed out, depends upon both the type of innovation activity and the overall capacity of educational systems to absorb ICTs-related teaching/learning innovations.

In the following subchapter discrepancies between experiential and R&D innovations in schools will be discussed. These two generic types are strongly related to different categories of key innovation agents in schools:

School practitioners in the case of experiential innovations and researchers/ developers in the case of R&D innovations. These two key innovation agents bring into innovation activities their own concerns, priorities, dispositions and capacities which shape the aims, the goals, the ways through which innovation is conducted, its outcomes and its capacity to sustain and diffuse. Focusing on these two generic types of innovations in schools six key dimensions are analysed: a) The innovation focus and key innovators, b) the innovation scale, c) the division of labour, d) the nature of knowledge and knowledge flow, e) the innovation sustainability, and f) the innovations' diffusion capacity.

The 'experiential' type of innovation activities

Focus and key innovators. Experiential innovations are conducted by innovators who mostly draw upon their own and other practitioners' experiences to implement teaching-learning activities that are new to the school context that these activities take place. The experiential approach often characterises ICTs-related teaching/learning innovations that emerge directly out of school-specific teaching-learning practices, needs and problems. In particular, this approach often characterises 'tailor-made' innovations which respond to school-specific needs and problems to effectively integrate ICTs in teaching and learning, and to support, enhance or reform existing teaching-learning practices.

Innovation scale. Because of their school-specific 'problem-solving' nature, experiential innovations tend to be limited in scale, involving, for example, a whole school, a few or just a classroom. A larger number of such 'nucleus' innovation contexts can be supported or coordinated by higher administrative units, such as local educational authorities or municipalities.

Division of labour. In experiential ICTs-related teaching/learning innovations in schools the key innovators undertake the responsibility to diagnose problems and needs, design the innovation strategy and activities, secure, if needed, the necessary funding, training and consensus (among colleagues for example, or parents), motivate the people involved (notably students), implement innovation, and ensure effectiveness and sustainability of the innovation. Experiential innovations, as implied by the above, show a low degree of division of labour (it is often an individual teacher or just a few that undertake the whole responsibility to carry out an innovative activity). Because of this, innovators are interacting mostly on the basis of mutuality and sharing of perspectives and tasks and less in terms of power and control.

Knowledge and knowledge flow. Knowledge in experiential innovations is based mostly on school practitioners' capacity to reflect upon and exploit the on-going informal experiential learning that take place during their everyday practice (mainly through learning-by-doing, learning-by-using and learning-by-interacting or generally learning-by-teaching) which leads to a wealth of tacit, non codified, situational and context-specific knowledge about the problem area and possible innovative interventions given the available means. The knowledge flow is based more on informal communication and tacit knowledge sharing among practitioners or even local school administrators (between breaks, for example, in the teachers' room or in teachers' meetings and workshops) and less on codified knowledge (in the form, for example, of records, reports or guidelines). Interpersonal communication between practitioners can be highly situational and context-specific, carrying within it all particularities of real-life situations that form the 'story' of how an innovation was implemented. When some form of research does take place (often informal or some sort of action research) this does not seek for generalisable evidence or theory formation but is driven by the need to gain a better understanding of the problems at hand; the data are used to inform decision making and to assess the effectiveness of the innovative activities.

Sustainability. Experiential innovations, because of their 'tailor-made' character, their very small scale and their dependence on the work of a single or just a few practitioners, can be highly sustainable as long as innovations are effective and the key innovators are enthusiastic and dedicated enough to keep doing what they do. In this sense, experiential innovations are bound to the people who implement them. Because of this, innovations are in danger of discontinuity when the innovators have to leave the school or their classroom.

Diffusion capacity. Perhaps the most important barrier to the diffusion of experiential innovations is the relatively low power of the actual innovators that are often behind such innovations (that is, individual teachers or school boards), in the field of education. This becomes more evident in centralised educational systems where bottom-up approaches to educational reform and change are facing bureaucratic barriers and hence are difficult to exert considerable influence on actual policy formation that would sanction their diffusion. Nevertheless, experiential innovations can gradually spread among practitioners and schools in informal ways through interpersonal communication and experience sharing. This way of innovation diffusion often depends on the physical proximity between practitioners or schools and is subject to some important limitations. As Hargreaves (2000) argues, one of the most characteristic features of teacher talk is the absence of a professional vocabulary that would allow for tacit knowledge to express with more precision and clarity. The lack of 'formal' codification of teachers' professional practice results in a low degree of cumulativeness of professional knowledge which is also true for experiential ICTs-related teaching/learning innovations in schools. As a consequence, teachers in their efforts to effectively integrate ICTs into teaching and learning often have to invent and reinvent pedagogical solutions to recurring problems. Beyond the low degree of innovation knowledge codification, the situational and context-specific character of effective experiential innovations can also prove important barriers to their diffusion. A wealth of 'best practice' innovation stories can be found archived in educational portals, but it is questionable whether they actually contribute to the diffusion of a particular innovation. Because no school is exactly the 'same', it is not at all straightforward that an effective 'tailor-made' innovation will work in a school as well as it did in the school that this innovation first emerged. 'Best practice' stories are likely to function more as official recognition of schools' and teachers' achievements and less as practical tools offering the necessary 'know-how' to other schools and teachers who would want to innovate.

The 'research and development' type

While experiential innovations are largely undocumented, innovations conducted in on the basis of formal research and development offer more opportunities for in-depth analysis and discussion.

Focus and key innovators. In contrast to the experiential innovations, the formal research and development type characterises ICTs-related teaching/learning innovations that emerge primarily out of wider scientific, pedagogical and technological concerns (for example, from the need to test hypotheses on the effectiveness of a new ICTs-based learning environment or the need to develop tools that support new forms of teaching and learning) which are not specifically related to the actual context where such innovations are implemented. In any case, seeking for generalisable evidence, formalisation of new knowledge and theory formation is of vital importance. Individual schools or teachers, as key innovators, are quite unlikely to adopt such an approach in conducting innovation because it is out of their traditional school practices and their institutionalised role. Furthermore, as Foray (2001, p. 1556) observes, formal R&D is considered by practitioners as of secondary importance in traditional professional knowledge-building in the educational sector. In formal R&D innovations research groups are very often the key innovators with schools or individual teachers serving more as those who put researchers' ideas into practice and as actual research subjects. This has some implications on how R&D innovations are perceived by schools. It is characteristic, for example, a point made by Van Der Meijden and his colleagues working in the CL-Net project that 'to a certain extent, schools perceive experimental projects like CL-Net as external, as originating from motivation of agencies that pursue objectives related with scientific investigation, as accepted by the head of the institute for the school prestige, but not as a really productive tool for the benefit of their own school community' (Van Der Meijden et al, 2000, p. 134). This may not be totally unjustified on behalf of the schools given that R&D projects are likely to embed within them concerns, research agendas and practices well beyond the scope and everyday reality of the schools that are invited to participate as 'research sites'. In many cases schools are involved in such projects because there exist some kind of formal or informal links between a school or individual teacher(s) and a research/academic institute. The development of higher reputation for the school is always an appealing idea among school administrators but there are other, more intrinsic, motives that seem to also play an important role. Very high in the agenda of the teachers who participate in European R&D projects are the opportunities offered to communicate and develop links with other schools, especially with teachers and pupils from other countries, to get back valuable feedback from researchers on how they can improve their ICTs-based teaching, as well as integrate ICTs in all teaching subjects, to develop a better understanding of the impact of ICTs use on pupils' learning, to motivate pupils and improve their levels of attainment, and to get training on educational uses of ICTs (Kollias and Kikis, 2002, p. 53). A conclusion that can be reached from the above is that innovation through R&D is seen only as auxiliary to schools' teaching and learning goals, not as an end in itself, something that also characterises schools' and teachers' involvement in experiential innovations. This is also evident in teachers' efforts to adapt R&D projects' activities to their own learning needs and to the demands of their teaching tasks (see Baron et al, 2000, p. 78-9).

Innovation Scale. Unlike experiential innovations, R&D-driven innovations need to go beyond singular cases and customisation of innovative solutions. The need to get generalisable evidence and to develop ICTs tools that are validated and can be proved useful to a great variety of school contexts and tasks requires the involvement of a large number of innovation contexts. The scale of an R&D innovation cannot be uniformly defined, however, because, in practice, a sample of schools may be large from a researchers' point of view and needs and at the same time very small in terms of the sample's actual weight considering the target population of the innovation.

Division of labour. In R&D projects the division of labour is largely dependent on the intentions and plans of the group of researchers that design and coordinate the project. Unlike experiential innovations where involved practitioners are cooperating on the basis of mutuality and sharing of perspectives and tasks, in the case of R&D projects researchers cannot avoid but adopt a more directive and interventionist approach in order to do research and 'transfer' their agendas into schools. Researchers can give away some of their power in ways that can support inspiration and creative action by engaging practitioners in action research and professional development activities, where teachers are expected to act as researchers and hence develop a sense of ownership of the R&D-based innovation. Teachers can genuinely enhance R&D innovation in schools by localising and contributing to the design and methodology of research projects, devising learning and research situations that better adapt to the reality of schools, extending the repertoire of anticipated uses of ICTs in pedagogically sound and grounded ways, offering invaluable insights into the limitations, strengths and applicability of research outputs in schools, localising research outputs to national and local levels, and disseminating research results in their schools and colleagues. Nevertheless, however valuable teachers' contribution in innovation through R&D that may be, teachers are facing considerable problems in their involvement and the effectiveness of their contribution in research-driven innovation. However, even in R&D projects where an action research methodology is adopted, collaboration between researchers and practitioners is often limited at the implementation phase with no or minimal teachers' and whole schools' involvement at the design and evaluation phase. For example, at the level of EU RT&D programmes, schools, is quite difficult to be involved as partners because of several reasons. One of them is that schools often lack the experience and the personnel to handle the formalities and practicalities of being part of a project consortium. Another reason is that consortia tend to invite schools at a later stage where they could serve as 'research sites' to avoid additional burdens regarding the management and coordination of several partners. Because of the above, schools cannot shape important aspects of the planned R&D innovation. Furthermore, they have limited involvement in the reviewing and evaluation process of projects' documents even when these are targeting to teachers' communities in Europe (i.e. guidelines for implementing an innovation, ICTs tools testing etc).

Knowledge and knowledge flow. Knowledge that triggers R&D-driven innovations is often highly codified up to the point that researchers need to go further in their codification efforts thus engaging in new research and development which is anticipated to extend the knowledge area as this is defined by state of the art reviews of existing research on ICTs-related teaching and learning. The knowledge flow in R&D-driven innovations in schools is largely dependent on the practices of the involved partners especially researchers which structure the conditions for project-related knowledge flow. While informal, tacit knowledge sharing is important, it is not as crucial as in experiential innovations. R&D-driven innovations are pursuing the codification of knowledge to achieve generalisation and hence increased applicability and greater capacity for diffusion in different and geographically spread school contexts. Researchers commonly do this job through research reports. However, teachers tend to understand research reporting as researchers' 'self-referential' activity because they are primarily interested to support their work to the scientific community, expert peer reviewers and the funding agents, but not to the European school communities.

Sustainability. The sustainability of R&D-driven innovations in the schools where they were initially implemented face considerable problems because of:

a) The nature of R&D-driven innovations: They often emerge out of scientific and technological concerns which do not necessarily respond to immediate school-specific problems, priorities, needs and actual practices.

b) The nature of research practices: R&D-driven innovations in schools require some control over research variables and conditions and it may actually be very difficult for R&D innovations to survive the crass-test of their transfer in 'ordinary' classroom situations.

c) The nature of research knowledge: Knowledge produced through formal research is abstracted from the specific school contextual characteristics and lack situativeness. Therefore research knowledge is often difficult to be directly applicable to real-life school contexts.

d) Schools' attitudes towards R&D and researchers' links with schools: Projects initiated by research teams are often perceived by teachers and pupils as external to school everyday life. This attitude may be strengthened when researchers and, more importantly, their institutes fail to develop long term links and cooperation with schools that would go beyond the demands of a single project. This is also not unrelated to the fact that schools and participant teachers very often do not get financial or other tangible support for their efforts.

e) The time-span of R&D projects: Experience shows that the actual time that can be devoted for the implementation of R&D innovation in schools is limited to a few months for R&D projects which run for two or even three years and that research institutes tend to cease supporting schools in their innovation efforts after the formal completion of a project.

f)   The nature of R&D innovation products: R&D projects in schools which also involve the development of prototype software is difficult to go as far as to produce a 'marketable' product ready to use by the teachers and pupils, because the consortia often lack expertise (market experience for example) and funding. Other products, such as teaching/learning materials which can be directly applicable to curriculum are often limited to small curricular areas because they are developed to support research needs.

Diffusion capacity. Diffusion of innovations in schools is affected by all of the issues discussed above, especially by the nature of knowledge created by R&D-driven innovations. The latter can greatly differentiate the patterns of innovation diffusion from those discussed in experiential innovations. In particular, innovation R&D-based knowledge, abstracted from the immediate contexts and situations where it was initially produced, has an immense potential since it can be applied for or enlighten and support innovation efforts of various agents such as practitioners, researchers and policy makers at local and, most importantly, regional, national and European levels. This potential is greatly enhanced by the codified character of such knowledge which allows for taking advantage the diffusion potentials of both printed and electronic media. On the other side, such knowledge, as already pointed out, is not immediately applicable and agents who decide to use it need to essentially transform or adapt it to specific school contexts and practices. A problem that needs to be faced is how such knowledge can be best utilised by practitioners and policy makers as well. New knowledge created through R&D projects has a limited diffusion capacity among school practitioners because research reporting and formal academic practices for the diffusion of such knowledge (publication of research papers, conferences etc.) do not constitute an important source for teachers' professional development (see also Foray, 2001).

Further discussion

In chapter 1 we suggested that researchers and teachers will benefit much in their collaboration for the implementation of ICTs-related teaching/learning innovations in schools if they worked together to develop strategic visions on the role of schools in technology-rich knowledge-based societies and define their roles and responsibilities in shaping the pedagogic innovation agenda. Our discussion on the concept of ICTs-related teaching/learning innovations stressed another important issue where researchers and teachers need to develop synergies and shared understanding: that of the relationship between new knowledge and praxis. The above steps are not isolated from one-another and require shifts in the ways researchers and teachers perceive their relationship. In chapter 2 we identified and discussed shared characteristics and discrepancies between teachers and researchers' practices when conducting innovations in schools; resolving tensions that may be created by these discrepancies in a constructive manner would greatly enhance the capacity of schools to innovate. All the above could be addressed and resolved through some basic but crucial steps for future action.

Identifying and studying effective experiential ICTs-related teaching/learning innovations that already happen in schools is both a great challenge and an opportunity for researchers to develop a better understanding of schools' needs, capacities, problems and expectations when engage in innovation, as well as to develop in-depth knowledge about teachers-innovators, about the social, cognitive, motivational and dispositional factors that may shape their innovativeness (or resistance to innovation) in schools. Researchers and pedagogues could also help to enhance the diffusion capacity of experiential innovations by conducting meta-analyses of experiential innovations which would offer schools abstracted but practical 'know-how' on effective innovative ICTs-related teaching/learning practices. As it was already pointed out, school communities often perceive R&D as external to school practices and mission. Such dispositions are likely to put considerable barriers to the emergence of ICTs-related teaching/learning innovations in schools and it is of vital importance for the schools' community to see in practice the advantages of participating in R&D projects. One measure towards this direction is to design, fund and implement R&D that will actually respond to real-life school problems and needs, especially those related to the improvement of pupils' learning and attainment in primary and secondary education curricula and learning targets. Such efforts should be adapted to the demands of everyday school life and provide for support mechanisms which will help schools sustain successful innovations well after the formal completion of an R&D project. The engagement of researchers in such types of 'school-sensitive' research and innovation also requires a considerable change in widespread dispositions among the research community, which often approaches schools as 'research sites' and rarely as partners in research and development. Overall, research institutes, universities and schools should develop long-term holistic forms of collaboration, expertise and resource sharing and professional development practices for both school practitioners and researchers. Developing long-term commitments between R&D institutes, universities and schools should also be accompanied by policy making efforts to implement large-scale R&D programmes which will particularly focus on whole school development, targeting to the enhancement of schools' capacity to transform into knowledge-based organisations. Furthermore, policy makers and researchers should put more power to schools and increase their capacity to play an active role in shaping the R&D agendas at various decision making levels (from EU to national and local levels), to involve as equal partners in the design and evaluation of research and innovation projects, and to integrate formal R&D into school-specific development plans. The above should also be complemented with concrete measures which would provide further incentives to schools and individual teachers to participate in formal R&D, for example through the direct allocation of project funds to school partners for buying new ICTs. On the other hand, schools should be encouraged to involve researchers and pedagogues in their own school development plans, as is for example required from Danish schools in order to get funding for ICTs projects from the latest 'IT, media and primary and lower secondary school' (IT medier & folkeskolen –ITMF[9] funding scheme).

While sustaining successful R&D innovations in the schools that were initially implemented can largely succeed through the dedication and the development of formal but also informal commitments between the institutions and the people involved, the diffusion and sustainability of successful R&D innovations in the wider school community is an issue of a different, much larger scale. At a primary level, the partners involved in an effective R&D innovation should seek for ways to enhance the capacity of a particular ICTs-related teaching/learning innovation to diffuse in schools by developing extensive documentation that will be of direct use by interested schools and practitioners. An inherent problem in developing such documentation is that R&D projects in order to get in-depth results need to narrow down their scope of research. Thus the documentation that can directly result from successful innovations is likely to be also narrow in scope. It is therefore necessary to devise strategies that will bridge the gap between a successful R&D innovation that is necessarily narrow in scope and its wider applicability potentials in schools. The provision of funding for follow-up R&D projects is sine qua non but this can only partly bridge such gaps because of the nature of research: It still needs to be narrowed down in scope in order to get in-depth results. What is suggested is the devising of funding and other support schemes which will aim to implement large-scale development and validation activities based on successful innovations. For example, such activities could include school networks which will implement and provide feedback on the effectiveness of such innovations in parallel with the development of validated learning materials that will exploit the wider applicability potentials of the innovation, the involvement of software houses in the further development, production and distribution of successful

ICTs products etc. Overall, the diffusion an innovation in schools is largely dependent on the innovation absorption capacity of the schools' community and it is therefore a great long-term challenge for policy making to ensure further development of favourable framework conditions and strategic support to innovation agents in schools.

Notes

1. Dr. Kathy Kikis is heading the Education and Training Group at the Foundation for Research and Technology-Hellas (FORTH- see). Dr Andreas Kollias is member of this group and visiting lecturer at the Department of Computer Science, University of Crete, Greece.
2. Sypredem: Synergy between Practitioners' needs and opportunities, Research orientations and Decision Making on the usage of ICT in primary and secondary education. See http://promitheas.iacm.forth.gr/sypredem
3. Panel on Transforming Learning, President's Information Technology Advisory Committee.
4. See http://www.ngfl.gov.uk/index.jsp
5. Adopted by the March 2000 European Council in Lisbon.
6. The European Round Table of Industrialists.
7. The Second Information Technology in Education Study: Module 2 (SITES: M2) is an international study of innovative pedagogical practices that use ICTs. The study is sponsored by the International Association for the Evaluation of Educational Achievement (IEA). See http://sitesm2.org/
8. 8. Merlin: Monitoring and Evaluation of Research in Learning Innovations. See http://www.ub.es/euelearning/merlin/
9. See http://www.itmf.dk/info/info-english.html

References

Bateson, G. (1979) *Mind and Nature: A Necessary Unity*. New York: Dutton.Bulletin EU 3-2000. http://europa.eu.int/abc/doc/off/bull/en/200003/i1013.htm

COM (2000) Innovation in a knowledge-driven economy. Communication from the Commission to the Council and the European Parliament, No. 567. eLearning Summit Declaration (2001). http://www.electranet.org/eLig/Downloads/declaration.pdf

eLIG (2003) Contribution of the eLearning Industry Group to the implementation of the 'eEurope 2005 Action Plan: an information society for all'. http://www.elig.org/

Ely, D.P. (1990) 'Conditions that facilitate the implementation of educational technology innovations'. *Journal of Research on Computing in Education*, Vol. 23(2), pp. 298-236.

Ely, D.P. (1999) 'Conditions that facilitate the implementation of educational technology innovations'. *Educational Technology*, Vol. 39, pp. 23-27.

ERT: The European Round Table of Industrialists (2001) Actions For Competitiveness Through The Knowledge Economy In Europe. ERT Knowledge Economy Task Force White Paper.

EUR (2001) Building an Innovative Economy in Europe, A review of 12 studies of innovation policy and practice in today's Europe. Enterprise Directorate-General, EUR 17043.

Foray, D. (2001) 'Facing the problem of unbalanced development of knowledge across sectors and fields: the case of the knowledge base in primary education'. *Research Policy*, Vol. 30, pp. 1553-1561.

Frade, C., Pedró, F., Velloso, A., Danau, D. & Boxelaar, T. (1996) Socio-Cultural, Economic and Policy Aspects of Education & Learning Innovations. The Delilah project, Deliverable 01.

Frade, C. (1998) Looking at Innovations in Education and Training: Framework, Results, and Policy Implications of the DELILAH project. The Delilah project, Deliverable 15.

Hargreaves, D. (2000) The production, mediation and use of professional knowledge among teachers and doctors: a comparative analysis. Knowledge Management in the Learning Society. OECD, Paris.

ImpaCT2 (2001) Emerging Findings from the Evaluation of the Impact of Information and Communications Technologies on Pupil Attainment. NGfL Research and Evaluation Series. Department for Education and Skills, UK.

Kollias, A. & Kikis, K. (2002) A framework for understanding teaching/learning innovations in primary and secondary education & policy recommendations. The SYPREDEM Project. Public Deliverable 02.

Kozma, R.B. (eds) (2003) Technology, Innovation, and Educational Change—A Global Perspective. ISTE Publications.

NGfL Pathfinders (2002) Preliminary Report on the roll-out of the NGfL Programme in ten Pathfinder LEAs. NGfL Research and Evaluation Series, No. 2. Department for Education and Skills, UK.

OCenW: The Dutch Ministry of Education, Culture and Science (2002) ICT Education Monitor 2000-2001.

PITAC (President's Information Technology Advisory Committee, Panel on Transforming Learning) (2001) Using Information Technology To Transform The Way We Learn. National Coordination Office for Information Technology Research & Development.

Rogers, E. M. (1995) *Diffusion of Innovations*. New York: Free Press.

Scheuermann, F., Kikis, K. & Barajas, M. (2001) Synthesis Report on Innovation Trends in ICT-based Learning. The MERLIN Project Deliverable No. 03. European Commission, DG XII/ TSER: SEAC-99-00066.

The Web-Based Education Commission (2000) The Power of The Internet For Learning: Moving From Promise To Practice. Report of The Web-Based Education Commission to the President and the Congress of the United States.

Van Der Meijden, H., Simons, R.J. & De Jong, F. (2000) Computer Supported Collaborative Learning Networks in Primary and Secondary Education. The CL Net Project, Final Report.